Baptism in the
Reformed Tradition

COLUMBIA SERIES IN REFORMED THEOLOGY

The Columbia Series in Reformed Theology represents a joint commitment of Columbia Theological Seminary and Westminster John Knox Press to provide theological resources for the church today.

The Reformed tradition has always sought to discern what the living God revealed in scripture is saying and doing in every new time and situation. Volumes in this series examine significant individuals, events, and issues in the development of this tradition and explore their implications for contemporary Christian faith and life.

This series is addressed to scholars, pastors, and laypersons. The Editorial Board hopes that these volumes will contribute to the continuing reformation of the church.

COLUMBIA SERIES IN REFORMED THEOLOGY

Baptism in the Reformed Tradition

A Historical and Practical Theology

JOHN W. RIGGS

Westminster John Knox Press
LOUISVILLE • LONDON

2010 paperback edition
Originally published in hardback in the United States
by Westminster John Knox Press in 2002.
Published by Westminster John Knox Press
Louisville, Kentucky

10 11 12 13 14 15 16 17 18 19—10 9 8 7 6 5 4 3 2 1

Scripture quotations are from the New Revised Standard Version of the Bible, copyright © 1989 by the Division of Christian Education of the National Council of the Churches of Christ in the U.S.A., and used by permission.

Book and Cover design by Drew Stevens

Library of Congress Cataloging-in-Publication Data is on file at the Library of Congress, Washington, D.C.

ISBN 978-0-664-22531-5
ISBN: 978-0-664-23182-8 (paper edition)

PRINTED IN THE UNITED STATES OF AMERICA

♾ The paper used in this publication meets the minimum requirements of the American National Standard for Information Sciences—Permanence of Paper for Printed Library Materials, ANSI Z39.48-1992

Westminster John Knox Press advocates the responsible use of our natural resources. The text paper of this book is made from 30% post-consumer waste.

For my beloved
Cindy, Andrew, and Abigail

CONTENTS

PREFACE

The basic issues that this book treats became clear to me in graduate school almost fifteen years ago. Teaching duties, other writing projects, family, and the normal, ambiguous course of life's events kept the ideas from ever coming to paper. When the Columbia Series in Reformed Theology (CSRT) Board suggested this study rather than the Calvin study I had originally proposed, the right moment had come for this project.

With the completion of this work, many thanks are due many people. There were scholars whose guidance and scholarship, in differing ways, helped form me as a scholar. Most of all I thank John Cook, Steve Ozment, Jim White, Brian Gerrish, and Phil Devenish.

The CSRT Board deserves thanks for this project and for the helpful comments on the manuscript that have kept me from making numerous mistakes. Don McKim of the CSRT Board, Academic and Reference Editor at Westminster John Knox Press, deserves thanks for his work in this project. His advice, encouragement, and editorial skills have been wonderful.

I thank the Eden community for all its help in so many ways. The board of directors and administration fully support faculty sabbaticals, without which writing projects such as this could not be done. My colleagues have been just that to me—colleagues who support, encourage, and challenge. In particular, I thank my two colleagues in New Testament, Steve Patterson and Deborah Krause, for their friendship and support. The Eden-Webster Library staff has been a tremendous help in this project. Thank you all; and thank you for the generous access to the James I. Good Collection, which contains many rare books of Reformed theology from the sixteenth century.

Finally, my deepest thanks go to my family. So often they have been the embodiment of God's presence for me, as both comfort and challenge.

INTRODUCTION:

THE LITURGICAL MOVEMENT AND BAPTISM AS CHRISTIAN INITIATION

The liturgical movement that began in Europe in the early nineteenth century and continued into the latter half of the twentieth century, spreading from Europe to various parts of the world, had historical methods and theological perspectives embedded in it. Not all these methods and theologies may necessarily fit with Protestant worship practices or theological perspectives. Basic problems can arise when a theological movement, with its own assumptions, is fitted to a tradition that may not share these assumptions. Recent Protestant scholarship has come to see this point when doing liturgical *history*. As James F. White observes:

> The study of Protestant worship has usually been conducted by methods derived from the study of Roman Catholic worship. In practice this has meant that the chief concerns addressed have been liturgical texts, and most of those were for the eucharist. These are properly the staples of Roman Catholic liturgical scholarship, and the methodologies for such research have been carefully developed during the last century and a half. Textual studies, especially for the mass, abound. . . . I contend that this gives a distorted image and is totally irrelevant to the worship of most Protestants in America and in many other lands as well.[1]

Section 1 of this chapter looks at the history of the liturgical movement so that the issues at stake become clear, particularly the replacement of the sacrament of baptism by the rite of Christian initiation of adults. Section 2 examines the theology lying behind the rite of Christian initiation. Section 3 then suggests difficulties reconciling this rite and sacramental theology with a Protestant perspective. Section 4 offers a comparison between Luther's baptismal rite in his 1526 *Taufbuchlein* (Baptism booklet) and the *Lutheran Book of Worship* (*LBW*), which was influenced by the modern liturgical renewal movement.

The turn to Luther and the *LBW* has features that make it a cardinal illustration. First, it helps show how the liturgical movement has affected liturgical material, which itself shapes congregations. In so doing, the discussion of the *LBW* addresses a possible objection against the course of the book as a whole: that one might borrow liturgical rites and structures without borrowing the theological perspective that was originally a part of the rites. Implied here is Karl Barth's idea that one must be sure that borrowed concepts appropriately fit the datum that the concepts are to analyze.[2] The central question asked, and tentatively answered in the negative, is whether the initiation ritual that the *LBW* adapted from the Rite of Christian Initiation of Adults (RCIA), the rite mandated for parish use by the Second Vatical Council, appropriately fits the Christian datum that Luther believed baptism to be exemplifying. Second, the section on Luther and the *LBW* baptism rite introduces the Reformation material of the next chapter and thus stands as a hinge in this chapter.

THE LITURGICAL RENEWAL MOVEMENT

The liturgical movement had its start within the Roman Catholic Church during the first half of the nineteenth century.[3] Here historians look to Prosper Guéranger, who in 1833 refounded the Benedictine monastery at Solesmes, France. Guéranger was interested in the recovery of more ancient worship traditions over and against (neo-Gallican) liturgical developments of his era. Guéranger's reforms sparked monastic liturgical renewal within the Benedictine order.

From these monasteries and their liturgical efforts came the development of concentrated scholarly endeavors in liturgical history and theology. In the nineteenth century, new approaches to the study of science, political philosophy, and textual criticism led to new research in liturgical studies. Great scholars such as Louis Duchesne (1843–1922), Pierre Battifol (1861–1929), and Fernand Cabrol (1855–1937) dominated the era. As the scholarship continued in the twentieth century, the effects of Guéranger's original movement continued. From the monastery at Maria Laach came Odo Casel, whose influential and controversial book *The Mystery of Christian Worship* has been much debated. From the monastery at Mont César came scholar and author Bernard Botte, who founded the Institut Supérior de Liturgie. Among other giants of liturgical scholarship have been Josef Jungmann and Jean Daniélou, whose works on the history of the mass and the origins and history of early Christian worship are considered classics.

By the middle of the twentieth century, the liturgical movement engaged not only academic interests but also pastoral practice that included bringing about changes in the worship life of the church. Within the Roman Catholic Church the movement had become a contending force. A notable landmark was the 1947 promulgation by Pius XII of *Mediator Dei*, the first papal encyclical devoted entirely to liturgical concerns. The encyclical encouraged participation in worship, and

it spoke of the worship life of the church as the work of the entire people. By the early years of the next decade, official worship reform had
begun to put the encyclical into action, attempting to encourage understanding, participation, and ownership of the liturgical life of the
church by the people. The important 1951 restoration of the Easter vigil
(*Ordo sabbati sancti*) was directly influenced by the liturgical movement,
many of whose scholars and activists had gathered the previous year
at the First German National Liturgical Conference around the topic
"The Sunday Celebration of the Eucharist." Yearly international study
weeks were held through 1959, on a range of liturgical topics, with
scholars, activists, and church leaders attending in increasing numbers.

In 1958 the international study week took up the topic "Baptism and
Confirmation." Less than a month later, on October 9, 1958, Pius XII
died and was succeeded by John XXIII, who was friends with Lambert
Beauduin (1873–1960), one of the founders of the liturgical movement.
As early as 1909, Beauduin had called for increased lay understanding, participation, and ownership of worship. John XXIII quickly
announced the summoning of the Second Vatican Council in January
1959, where significant liturgical change was clearly on the horizon.
Most of the leading scholars of the liturgical movement assisted the
worship reforms by working with various Council committees. The
liturgical movement itself by direct involvement, as well as by its
century-long indirect raising of liturgical consciousness, profoundly
affected the worship changes that were mandated by the Council.

In October 1962 the Council began work on the *Constitution on the
Sacred Liturgy* (*De sacra liturgia*). After many sessions it was passed
overwhelmingly in 1963 and promulgated by Paul IV in December of
the same year. Its contents were to affect profoundly the Roman
Catholic Church and other faith traditions as well. Both academic and
pastoral in content, the *Constitution on the Sacred Liturgy* exemplified
the principles of the liturgical movement: to encourage understanding,
participation, and ownership of the worship life of the church, in ways
ecumenical, mission oriented, and appropriate to the work of the
church in the world. Implementation of the *Constitution* began thereafter with vernacular eucharistic rites and a complete revision and
issuing of the various rites of the church. In 1972 the new order for
Christian initiation (Rite of Christian Initiation of Adults) was issued.
With the RCIA came a sweeping reform of baptismal practice, as well
as the vision that the ministry of the church lay fundamentally in the
ministry of every baptized member of the church.

Liturgical historians had long been studying the history of Christian initiation. The patristic development of and the late patristic and
medieval dissolution of a rite of Christian initiation has been well studied and can be summarized.[4] During the second century, a general

pattern for initiating people into the church appeared for which there is little or no prior evidence.[5] This general pattern developed in the West, with some variation in the East. Its shape became relatively standard by the late fourth century:

> lengthy prebaptismal catechesis
> baptismal preparation including (typically Easter) vigil
> baptism on (typically Easter) Sunday morning
> anointing with oil
> first communion with the gathered community

By the beginning of the fifth century this rite had become compressed and was usually administered all at once to those who were most often being baptized—infants. Not only had Augustine's debates with Pelagius produced the belief in original sin that inhered with every human birth, but the compressed rite of initiation, with exorcisms once done for adults now being done for infants, also reinforced the idea of the infant's guilt.

Baptism as the patristic, unitive rite of Christian initiation was gone by the fifth century, and in the coming centuries the episcopal anointing with oil (to be called confirmation) was separated from the rite. The event of first communion also was split from the initial, unitive initiation rite. What were left were infant baptism, confirmation, and first communion, all unconnected and drifting in the liturgical life of the Western church. By the late medieval period, infants were baptized soon after their birth; they might or might not receive episcopal confirmation around the age of seven; and then, at the age of discretion, they had the opportunity to take first communion, whether confirmed or not.

The Reformers dealt with the problem in a way well known to Protestants. Confirmation became a rite of training young adults and the time of their acceptance of Christian responsibility, after which they received their first communion. The Roman Catholic Church continued with the practice of three separate rites (baptism, confirmation, first communion), unaided by the reforms of Trent, until the decree of Pius X in 1910 that lowered the age of first communion (and thus communion penance). The Roman Catholic Church at the time of Vatican II therefore had the pattern of baptism, penance, first communion, and confirmation. This pattern, with its indiscriminate baptism of infants to secure their salvation, was seriously questioned in some areas of the church, most notably in France during the postwar period.[6]

A brief mention is needed concerning the theological climate that surrounded baptism prior to the Second Vatican Council. The old Augustinian emphasis on infant original sin and the need for immediate baptism and entry into the sacramental life of the church dominated popular and ecclesial piety. As Kavanagh pointedly observed:

Roman Catholics could not simply jettison an Augustinianism that ran through the medieval scholasticism to which their Church had given normative theological value. This meant that whenever the baptismal core of the discussion and possible reform were touched, the matter of baptism's absolute necessity and its immediate (*quam-primum*) administration in infants came quickly to the fore. In turn, the question of the meaning of original sin had to be broached as the setting within which conventional Catholic theory and practice could be reviewed. The ensuing debate revealed that some liberalization had taken place among Catholic scholars since Herman Schells' *Katholische Dogmatik*, which suggested in 1893 that unbaptized infants might attain to some state more exalted even than limbo, had been put on the Index of Forbidden Books.[7]

Such was the state of the Roman Catholic baptismal rite and theology prior to the Second Vatican Council. From the Council's *Constitution on the Sacred Liturgy* and its new rite of initiation came a new vision of baptism.

THE RITE OF CHRISTIAN INITIATION OF ADULTS

The RCIA reaches back to the patristic model of initiation.[8] First is the precatechumenate, when inquirers about the Roman Catholic Church enter conversation with a local church. When it is thought that the person has the desire to convert and commit to a new life, the candidate moves on to the catechumenate. In this second stage, the candidate for baptism undergoes formation that may take a year or more. Such formation includes instruction, involvement in mission, and participation in worship up to, but not including, the prayers prior to the Eucharist. When those responsible for the candidate's formation understand the person to be ready, the candidate moves to the period of "purification and enlightenment," which is marked by the liturgical event of enrollment that takes place at the beginning of Lent. At the end of this period, the sacrament of initiation itself occurs—baptism, confirmation, first communion—which marks the entrance of the candidate into the body of Christ. This leads to the fourth stage of the RCIA, a period of post-baptismal education usually called the "mystagogical catecheses." This phrase comes directly from the fourth century when it was the name given by the bishops to the sermons that they preached to the newly baptized in order to explain to them the mysteries they had undergone during the initiation rite. For the RCIA mystagogical catecheses signifies the stage when the newly baptized learn further from their event of initiation, and they are strengthened in their new life. The Roman Catholic church in the United States has extended this period of mystagogy through the following Easter, with monthly meetings, in order to incorporate the new member fully into the church.

The RCIA thus envisions both a renewed sacrament of baptism and a renewed vision of the ministry of the laity. Not only does each person newly engrafted into Christ take up her or his ministry, but so also do the members of the worshiping community as they participate in the RCIA along with those to be baptized. The rite thus expresses a long-standing desire of the liturgical movement for the renewal of the church. In 1914, Beauduin published his *La Piété de l'église*. There he argued that worship is the work of the gathered community, continually incorporating them into the saving work of Christ. Being the mystical body of Christ, the faithful are renewed inwardly in spirit and outwardly in mission.[9]

If the rite of Christian initiation brings to partial fruition long-standing goals of the liturgical movement, so too the best of current liturgical theology exemplifies these goals. Although liturgical theology has taken many forms in recent years,[10] I take the liturgical theology of Aidan Kavanagh and his student David Fagerberg to represent the most consistent current articulation of the theology operative in the liturgical movement and thus in the RCIA.[11] Here liturgical theology is conceived as part of the entire theological project:

> Liturgical theology involves ecclesiology, for this identifies the assembly which celebrates; ecclesiology involves Christology, for this confesses whose body the Church is; Christology involves soteriology because this reveals the (functional) identity of the incarnate one into whose Paschal mystery we are engrafted; and why do soteriology without a doctrine of sin? and how can one understand what sin is without a doctrine of creation which reveals what humanity was meant to be?[12]

Within these "facets on the single diamond" that the church enacts in word and deed during worship, three aspects particularly reflect the goals of the liturgical movement so well expressed by Beauduin and others: the worship event itself (what Fagerberg calls "leitourgia"), ecclesiology, and ministry.

The foundational premise of liturgical theology so conceived is that God encounters us in and through worship itself; better still, worship *is* divine encounter, for therein God self-reveals and establishes the church again and again:

> Leitourgia is ontological (not just esthetic) because leitourgia reveals how God sees the world. It shapes us and changes us to fit God's vision of what a human being is, it is not a series of snap-on liturgical formats which express the theological ideals of one generation or another, one culture or another. Leitourgia is revelation-in-motion.[13]

Worship in this sense (leitourgia) is not the mere expression of some idea or ideas but is itself "epiphanic" since there we are encountered and become who we are. As Kavanagh puts it, in a passage cited at length by Fagerberg, "In this sense a human community does not merely use a language; it *is* the language it speaks. Similarly, a Christian church does not merely use its liturgy; it *is* the liturgy which it worships."[14] Regarding secondary or reflective theology, "liturgy is the ontological condition for theology because the kingdom is rendered present in the Divine Liturgy (it is 'symbolized' in Fr. Schmemann's sense of a verb). Liturgy is foundational for theology because in liturgy's sacramental axis, what happened by Jesus happens to us."[15]

Ecclesiology is second-order reflection on the *ekklesia* so formed in this divinely epiphanic event, this revelation-in-motion. Here ecclesiology recognizes that leitourgia forms believers both separately and corporately. The individual *becomes theological, becomes doxological,* in the divine encounter, and likewise the gathered people actually become what they had not been previously, the body of Christ.[16] The formative event of individual and community that happens in the epiphanic encounter, happens within given ritual structures. These structures are for us the very grammar of the epiphanic encounter because they are the means by which God is communicated to us and shapes us and in which we adjust ourselves to that divine encounter, This grammar, however, like the grammar of language, is something we do not invent but inherit. Theologically speaking, we inherit this grammar through the liturgy itself.[17] Kavanagh speaks plainly about the grammar of the initiation rite:

> Christian fellowship in the fullest and most unqualified sense is the result: it is life "in the Holy Spirit in the holy Church." A web of intimately articulated meanings has been matched with a multiplicity of closely coordinated acts. The liturgical genius of this arrangement is remarkable. Yet its genius consists in the mutual dependence of each of its parts: like an ecological system, it is robust only to the extent that its parts remain both whole and in vital harmony. Disrupt that harmony and the whole system mutates.[18]

Worship that is epiphanic, and the church so constituted in this epiphany, leads to a view of ministry that is crucial for the renewal of the church. When the entire body of the faithful reenters the paschal mystery, the very life and mission of the church then rests on the ministry of all the baptized:

> In the liturgy the laos do the *ergon* of believing, hoping, grieving, rejoicing, repenting, making glad noises, etc. The Word is proclaimed, and the people do the Word; it grips them, and they exercise it. The mouth can speak "theos-logos" because the heart is filled with Christ, the logos of God.[19]

The life of the church and its ministry are conceived not as a flowing downward of the Spirit from the clerics to the laity but rather as a building upward from the Spirit-inspired common ministry, and this through leitourgia itself.[20] In short, the long-standing goals of the liturgical movement find exemplification in the RCIA and well-articulated second-level reflection in the best of current Roman Catholic liturgical theology.

A PRELIMINARY APPRAISAL: ECCLESIOLOGY

The question arises for Protestants whether this perspective can be called Protestant.[21] To some, this may seem to beg the real question: whether we ought to be still holding to divisions such as Protestant and Roman Catholic, instead of moving toward a truly catholic perspective based on our catholic roots. This question can hardly be answered here. It must suffice for now that I find such distinctions important, not least because some of the positions the Reformers held over and against the late medieval church I find to be positions that still distinguish the traditions. Take one brief example that comes directly from the prior liturgical discussion—the question of ecclesiology.

The liturgical movement speaks of the church as the body of Christ epiphanically constituted in its leitourgia. As such, the church continues the incarnation, inwardly by the members becoming engrafted into the paschal mystery (Fagerberg's "what happened by Jesus happens to us") and outwardly by becoming once again Christ's mission to the world. Now, while Luther and Calvin spoke of the church as the body of Christ, and at times spoke of the members of the church participating in this mystical body, nowhere did they intentionally speak of the visible, historical church and its members in such an unqualified manner. Most frequently, Luther and Calvin understood the church, which is the mystical body of Christ and in which believers are engrafted, to be the invisible church.

Luther more usually called the church "hidden" rather than invisible: the church is hidden away; the saints are out of sight.[22] Because no one can determine whether another person has faith, the true believers simply are not visible to the human eye.[23] They indeed are known by God, who has preserved them within the historical church, but at times they may have been a distinct minority.[24] This view has two important consequences. First, the visible historical church is a mixed body in which exist both sheep and goats, where sometimes the goats are called sheep and those who are sheep are not even known as such.[25] Second, although the true church does show forth amid the visible church, it does not do so by human response. The true church shows by way of the divine offer of Christ (objective and subjective genitive) given through preaching and sacraments. So it is that the historical church had continuity to Luther's day, but only insofar as it bore the means of grace, offering Christ through preaching and sacraments.

It should be noted that most of these references to the hidden aspect of faith and the true church occurred when Luther wrote against the Roman Church, with its claim that its hierarchy was the true church, and when Luther wrote against the Anabaptists, with their claim that they were the true Christians confessing the true faith. The context for Luther's language is important because it reminds us that the doctrine of the "invisible church" was primarily prophylactic. It guarded against the attempt to draw the exact boundaries of the church insofar as human participation occurred, because faith as the heart's trust in God could not be seen by human eyes. The visible boundaries for the church *strictly speaking* did not center on God's Word *and* the human response but only on God's Word, which was sure.[26] Here we see Luther's strictly theocentric focus on God's graciousness, a theme repeated through Luther's theology and sacramental theology, that contradicts the sometimes popular notion that Luther was merely "subjective" and focused on human faith.[27]

Calvin's assertions about the invisible church follow Luther's ideas; subsequent chapters of this book trace some of this material. When we turn to the 1536 *Institutes*, we find that Calvin began by defining the church as the whole company of the elect, angels and people, the living and the dead, one people of God, and one body whose living head was Christ, comprised of all those who, since the beginning of the world, have been called and united according to God's eternal providence.[28] Calvin insisted on God's election as the constitutive essence of the church. This argument meant, of course, that the church existed beyond the sight and control of any visible means. In fact, in his dedicatory letter to the 1536 *Institutes*, written to Francis I, king of France, Calvin said that we "affirm that the church can exist without any visible appearance, and that its appearance is not contained within that outward magnificence which they foolishly admire."[29] Calvin here attacked the Roman Church with its organized outward structures.

Calvin quickly realized that such a position raised difficult questions. Who was elect and who was reprobate? In short, who belonged to the church and who did not? This question itself parsed into two parts: How am I to tell whether I am elect, and what can I say about my neighbor? As for the first part, knowledge of self, Calvin as always did not care to discuss the matter intellectually, for that was not the issue. And so he declared that intellectual debates were out and that the real issue was in whom one trusted in life.[30]

But what about our neighbors? This answer had two parts. First of all, insisted Calvin, there were visible marks of the church. In his dedicatory letter to Frances I, immediately following the remark that the church can exist without any visible form whatsoever, Calvin said that the church did have a visible mark, although compared to Rome "it has quite another mark: namely, the pure preaching of God's Word and the lawful administration of the sacraments."[31] Calvin repeated this in the 1536 *Institutes* themselves, penning a phrase that would hardly change over all the editions of the *Institutes*. Calvin said that the church existed where the sacraments were rightly administered and God's Word properly preached and heard.[32]

Just like Luther, Calvin spoke of the invisible church entirely in context of those who claimed to know the precise boundary of the church; and he maintained the distinction between the visible and the invisible church throughout his theological career, even though he realized early on the difficulties that such a position entailed. This did not mean there were not real points of contact between the visible and invisible church. Again, like Luther, Calvin identified marks of the church: the Word preached (and heard) and the sacraments properly administered, for there the one true foundation of the church existed—the present offer of Christ (as both objective and subjective genitive). More is said about this last point as the discussion advances. For now it should be clear why, at the least, I think the theology behind the liturgical movement's rite of initiation is problematic for Protestant traditions insofar as they trace their roots to Luther and Calvin. Before I meet a possible objection, and in so doing turn to Luther and the baptism rite from the *Lutheran Book of Worship*, one more comment can be made by way of distinguishing between the rite of Christian initiation and Protestant theology, at least as represented by Luther and Calvin.

The theology operative for the rite of Christian initiation argues for the epiphanic encounter with God as the worship that constitutes the very life of the church and its members. Such epiphany occurs within a rite that has structures that are passed on as the means of exemplifying the tradition from generation to generation.[33] Now, were this to be so, then anyone who wanted to be part of the particular church that embodied the epiphany of God would want to enter into the church that has concrete *liturgical continuity* from apostolic times to the present. There lies the church that truly continues the incarnation. The ecclesiology of such a church would understand that it is continually established *in and as* the *leitourgia* that is divinely epiphanic. In short, would one not want to become Roman Catholic? And does this logic itself not speak difficulties that arise when considering the theology of the liturgical movement and Protestant traditions?[34]

Here a possible objection must be met. Might it not be possible to learn from liturgical history and borrow a liturgical form without also borrowing a liturgical theology along with it? The tempting, quick answer is that were one to take seriously the liturgical movement in both its historical research and theological approach (which I have argued from a more or less unified perspective), then one would understand that to "borrow" a liturgical form would be to borrow the grammatical structures of the community that used that form and thus to enter into that community. In fact, some Protestant liturgical scholars have argued that is exactly the point, because it moves beyond Reformation divisiveness and ecumenically returns us to a period of catholic unity.[35] But what then of retaining the Protestant name and the specific denomination: why not simply become Catholic?

The common direction for the liturgical movement among American Protestantism has been different. There have been a number of mainline American denominations whose liturgical life has been influenced by the liturgical movement but who still want to retain their Protestant tradition. If we look at their liturgical material, however, we see the difficulty that this poses; and here I propose to look at the *Lutheran Book of Worship* and compare its baptismal rite with the rite and theology of Martin Luther. One word about method before we begin.

I take Kavanagh to be close to target when he asserts that myth is how a group conceives of its values and that ritual is that which enacts the myth, myth and ritual together making cult.[36] My preference is to put the matter a bit differently by saying that Christian worship reenacts the central datum of the community's life.[37] By "central datum" I mean the group conception of how its life and lifestyle is authorized.[38] With that said, I turn to Luther and to the *Lutheran Book of Worship* in order to identify what, in their prayers and ritual, the central datum might be.

A PRELIMINARY TEST: THE *LUTHERAN BOOK OF WORSHIP*

In late 1527, Luther wrote a treatise that responded to the challenge from Anabaptists that only believers ought to be baptized since only believers had faith; infant baptism would thus be no baptism at all. As Luther defended infant baptism, he spoke pointedly about the nature of baptism itself. First, said Luther, baptism was not fundamentally human activity, which itself was no more than shifting sand. Baptism was God's sure and dependable activity. In baptism, God gave the word of promise that offered forgiveness of sin; and God's promise could be trusted. Second, said Luther, no one else's faith could be determined. "Have they now become gods," Luther rhetorically asked about the Anabaptists, "that they can see in people's hearts whether they believe or not?"[39] The one and sure foundation of baptism was also the one sure foundation of the church and the one sure foundation for all life: God's gracious word of promise.

When we turn to his 1523 *Taufbuchlein*, we see how consistently Luther enacted this datum in the structure and central prayer of the rite, the so-called *Sintflutgebet*, or "Flood Prayer." The sources that Luther used for this prayer are not entirely clear, and the secondary literature is extensive.[40] Whatever Luther's sources, his Flood Prayer influenced the baptismal invocation prayers of the early Reformed tradition, and it has had stronger influence on such prayers in modern Protestant worship books.[41]

Within Luther's 1526 baptism rite,[42] the Flood Prayer followed the signation and set the stage for the exorcism and Gospel reading. It proclaimed that new birth came through the direct relationship between the God of groundless mercy and the person addressed:

> Almighty eternal God, who through the flood condemned the untrusting world according to your righteous judgement and preserved the trusting Noah and his family according to your great mercy, and who drowned hard hearted Pharaoh with all his men in the Red Sea and led your people Israel through there dry, thereby signifying for the future this bath of your holy baptism; and who through the baptism of your beloved child, our Lord Jesus Christ, sanctified and instituted the Jordan and all water as a blessed flood and plentiful washing away of sins; we pray through your same groundless mercy that you will look on this N. and bless him with right faith in the spirit so that everything may be drowned and go under which was born in him from Adam and to which he himself contributed; and that he may be torn from the number of the untrusting and kept dry and safe in the holy ark of Christendom, at all times burning in spirit and cheerful in hope serving your name, that he with all who trust may be worthy to attain eternal life, according to your promise, through Jesus Christ our Lord.[43]

Notice how Luther made no references to creation and began instead with faithful Noah, even though Luther himself understood a fundamental connection between God the Creator and baptism.[44] The allusion to Noah began the first of two typological moments that gave meaning to the present moment of baptism. First, the world was challenged to trust God. Noah trusted and he passed into life; but the world did not trust and it passed into death. Luther's *chiasmus* (in German) is striking:[45]

> condemned the untrusting world according to
> your righteous judgement
> and preserved the trusting Noah and his
> family according to your great mercy

Next, Luther used the story of Israel and Pharaoh to portray typologically the same decisive moment. Pharaoh hardened his heart and went unto death, while God's people Israel trusted God and passed through into life. Here (again in the German) Luther paralleled the two options that confronted a person:[46]

> drowned hard hearted Pharaoh with all his men in the Red Sea
>
> and led your people Israel through there dry

This moment in which one did or did not trust God, the moment of life or death, prefigured the present moment of baptism. Just as biblical characters had stood either for or against God, so also the person to be baptized would have a lifetime of standing for or against God.

Furthermore, Luther's prayer resulted in a highly theocentric prayer in which God personally and directly met the one addressed. For example, Luther mentioned neither the Spirit nor Christ and an atonement; there was simply the God of groundless mercy. Lorenz Grönvik's research confirms this point: In baptism, God's own self was present "for us" (*pro nobis*) with the promise of grace.[47] We see the same thing when we turn to the structure of the 1526 baptism rite.

Here Luther's revision of his 1523 translation of the late medieval baptism rite rendered a striking structure:

Cleansing
Signation
Prayer

Exorcism
Gospel
Lord's Prayer

Renunciation
Profession
Baptism
Lord's Prayer

However much the pruning of the rite, especially its exorcisms, reflected a late medieval pattern, the structure of the 1526 baptism rite that remained echoed the same crucial theme that Luther's baptismal theology and Flood Prayer proclaimed: turn from the old (cleansing), turn to the new (signation), then pray (prayer). The pattern repeated with exorcism—Gospel reading—Lord's Prayer, and the rite finished with renunciation—profession—baptism—prayer. Simply put, both in his Flood Prayer and in his edited 1526 baptismal rite, Luther liturgically reenacted the central datum of Christian life. Grounded in God's grace, we turn *from* death, turn *to* life, and then offer our prayers to God.

The *Lutheran Book of Worship* presents us with a very different prayer and rite because its central datum is different.[48] Luther's carefully constructed Flood Prayer was used as model for a narrative theology prayer in which the believers are urged to "find their story."[49] Compare the main baptism prayer from the *Lutheran Book of Worship* with Luther's Flood Prayer:

> Holy God, mighty Lord, gracious Father: We give thanks, for in the beginning your Spirit moved over the waters and you created the heaven and earth. By the gift of water you nourish and sustain us and all living things. By the waters of the flood you condemned the wicked and saved those whom you had chosen, Noah and his family. You led Israel by the pillar of cloud and fire through the sea, out of slavery into the freedom of the promised land. In the waters of the Jordan your Son was baptized by John and anointed with the Spirit. By the baptism of his own death and resurrection your beloved Son has set us free from the bondage to sin and death, and has opened the way to the joy and freedom of everlasting life. He made water a sign of the kingdom and of cleansing and rebirth. In obedience to his command, we make disciples of all nations, baptizing them in the name of the Father, and of the Son, and of the Holy Spirit.
>
> Pour out your Holy Spirit, so that those who are here baptized may be given new life. Wash away the sin of all those who are cleansed by this water and bring them forth as inheritors of your glorious kingdom.
>
> To you be given praise and honor and worship through your Son, Jesus Christ our Lord, in the unity of the Holy Spirit, now and forever.

Luther's baptismal theology of God's Word, which met each person with the choice between life or death, has been lost when the *Lutheran Book of Worship* describes scriptural people from the flood story as "chosen" or "wicked" rather than as "believing" or "unbelieving." Next, the *LBW* omits Luther's carefully constructed reference to Pharaoh and Israel, in which Luther had again posed the religious problem of choosing for life or death. The *LBW* Thanksgiving Prayer then fleshes out the story of salvation history, adding parts Luther did not mention or even avoided, such as the creation motif, which were present in some of the prayers that may have served as models for Luther's Flood Prayer.[50] We do not know why Luther omitted the creation motif, especially since he saw a connection between creation and baptism, but one might make a guess: Water cannot choose for or against God, and so the reference to the waters of creation was not relevant to the central datum of Christianity, baptism, and the baptism prayer—encounter with a gracious God in which we choose for either life or death.

When the *LBW* returned this detail to the baptismal rite, it offered a small but valuable insight into the difference between the two theologies at work: The central datum for the *LBW* is the narrative that the community tells about itself and its God. This is the narrative in which "we find our own narrative," to use the idiom of the liturgical movement. Central now is not the existentially present God but the story about this gracious God.

The structure to the *LBW* rite confirms this analysis. Whereas Luther's rite opened with an address by God to the one being baptized, occurring when the minister reenacted God's initiative and met the candidate at the front of the church, the *LBW* rite begins with the pastor addressing the community about the meaning of baptism. The Thanksgiving Prayer soon follows and recounts God's story, in which the believers find their story. In keeping with the meaning of Christian initiation, the *LBW* sees baptism primarily as entering the Christian narrative, wherein one enters the "paschal mystery." Among Protestant worship books, the *LBW* rite stands as an exemplary model of Christian initiation, coherent in prayer, structure, and theology.

Does this prayer appropriately reflect Luther's theology, especially his theology of baptism? How far might it appropriately reflect Lutheran tradition and adaptation of Luther? To what degree are the *LBW* rite and prayer advances over the prior liturgical material, such as that in the *Service Book and Hymnal*? These are complex questions that cannot be entertained here. Answering such questions would require a more detailed look at Luther's theology of baptism as it developed in context; greater clarity about the relationship between Luther's thought and that of the Lutheran tradition(s); and a more detailed examination of the relationship between Luther and Lutheran theologies of baptism. More discussion would also be needed about the relationship between American Lutheranism, as represented by the *LBW*, and the theology of the modern liturgical movement. And all these matters would have to be taken up within a more detailed discussion of the *LBW* baptism rite itself. For now, it should be clear that serious questions arise about any "mere" borrowing of a liturgical rite with its structures and prayers. At the least, this partial look at Luther and the *Lutheran Book of Worship* suggests that something was lost from Luther that was central to his theology and baptismal theology.[51]

THE SCOPE OF THIS STUDY

The subsequent chapters are intended to contribute to such an analysis of Reformed baptismal practice, specifically the revised sacrament of baptism in the *Book of Common Worship* (Presbyterian Church (U.S.A.) and Cumberland Presbyterian Church). This rite of baptism potentially affects the largest number of Reformed Christians in the

United States. The rite, as well as the worship book itself, has developed out of the current liturgical renewal movement. *How* to approach this study is, however, a much more difficult question than *what* rite or worship book to study.

What defines the "Reformed tradition"—or would it be "traditions"? Does the Reformed tradition itself carry the seed of further reformation, so that the only way a later tradition can be faithful to the meaning of an earlier tradition is to express that meaning in a new way? What theologians, churches, and liturgies ought to be examined? What to do with theologians who otherwise seem quite Reformed but on the issue of baptism seem not so Reformed? (Karl Barth and his repudiation of infant baptism comes to mind here.) This study proposes a very pragmatic approach in order to contribute to the discussion of current Reformed baptismal practice in the United States.

The largest part of this book is a historical-theological analysis of the foundations and trajectory of Reformed baptismal theology. Furthermore, within this study of Reformed theology, Calvin's teaching on baptism will receive more treatment than those of other Reformed theologians. First, Calvin's theology of baptism remains one of the surprisingly neglected aspects of his thought.[52] Second, Calvin's influence on Continental Reformed churches and their confessions is well known, and lessons learned in studying Calvin will aid the understanding of the twentieth-century Reformed debates on baptism. Third, to study the development of Calvin's theology of baptism is also to engage the theology of two Reformed theologians who directly influenced Calvin here, Huldrych Zwingli and Martin Bucer.

Chapter 1 turns to the foundations of Reformed baptismal theology by looking at the thought of Zwingli, Luther, and Bucer. Chapter 2 turns to Henrich Bullinger and Calvin, with chapter 3 continuing the thought of Calvin on issues of divine power and baptism.

Chapter 4 moves from these foundational theologians to trace the trajectory of Reformed discussions on baptism. The Reformed confessions comprise a long first section and lead to a section on Reformed orthodoxy. Section 3 in this chapter then takes up the baptismal theology of Friedrich Schleiermacher, which has some striking similarities to that of Barth. Next, chapter 4 turns to the twentieth century, when the Reformed debates over infant baptism raised the issue of baptism to a place in theology it had not had since the Anabaptist challenge at the time of the Reformation.

Chapter 5 then brings to bear the pragmatic task of holding together the views from both the first two generations of Reformed thinking and the larger sweep of Reformed baptismal theology, in order to see what views might be shared concerning baptism. This would seem a fair enough summary of Reformed thinking on baptism and thus a standard against which to compare the current liturgical material in the *Book of Common Worship* (*BCW*). At the least, one surely can make that claim that if Zwingli and Bucer, Bullinger and Calvin, the Reformed confessions, Reformed orthodoxy, Schleiermacher, and the twentieth-century Reformed theologians who debated baptism all agree on a particular point, and that point is clearly denied by liturgical material in the *BCW*, then such liturgical material can hardly be considered Reformed. That such an approach is historical and commonsensical rather than systematic and logical in the way one might otherwise want is to be admitted. But pending improvements in method, which are much welcomed, this approach will have to do.

Chapter 5 therefore has three sections that move from historical theology to practical theology. Section 1 summarizes and organizes the historical-theological material. The next section examines the actual baptismal rite in the *BCW*. Section 3 then offers suggestions that gently reshape various structures and prayers so that what Reformed congregations do might actually reflect and appropriately shape who they are and how they think theologically. Chapter 6 concludes this study by briefly suggesting the overall shape to Reformed baptismal and sacramental theology.

PART ONE

THE FOUNDATIONS OF
REFORMED BAPTISMAL THEOLOGY

1

THE FIRST GENERATION:
ZWINGLI, LUTHER, BUCER

The introduction provided the warrant for this book's inquiry. The century-long liturgical renewal movement had liturgical and theological goals reflected in the reforms of the Second Vatican Council. In particular, the Rite of Christian Initiation of Adults (RCIA) liturgically and theologically represented the harvest of the liturgical movement. Serious doubts arose about the fit between this liturgical project and the classical Protestantism of Luther and Calvin, as a brief discussion of ecclesiology showed. When such Protestant traditions borrowed from the liturgical movement, what was borrowed even innocently may well have imported unwanted theology as well, as we saw with the *Lutheran Book of Worship*. Has this happened to the Reformed tradition? The remainder of this study takes up that question in some detail. This chapter looks at Zwingli and the development of his baptismal theology, then it turns to Luther and Bucer to look at the same material.

HULDRYCH ZWINGLI

Huldrych Zwingli was born on New Year's Day, 1484, to a solid, rural family of some substance and influence in the village of Wildhaus.[1] At about the age of ten, Huldrych went to Wesen to study with an uncle. His more formal education then continued under the tutelage of Heinrich Wöfflin, a humanist, musician, and renowned schoolmaster in the area. Zwingli went on to study at the Universities of Vienna and Basel, receiving from the latter his bachelor's and master's of liberal arts degrees (the latter in 1506). While at Basel, Zwingli would have been formally schooled in the *via antiqua*—the (realist) theology of the early scholastics—rather than the *via moderna* of the late medieval nominalists. At Basel, Zwingli would also have had contact with humanists and reformers such as Beatus Rhenanus, Conrad Pellican, Caspar Hedio, Thomas Wyttenbach, Caspar Megander, Conrad Grebel, and Leo Jud.

Zwingli's first parish was in Glarus, where his interest in humanism and the church fathers grew.[2] He learned Greek, purchased Erasmus's critical edition of the New Testament, and traveled to Basel to meet Erasmus. When, in 1516, he took the call as people's priest at Ein-siedeln, Zwingli brought with him annotated copies of many of the church fathers, showing a preference for Origen, Jerome, and, later on, Augustine. By this time at Einsiedeln, Zwingli had come to important reforming principles: the return to Scripture, where God's Word could be found; the close study in Greek of the Pauline epistles; and the all-sufficient and all-inclusive atoning death of Christ the sole mediator.[3]

With his call to Zurich in 1519, Zwingli, both humanist and biblical scholar, quickly became involved in the Reformation of Zurich.[4] Within three years, his writing and preaching challenged a number of late medieval worship practices such as penance and indulgences, fasting, veneration of the saints, clerical celibacy, and pilgrimages.[5] In January 1523 the town council called for a public disputation on the issue of worship. The disputation was to be held in German, and the norm for adjudicating issues was to be the Word of God found accord-ing to the Scriptures. The four representatives of the bishop of Con-stance basically withdrew from theological dialogue and appealed to procedure: Such weighty matters could not be decided in a town like Zurich without the great doctors of the church present. Zwingli, how-ever, arrived with the Greek New Testament, the Hebrew Bible, the Vulgate, and a sharp mind with prodigious memory. The outcome was never in doubt. The council agreed that Zwingli was to continue his preaching according to Scripture and that all other preachers were to follow the same norm.

By June of that year, Zwingli had rejected the concept of transub-stantiation and had rethought the eucharistic section of the mass (the canon), both according to a scriptural norm. Some local citizens who thought that the scriptural norm was not being taken seriously enough in matters of worship began public demonstrations against idols and images. When, in September, a cobbler was arrested for tearing down a much-revered crucifix that the local miller had erected on his own, private property, the city council called for a second disputation, which was held in October. The outcome was disappointing to many, since the mass was still to be said in Latin, Communion using only bread was continued, and private parties and particular congregations were allowed to remove images discreetly.

From 1524 through 1525, Zurich saw considerable tension between those who wanted measured reform for the sake of piety and peace and those who thought the evangelical principle of Scripture as the norm in worship ought to be taken seriously, even if it meant a clear break with Rome. The slow reform of the mass was contended, as was paying tithes and the issue of images. A vocal minority of Zwingli's followers and friends comprised these radicals and met regularly to discuss new religious ideas. The question of baptizing infants was

raised and challenged on scriptural grounds. By August 1524, local citizens began to refuse to have their children baptized, and the practice
spread in Zurich and into neighboring towns such as Zollikon, where
the batismal font was broken. In January 1525 the council ordered all
unbaptized children to be baptized, all secret religious meetings to
stop, and the Zollikon church font fixed.

What happened next is well known. On January 21, 1525, a group
of evangelicals dissatisfied with Zwingli and the town council met at
the home of Felix Mantz. Conrad Grebel, who had studied at Vienna
and Basel and who had known Zwingli at Basel, was there. After
prayers, George Blaurock asked Grebel to baptize him, which Grebel
did. Blaurock then baptized fifteen more adult confessors. This simple
practice of religious devotion and political defiance soon spread
throughout the greater Zurich area, and by the first half of 1525 this
"baptist" teaching had spread through a large number of Swiss towns.
The religious and political practice of adult baptism continued to spark
controversy, and by March 1526 the Zurich council forbad rebaptism
on penalty of death by drowning. Within a year Felix Mantz, with
hands bound, was lowered from a boat into the icy January waters of
the Limmat River and was drowned.

With the challenge of the Zurich radicals for a fuller and speedier
Reformation in Zurich and the spreading religious and political influence of this baptism movement, Zwingli was forced to think carefully
about baptism.[6] In the early period, through 1524 and prior to the controversy with the so-called Anabaptists, Zwingli's idea of covenant
remained fairly constant. There was a basic discontinuity between the
old and new covenants. Zwingli argued from the lesser to the greater:
the one temporal and of law, ordinances, and animal blood; the other
eternal and of gospel, freedom, and the atonement of Christ. Lying
behind both covenants was God's pledge to humanity, ultimately confirmed and grounded in Christ. Through this covenant was eternal
access to God and the remission of sins.[7] One change in Zwingli's
thought did begin during this first, pre-Anabaptist period. In his *Proposal concerning Images and the Mass*, Zwingli added the idea that the
sacrament was not only God's covenant toward humanity but also the
believer's pledge and confession toward fellow believers. The believers remembered with one another and renewed one another, thus
becoming one.[8]

Zwingli's emphasis on the believer's pledge intensified in the
period after he wrote the *Proposal*. Within the year the issue of baptism,
infant baptism, and rebaptism appeared in Zurich, and Zwingli wrote
a number of important works on the subject, among them his *Commentary on the True and False Religion* and his *Baptism, Rebaptism and the
Baptism of Infants*.[9] During this period Zwingli asserted even more

strongly that the sacraments were human covenants that pledged a life of obedience to Christ.[10] Infant baptism was also a pledge sign (*pflichtzeichen*), since it was the parallel to circumcision by which the children of Abraham were to be raised in the covenant (*pundt*) of the one true God.[11] Zwingli did not, however, lose the christological pole of the covenant, since Christ was still described as the "pledge of God's grace."[12] In short, responding to the Anabaptist movement, which Zwingli believed elevated the believer's subjective experience above the objective Word, Zwingli emphasized baptism as a confessional pledge. Zwingli meant, however, not a pledge from the subjective standpoint of a person's faith. Instead, baptism was an objective sign of membership in the Christian community that found fulfillment in God's blessings and promises. Especially troublesome to Zwingli was seeing rebaptism as the entire sum of faith rather than an objective pledge dedicating one to leading a life of discipleship according to God's objective Word.[13]

From 1525 through 1527, Zwingli made his fullest defense of infant baptism and developed the idea of covenant unity.[14] Beginning with his *Commentary on Genesis*,[15] which developed from the *Prophezei* lectures,[16] Zwingli emphasized the unity of God's covenant, given to Abraham and continued through the Christian dispensation. In his *Essay on the Eucharist*, for example, Zwingli described God's covenant to Abraham as the true covenant. Further, just as circumcision was the sign of the old covenant, so baptism marked the new covenant.[17]

Zwingli's *Reply to Balthasar Hubmaier's Baptism Book* continually emphasizes the covenant as God's gracious promises toward humanity, which comprise the whole of salvation.[18] Replying to Hubmaier, Zwingli argued at length that Christian children were God's children, just as the children of the old covenant were God's children.[19] He concluded this argument with the simple deduction that as the sign of the old covenant, circumcision, was given to Israelite children, so the sign of the new covenant, baptism, ought to be given to Christian children.[20] Significant for Zwingli was grounding this argument in the concept of covenant unity from old into new. Not only were Christian children "equally in the testament, church or covenant (*pundt*) as were Israelite children, but the covenant itself was a "covenant of grace" (*gnädigen pundt*).[21]

Zwingli's *Refutation of the Tricks of the Anabaptists* was his crowning work against the Anabaptists. There he provided a theological basis for baptism and infant baptism within the idea of covenant. Zwingli emphasized the one covenant as God's "testament of promise."[22] Addressing the Anabaptists, Zwingli said that his grounding for infant baptism had been the same since he wrote his reply to Hubmaier two years earlier (1525). "Don't you read in that book," Zwingli began, that infant baptism was based on: (1) Christian children being children of God just as Israelite children were God's children. Therefore, who would forbid baptism? (2) As far as circumcision was sacramental (*quod ad rationem sacramentalem adtinet*), it was the same as baptism, and as children received circumcision, so they ought to receive baptism.[23] Underlying this argument was the idea of a single, unified covenant that God had first made with the fallen Adam.[24] This covenant was renewed with Noah and then with Abraham, when the content of the covenant was made even clearer.[25] This covenant then embraced the Israelites, who were "God's people with whom he entered into covenant . . . and gave a sign of his covenant" (*foederis sui signum*). They were God's "people and were of his church" (*de populo eius, de ecclesia eius essent*).[26] Zwingli then concluded this historical narrative by saying that God had entered into the same covenant with us, "that we may be one people with them [i.e., the Israelites], one church, and also may have one covenant."[27]

In sum, from 1524 to 1525, Zwingli emphasized the idea of the human response by talking about baptism as the human covenant with God. His attempt was to move the growing Anabaptist discussion away from the subjective confession of a so-called believer to the objective pledge to join the Christian community and to live by, and raise children by, God's objective Word.[28] By 1525 it became clear to Zwingli that to defend his position on baptism and infant baptism against the Anabaptist arguments, he needed to speak about the nature of baptism itself, not about the believer's (even objective) pledge in baptism.[29] Therefore he spoke strongly about covenant unity and continuity. The grace of God offered was offered in the sign of the one eternal covenant, regardless of the sign itself.[30] This shift was not, as some Catholic scholars have suggested, a shift from a pledge sign to a more sacramental view of the baptismal sign[31] but the attempt to ground baptism in God's grace rather than in the human response given in baptism.[32]

MARTIN LUTHER

Martin Luther was born November 10, 1483, in Eisleben and grew up a few miles away in Mansfield, where his family moved during his first year.[33] There his father mined copper and soon managed his own mine, later owning several mines and becoming a leading citizen of Mansfield. The desire for upward mobility by the parents was passed to the children, who were raised with love, discipline, and an eye to the future.

In keeping with his father's entrepreneurial spirit and his maternal lineage of means and education, Luther was destined for a lawyer's degree from the University of Erfurt. At Erfurt, Luther matriculated with a bachelor's and a master's of arts by 1505 and was ostensibly on his way to becoming a lawyer. After an atypical encounter with a thunderstorm near the village of Stotternheim, on his way back to Erfurt for his law studies, Luther had a typical reaction for a person of his time: "Help me St. Anne. I will become a monk." St. Anne was the patron of miners and those threatened by storms; devotion to Anne was already widespread in Germany; and Luther reacted as people of that age did.

At Erfurt, Luther decided to become an Observant Augustinian friar. His study and spiritual growth progressed sufficiently, and at the occasion of his first mass in 1507, Luther's father attended with friends. His father made a generous gift to the monastery. Luther continued his education at Erfurt, where he also worked on behalf of his monastery, and he received his doctorate in 1512. Soon thereafter, the vicar general of Luther's order, Johann von Staupitz, who had become overwhelmed by his many and varied duties, handed over to Luther his chair in biblical theology at the University of Wittenberg. In the ensuing decade, Luther would lecture on the Psalms twice (1513–15 and 1518–21), as well as on Romans (1515–16), Galatians (1516–17), and Hebrews (1517–18). Sometime during this period Luther had his "breakthrough"—his move to a new evangelical perspective rooted in, and growing from, his own late medieval formation. Scholars now understand this breakthrough to be a process more than a single moment. Debate continues, however, over what "insight" marked the culmination of this process, and thus the search for a breakthrough date continues.[34]

Regardless of the precise dating of Luther's breakthrough, the complex political, cultural, ecclesial, and theological event known as the Protestant Reformation publicly began with the 1517 indulgence peddling in Germany by the Dominican John Tetzel. In Luther's ensuing debates with Cardinal Cajetan in Augsburg (1518) and especially with Johann Eck in Leipzig (1519), Luther came to regard faith (trusting God) and Scripture as the two reforming principles for the church. And Luther indeed worked on reform. Between 1518 and 1520, the curriculum at Wittenburg was revamped according to scriptural and humanist guidelines.[35] Luther also began what would be the greatest literary output of the sixteenth century.

One of Luther's most productive and influential literary years was 1520. Among his important works that year were his *Sermon on Good Works, To the Christian Nobility of the German Nation, On the Freedom of a Christian,* and *The Babylonian Captivity of the Church.* The *Babylonian Captivity* struck at the very sacramentality of the late medieval church by arguing that sacraments were signs to which adhered divine promises of grace. The medieval church, with its sacramental system and perspectives on grace and faith, had been carried into exile not by the Babylonians but by the papacy, which exercised sacramental abuse.[36]

The theme throughout *The Babylonian Captivity of the Church* was the *proper appropriation* of the sacraments. Luther began by discussing the Lord's Supper, and he insisted:

> Where there is a divine promise, there every one must stand on their own; their own personal faith is demanded, all will account for themselves, and bear their own load, as it is said in the last chapter of Mark, "He who believes and is baptized will be saved; but he who does not believe will be condemned." Thus from the mass each one is able to benefit personally only by their own faith.[37]

Concerning baptism, Luther said:

> Baptism never becomes ineffective, unless despairing you refuse to return to its salvation. Indeed you can wander away from the sign for a time, but the sign is not on that account ineffective. Thus, you have been sacramentally baptized once but you ought to be baptized by faith continually, continually to die and continually to live.[38]

So also, throughout the discussions of ordination, confirmation, penance, marriage, and extreme unction, Luther explained how one appropriated the sacraments by appropriating the gospel promise contained therein. "All sacraments," asserted Luther, "were instituted to feed faith."[39]

In the *Babylonian Captivity*, Luther argued that the correct sacramental structure ought to be divine promise, attached to the outward sign, which was trusted by the one receiving the sacrament. On the one hand, the significance of the sacrament had become God's direct word-of-promise (*Verheißungswort*). On the other hand, this meant that faith was properly trusting God rather than believing certain sacramental ideas.[40] Naturally, then, when Luther wrote his Small Catechism (1529), he carefully distinguished all these issues. In the second section on baptism, Luther discussed the effect of baptism; then, in the third section, he said:

> It is not the water that produces these effects, but the Word of God connected with the water, and our faith which relies on the Word of God connected with the water. For without the Word of God the water is merely water and no Baptism.[41]

Luther followed this section with a fourth and final section in which he described the significance of baptism as drowning the old Adam every day, so that every day the new person arose, "cleansed and righteous," to live in God's presence.

In a similar manner, though in more detail, Luther described these aspects of baptism in his Large Catechism. Quoting Augustine, Luther said that "the Word is added to the water or natural element and makes it a sacrament."[42] Only faith, therefore, could appropriate the Word that attached to the water, and the faithful reception of the Word brought with it the benefits of baptism.[43]

The triad of divine promise–sign–faith became Luther's classic sacramental structure and influenced almost all Reformation sacramental theology, that of the Lutheran churches and that of the Reformed churches. Chapter 1 gave an analysis of Luther's 1526 baptismal rite and his famous and influential Flood Prayer. There is now sufficient context to see exactly how clearly this rite and prayer reflected Luther's baptismal theology. Through their structure and content, both the rite and the prayer show the central datum of Christian life to be standing before the God of grace, choosing for life or for death. Here Heiko Oberman's comment seems apt:

> It is crucial to realize that Luther became a Reformer who was widely heard and understood by transforming the abstract question of a just God into an *existential quest* that concerned the *whole* human being, encompassing thought and action, soul and body, love and suffering.[44]

But if baptism was the outward sign of the divine promise of grace attached to the sign, so that baptism had effect only when faith grasped the promise of grace inhering to the sign, what about the baptism of infants? Luther's position on infant faith can be divided into three periods.[45]

From 1518 through 1520, Luther maintained an idea long prevalent in the medieval church. A child was baptized into "the faith of others" (*fides aliena*), which meant the faith of the church and the faith of the child's parents. Such faith was sufficient to warrant the administration of baptism but not to account for the future faith of the child itself. As the Anabaptist challenge was heard through the mid-1520s, Luther's position on baptism began to develop.

From 1525 through 1526, Luther began to speak of infants having their own faith and being baptized into such faith. The story of John the Baptist, for example, proved that infants could have faith because John "leaped in his mother's womb" on Elizabeth hearing the greeting by Mary. Although the infant could itself have faith, the faith of the parents and that of the church helped develop the faith of the child.

Beginning in 1528 and 1529, Luther developed his primary defense of infant baptism. Without repudiating his earlier positions on infant faith, Luther appealed instead to infant baptism as grounded on God's gracious promise attached to the sign and God's command to baptism with that sign. Luther denied that one should baptize because of the faith of the baptismal candidate. Such was Luther's basic position in the Large Catechism and especially in *Concerning Rebaptism* (1530), after he saw that radical reformers such as the Anabaptists took the demand for faith and declared that there was no sacrament without faith.[46] Those baptized as infants, they argued, received no baptism at all, and they needed to be baptized when they did profess their faith.

In *Concerning Rebaptism*, Luther argued that the mistake the Anabaptists made was to ground baptism in human faith. That one should have faith was indeed true, but to ground baptism in the presence of human faith was to commit a grave error. First, said Luther, baptism was God's activity. Our faith may come and go, but God's promise and command to baptize always remain. Baptism was still baptism, even if it was incorrectly received, because our impropriety could not negate God's work any more than bad faith by the Israelites could negate the covenant.[47] "Abuse does not take away the substance," said Luther following a scholastic dictum; "rather it establishes the substance."[48]

Second, Luther argued that faith itself cannot be proved. "Have now they become gods," Luther challenged the Anabaptists, "that they can see in people's hearts whether they believe or not?" Receiving someone's confession, Luther said, is "neither here nor there" because

> [t]he text does not say "Whoever confesses," but "Whoever believes." To have someone's confession is not to know their faith. . . . Therefore, whoever grounds baptism in the faith of the one to be baptized, can never baptize anyone. Even if you baptized a person a hundred times a day, in no way would you know whether he or she believes.[49]

Lorenz Grönvik has given a helpful analysis of Luther's baptismal theology in dialogue with his varied opponents. Grönvik has shown that, for Luther, the divine word of promise *(Verheißungswort)* and human faith were intimately connected in his baptismal thinking, and the promise, as God's promise, was also bound to the institutional sign of the promise. There was, therefore, a double aspect to Luther's baptismal theology: The sign was one aspect, and the human faith that grasped the promise offered through the sign was the other aspect.[50]

Luther always retained this double aspect, even though the question he faced varied. The theme in the *Babylonian Captivity* (1520) was the right use of the baptismal promise throughout one's life. Thus Luther discussed confession, penance, and monastic vows as a second baptism. Five years later, after challenges from Thomas Müntzer, Andreas Carlstadt, the Zwickau prophets, and Zwingli, the question shifted from the right use of baptism at the nature of baptism itself. In neither period did Luther hold to one aspect of baptism at the expense of the other. In the *Babylonian Captivity*, Luther held to the faith-promise relationship without denying the sign; and the later Luther did not hold to the exterior sign at the expense of overlooking the faith-promise relationship in the sacrament. This double aspect, which Luther carefully maintained, can be clearly seen in the Large Catechism, where both aspects receive attention. There is, therefore, no essential change between the *Babylonian Captivity* (1520) and the Large Catechism (1529), even though the writings after 1520 emphasized the exterior sign much more because of the questions Luther addressed.[51]

In short, where in 1520 the question with Rome was how rightly to *appropriate* baptism, the question Luther answered in 1527, conversing with the Anabaptists, concerned the *nature* of baptism itself. Whereas earlier Luther emphasized *faith* in God's promise, represented by the sign (e.g., *The Babylonian Captivity*), later he emphasized the *sign itself* as the bearer of God's immutable promise (e.g., *Concerning Rebaptism*).[52]

MARTIN BUCER

In 1491, Martin Bucer was born in the city of Sélestat (Schlettstadt), in the Alsace, to a working-poor family.[53] He joined the Dominican order, seeking to continue the education he had begun in the town's Latin school. Bucer's studies at the University of Heidelberg furthered his interest in both theology and humanism. He attended the famous 1518 Disputation there and also found himself agreeing with Luther. After his Heidelberg education, Bucer was laicized, became a secular priest, and got married. When his Reformation efforts at Wissembourg resulted in his excommunication, he migrated in 1523 to Strasbourg, where his father had moved many years before.

Within a year, Bucer had been appointed pastor of the church of St. Aurelien, and for the remainder of the decade he worked to advance the Reformation in Strasbourg. By the 1530s he was active in theological discussions and political advising throughout the continent. His labors in Strasbourg focused on the organization and discipline of the Strasbourg church. By the 1540s, Bucer was one of the leading Protestant theologians and statesmen, with far-ranging theological and political influence. When, in 1549, the military power of Charles V forced the Augsburg Interim on Strasbourg, Bucer left for England. There his mediating temperament and approach to theology fit well with the reform efforts of Thomas Cranmer and Nicholas Ridley. Bucer was made professor of theology at Cambridge. He worked on the *Book of Common Prayer,* and he wrote *On the Kingdom of Christ*, which outlined a process for theological and social reform according to the gospel.

In a curious way, the religious and political location of Strasbourg was not unlike Bucer's own theological efforts: a generally mediating position between Zwingli and Switzerland to the south and Luther and the region of Germany to the north. The secondary literature on Bucer that appeared in the "Bucer renaissance" during the second half of the twentieth century typically praised his theological approach as mediating, pragmatic, irenic, aimed at the edification of the church, and oriented toward a true ecumenical and catholic church.[54] More recently, Greschat has argued that Bucer's ecclesial and theological projects were grounded in a dialogical approach. Theological insight, for the benefit of theology, ethics, and church and civil society, happened within communities where people stood in mutual support, challenge, and conversation.[55]

When the young Bucer came to Strasbourg, his theological skills for dialogue and community edification were quickly used on behalf of the new evangelical faith.[56] Although Bucer had entered the city only in May 1523, by late December 1524 he published his *Grund und Ursach*. Dedicated to Count Frederick of the Palatinate, this document had several purposes, among them giving the justification and reason (*Grund und Ursach*) for the evangelical reforms in Strasbourg. At the end of the document were the signatures of the leading Strasbourg Reformers, including the renowned humanist and Hebraist Wolfgang Capito (1478–1531), his student and continual colleague Caspar Hedio (1494–1552), and the popular preacher Matthias Zell (1477–1548).

The baptism material in the *Grund und Ursach* shows the same concern for correct appropriation of the sacrament that we have seen in the early baptism writings of both Luther and Zwingli.[57] Baptism as such did not produce salvation, and children were not to be baptized because the "chrism, oil, salt, bread, candles and consecrated water" would save them. Such late medieval superstition only insulted the sacrifice of Christ, which was the source of all sanctification.[58] Children were to be baptized because they already possessed the covenant,[59] and because children were beloved by God and Christ.[60] Baptism had effect on salvation only through the Spirit and human faith.[61]

By the 1530s, Bucer began to emphasize the grounds for baptism's sacramental validity rather than baptism's effect through the Spirit and human faith. In 1530, Bucer and Capito composed a confession of faith for the cities of Strasbourg, Constance, Memmingen, and Lindau that was to be presented at the Diet of Augsburg that same year. The Tetrapolitan Confession attempted a compromise between Lutheran and Zwinglian positions on sacramental presence in the Lord's Supper, in the end satisfying neither side on this issue. More broadly, the confession took up a classical Augustinian position on the validity of the sacraments.[62] The sacraments were "visible signs of invisible grace, as Augustine says."[63] As such, baptism could indeed save because it was the sign of God's saving covenant, made with Abraham, extending through his seed, and including within that covenant all the people of God from Moses through Christian infants.[64] Likewise, in his *Apology*, Bucer said with Augustine that the same gospel offered in words was also visibly offered through the signs.[65] When Bucer no longer needed to address the issue of proper appropriation and discuss what the sacrament did not do, he stood with the long tradition of sacramental validity and asserted that divine grace inhered to the external sign.

Three years later, Bucer continued the same arguments in his pamphlet *On Infant Baptism*, which was written as a defense for infant baptism.[66] Bucer's theological opponent was Bernard Rothmann, whom Bucer had never met but whose theological gifts Bucer respected. Rothmann had ties to the Strasbourg Anabaptist community, as well as to Caspar Schwenkfeld, who was still residing there. When Rothmann raised the question about infant baptism so acutely in Münster that all the churches were closed, save the one in which Rothmann preached, Bucer intervened with his baptism tract that was addressed to the city of Münster—Rothmann was left unnamed.[67] Bucer asserted that "our regeneration and our renewal through the Holy Spirit are offered and showed us, revealed through words and washing in water."[68] This was so because baptism itself "is a sign of the promise of divine good-will" that was offered in the covenant to Abraham (Genesis 17) and his seed, now including the church (Genesis 3) and its children.[69]

Bucer realized that his short essay to Münster was inadequate to address the questions raised there, and from the start he intended a more detailed reply about baptism and the sacraments. In 1534 he published his *Account from Holy Scripture* to provide the more detailed reply that was needed in Münster.[70] There he explicitly connected the covenant of grace and its sign of circumcision (Genesis 17) with Christian baptism: Circumcision meant dying to sin, as did baptism, and by both one entered into the covenant of grace already given by God.[71]

Soon the pastors in Strasbourg wanted to regularize the teachings of the new faith, both for community formation and as defense against Anabaptist inroads. In 1534, Bucer published his first catechism, which stood in a decade-long tradition of catechetical interest for Strasbourg.[72] In his catechism, Bucer again asserted the validity of the sacraments and baptism. The opening question on the sacraments ("Why are they called sacraments?") elicited the response: "*In and with* these visible signs God delivers and gives over his invisible and hidden grace, and the redemption in Christ." Just a bit further came the question "How can the water and outer word, with which baptism is administered, renew with the Holy Spirit, incorporate into Christ, clothe with Christ, and make participation in his death?" To this the child answered:

> Our Lord Jesus, our high priest and savior, acts and accomplishes everything through his Holy Spirit. He uses for this work the service of the ministry of the church, in outer words and signs. Thus they are called sacraments and *mysteria*, holy secrets: while one thing happens inwardly through the power of Christ, another thing appears and happens outwardly in the ministry of the church.[73]

By the middle of the decade, Bucer had come to a more or less consistent position on baptism that then showed little change for the rest of Bucer's career.[74] The exterior sign of baptism, administered by the pastor, indicated the interior gracious activity accomplished by God through the Spirit. The faith of the one being baptized was needed for the sacrament to have efficacy—this was Bucer's emphasis during the 1520s. But the sacrament remained a means of grace, not dependent on human faith for its validity, since it signified God's steadfast promise of grace—this was Bucer's argument against the Anabaptists and spiritualists during the 1530s. The divine promise came as the covenant promise offered to Abraham and his seed (Genesis 17). It included those in the new dispensation whose children were to receive the covenant sign (baptism) just as the child of the old dispensation received the covenant sign (circumcision).

The question of election in Bucer's thought deserves a brief comment as it relates to baptism. W. P. Stephens devotes long attention to the topic of predestination in Bucer's thought, asserting from the start:

> The doctrine of predestination or election is one that shapes the whole of Bucer's theology. Even where it is not expressed explicitly, its stamp is to be found. The centrality of this doctrine and the way Bucer interprets it distinguish him from Luther on the one hand, and from his catholic and radical opponents on the other.[75]

It would not appear that Stephens makes the case that predestination "shapes the whole" of Bucer's theology and so is "central" to his thought. There are indeed many references to predestination throughout the course of Bucer's writings, and Stephens can show that, for Bucer, predestination secured not only the divine gift of grace but also human sanctification unto the glory of God. But how did predestination *shape* Christology, ecclesiology, sacraments, baptism, and the connection between the church and the civic realm? These questions remain unanswered by Stephens.

Again, Johannes Müller, in his discussion of Bucer's scriptural hermeneutic, devotes a chapter to the importance and presence of the doctrine of predestination lying behind Bucer's approach.[76] He shows that, for Bucer, proper scriptural understanding came from the inner gift of the Spirit and thus to those who were elect. This inner, pneumatic enlightenment of the meaning of Scripture made for the renewed self, and thus predestination undergirded this part of the sanctification process. Müller, however, does not make the sweeping claims that Stephens makes about predestination in Bucer's thought.

In sum, the work on predestination in Bucer's thought indicates its *religious* importance for the Christian life: Predestination grounds the beginning and end of Christian life and helps nurture its spiritual growth.[77] How far Bucer integrated predestination *theologically* as an organizing principle for Christ, church, and sacraments is another issue. Such work was yet to come in the Reformed tradition.

SUMMARY

In the course of this chapter, the baptismal theologies of Zwingli, Luther, and Bucer became clear in specific contexts. To anticipate future discussion, a key problem for these Reformers was to find a consistent theology of baptism that distinguished itself from both Roman Catholic and Anabaptist positions and yet could credit insights from both positions. In different ways, all three Reformers distinguished the institutional sign of God's grace from the subjective appropriation of the grace signified by the sign. The distinction made by Augustine between the validity of a sacrament and its efficacy proved important. Second, covenant baptismal theology became central to both Zwingli and Bucer. Covenant baptismal theology would be given even more attention by Henrich Bullinger and John Calvin, as would also the issues of covenant and election as they related to baptism. The next two chapters study the baptismal thought of two second-generation Reformers, Bullinger and Calvin. Chapter 2 discusses issues of covenant, election, and baptism in the thought of both Reformers, and chapter 3 then looks at these issues as they arose later in Calvin's ministry and produced unresolved tensions in his theology.

2

THE SECOND GENERATION:
BULLINGER AND CALVIN

Chapter 1 examined the baptismal theology of Zwingli, Luther, and Bucer, first-generation Reformers whose work influenced those Reformers who succeeded them. Several lessons were gained. First, in baptismal debates both with Rome and with the Anabaptists, it was important to distinguish between the validity of a sacrament and its efficacy, between its right administration and its usefulness for Christian life.

Second, historical context was crucial for sorting out exactly what the Reformers were saying. For instance, it was important to see in the 1520 *Babylonian Captivity* that Luther argued with Rome about the conditions under which sacraments had their effect. By 1530, Luther had discussed with the Anabaptists and other radical reformers what made a sacrament valid. Analogous discussions about efficacy and validity were seen in the baptismal theology of both Zwingli and Bucer.

Third, we saw two distinct but not incompatible ways of doing sacramental theology, and particularly baptismal theology. Luther preferred a sign-promise theology in which the divine promise of forgiveness inhered to the outward sign. Zwingli and Bucer, who had much firsthand contact with Anabaptists, preferred a covenant baptismal theology: As it was for the children of the old covenant, so too with the children of the new.

Fourth, there was discussion about the place of human responsibility in the sacraments and therefore in the definition of the sacraments. What role did faithful reception, or at the least publicly loyal reception, play in the sacrament?

This chapter turns to two key second-generation Reformers who stood at the headwaters of the Reformed tradition along with Zwingli and Bucer. The first section studies the baptismal thought of Heinrich Bullinger (1504–75), and the second section studies baptism in the theology of John Calvin (1509–64).

HEINRICH BULLINGER

Heinrich Bullinger was the youngest of five sons born to Heinrich Bullinger, a priest in Bremgarten (just west of Zurich), and Anna

Wiederkehr, the daughter of Bremgarten's miller.[1] He studied at the University of Cologne, where he received both bachelor's (1519) and master's (1522) degrees. While there he developed an interest in theology and read both Luther and Philip Melanchthon, as well as the early church fathers. By the time of graduation he had a new understanding of justification by faith. The year after attaining his master of arts degree, he took a job in Kappel as the head teacher at a Cistercian monastery, where he taught New Testament. Within two years the monastery had abolished the mass, and in 1526 the Lord's Supper was celebrated in a Reformed manner.

Bullinger went to Zurich in 1523, where he met Zwingli. The two shared ideas and found enough commonality that this meeting started a partnership that would last until Zwingli's death in 1531. Bullinger attended the first Zurich disputation in 1525, and he clerked for the second and third Zurich disputations.

After the Catholic forces defeated the Swiss at Kappel in October 1531, Bullinger and his family fled from Bremgarten (Aargau) where he was pastor, arriving in Zurich in November. Within a month he became head of the Zurich church and set about stabilizing and revitalizing a city that had been devastated by the losses at Kappel. For the next four decades, Bullinger oversaw the religious and theological life of the city of Zurich, acting as its head pastor and theologian.

Bullinger scholarship over the last forty years has come to appreciate the theological differences between Bullinger and Zwingli and the theological insights of Bullinger himself.[2] Scholars have rehabilitated Bullinger from the status of "Zwingli's successor," and some have argued that Bullinger stood at the headwaters of Reformed covenant theology.[3]

Sacraments and Baptism

In Bullinger's thought, covenant is closely tied to both baptism and predestination, and to begin discussion of one topic is to entail discussion of the other two. Perhaps the best place to begin is by giving Bullinger's definition of a sacrament and of baptism.[4] In his 1559 *Catechesis*, Bullinger asserted that a sacrament

> is a sacred symbol, or a holy rite, or a sacred action, instituted by God through words, signs, and things, by which he retains in the memory of the church his greatest blessings, and he continually renews them. By these he also seals and represents what he executes for us and what he in turn requires from us.[5]

The sacrament represented and sealed on us what God did on our behalf. At the same time it indicated for us what our duties were in response to the divine activity. Bullinger's definition of baptism fit within this scheme, and it remained constant from his earliest writings to those at the end of his career. For example, in a letter to Heinrich Simler of Bern, now dated between November 5 and December 10, 1525,[6] Bullinger concluded by saying:

> Now my dearest Heinrich, from both testaments you have heard about the true grounding for baptism: how humankind has a covenant with God, in which the high God gives himself a duty towards us miserable people to be our highest good, our fullness and sufficiency; and he therefore wants to gift us with his Son for a firm foundation, who had to seal with his blood the testament or covenant for the young and the old; and how this testament has no difference, but that for us Christ fulfilled that which was promised to them; and also that this covenant was made with a new people and all blood was stopped (*gestellen*) . . . as circumcision at first bound us to God from the cradle onward, so also baptism binds us by the power of the God who accepts us by grace through his Son.[7]

Here are themes that repeated throughout Bullinger's career. There was a continuity of covenant from old to new, whose character was that of divine grace, promised and fulfilled in Christ. The covenant sign of circumcision was carried over into the nonbloody sign of baptism, and both signs were to be given to those infants born into the covenant.

In the article on the sacraments (art. 8) in his *Summa* of 1556,[8] Bullinger again called sacraments "holy actions" (*heilige actione*) that reminded us of our covenant and thus reminded us of the two sides of the covenant: the salvation offered us and our duty to God.[9] In the baptism section of his 1559 catechism, Bullinger said that Christian infants ought to receive baptism as the sign of their adoption into God's family just as the "children of old" received circumcision to mark their membership "in the eternal covenant of God."[10] In his 1561 treatise *Against the Anabaptists*, Bullinger dwelled on the theme of covenant unity, with the covenant sign changing from circumcision to baptism.[11] There was one eternal covenant from Abraham (Genesis 17) through Christ. The sign of the covenant in the new age passed from John the Baptist through Christ to the church.[12] And so Bullinger asserted in his Second Helvetic Confession, written in 1561 and published in 1566, that "to be baptized in Christ's name is to be enrolled, entered, and received into the covenant, and family, and thus into the inheritance, of God's children."[13]

Covenant, Predestination, and Baptism

Bullinger's otherwise straightforward teaching on baptism becomes more complicated, perhaps supple, when considered in the context of his idea of covenant. Among the intriguing aspects of covenant is Bullinger's assertion that the covenant began with Adam. In his letter to Semler, Bullinger began by asserting that out of divine mercy God made a covenant that began with Adam, then continued on with Noah, Enoch, and Abraham, followed by Isaac, Jacob, Moses, Joshua, Gideon, Samuel, David, Solomon, Josiah, Hezekiah, and Judas Maccabee.[14] In the same letter, Bullinger said to Semler that "when a child is young and lying in the cradle, it is not disinherited; but it is disinherited if, upon growing up, it acts against the will of the father which was expressed in the written will."[15]

These ideas suggest a universalism to Bullinger's concept of the covenant, at least in this restricted meaning: God is disposed kindly toward all humankind, wanting their salvation and thus wanting them to take up responsibly their side of the divine-human relationship.[16] If we look at the human responsibility to the covenant, Bullinger noted that what was required of anyone was to follow God's commandments, love one's neighbor, and delight lifelong in the duties that went with being a person of the covenant.[17] In short,

> [b]aptism was the sign of belonging to God's people and a seal of justification. Having accepted this covenant sign, the individual was obligated to love and trust God through faith in Christ and to love and serve his neighbor. These were the human conditions of the covenant, and if the individual met them he was one of the elect. Election was a positive matter of inclusion and assurance.[18]

We can easily understand why the Dutch Arminians appealed so often to the work of Bullinger. The Arminians were followers of the Calvinism offered by Jacob Arminius, who was professor at the University of Leiden from 1603 until his death in 1609. They rejected the ideas of complete divine omnipotence, absolute divine election to salvation or reprobation, and the atonement of Christ as effective only for the elect. Arminian Calvinists argued instead that Christ died for all, and that God's prevenient grace was sufficient for sinners to turn to Christ, although human free will could resist such grace and reject Christ. In Bullinger's theology they heard the clear overtone of a single gracious covenant, embracing all people, which when taken upon oneself made effective the salvation offered in that covenant.

At the same time, Bullinger clearly asserted that God had predestined some unto election,[19] and at times Bullinger even sounded double predestinarian: "God's election, by which God indeed elected some for life and some for death, is eternal."[20] No wonder then that some defenders of the Synod of Dort (1618–1619) also appealed to Bullinger. The Synod of Dort explicitly rejected Arminian Calvinism. It upheld ideas such as divine double predestination, divine grace as irresistible, and Christ's atonement as effective only for the elect. Although the issues go beyond the scope of this study, some points seem clear.[21]

On the one hand, Bullinger argued for a single predestinarian view of God's election. Out of God's free mercy, God chose to save some. Bullinger thought that this secured the idea of *sola gratia*—God's grace was given in absolute freedom. He also thought that Scripture supported this view. On the other hand, pragmatically speaking in the life of the church, as men and women work out their lives during the course of human history, covenant functions far more to the side of the universalism described above. God's covenant embraced all people; those who accepted the divine offer of salvation then took upon themselves the duties of the covenant and so rightly were counted among the elect.[22]

Baptism thus meant taking upon oneself, in personal responsibility, the covenant already embracing humankind, so that while from the human side baptism entered us into the covenant, from the divine side we were already included in that covenant.

JOHN CALVIN

John Calvin was born July 10, 1509, in Noyon, France, one of four or five sons born to Gérard and Jeanne Cauvin.[23] Calvin's mother died when he was a young boy, and his father remarried and had two daughters by his second wife. Calvin likely lived his early life and received his early tutoring with the three sons of local nobility, the Montmor family. Since Calvin's father had a position of responsibility within the cathedral chapter, he was able to secure cathedral positions for John and his older brother Charles, which would pay for their education. In 1523, Calvin and the three Montmor boys went to study at the University of Paris.

At the Collège de la Marche, Calvin finished basic liberal arts training, mastering Latin grammar and syntax with great skill. He studied Latin with the renowned Mathurin Cordier, whose piety was that of the *devotio moderna* and whose Latin textbook was used for nearly three hundred years. Cordier ended his career as teacher of Latin at the academy in Geneva at the age of eighty-five. Calvin went on to study at the Collège de Montaigu, which was a school known for its stern discipline and even sterner food. The school had been founded in 1314, had gone through some decline, and was more recently renewed as a center for clerical education and development. The ethos was that of the *devotio moderna* and the spirituality was that of Geert Groote and Thomas à Kempis. By the time of Calvin, however, the original missionary, heartfelt zeal of the school had diminished toward an emphasis on sheer discipline and obligatory formation.[24]

Education at Montaigu was in two divisions: the Faculty of Arts taught the grammar and arts, the Faculty of Theology taught the theology division. Calvin studied in the arts section, where his four-year course of study included "logic, metaphysics, ethics, mathematics, physics, astronomy and psychology." Although he had no formal training in scholastic theology during this period—his first edition of the *Institutes* shows only a cursory knowledge of scholastic authors— the young Calvin was educated in an intellectual and cultural environment that provided late medieval resources from both piety and scholasticism that facilitated his own theological enterprise.[25] While at Paris, Calvin also became conversant with the evangelical humanism of Erasmus and the native French Christian humanism of Jacques Lefèvre and Bishop Briçonnet, who was the spiritual adviser to Marguerite of Navarre (eldest sister of Francis I).[26]

Having completed his bachelor's and master's degrees in the arts course, which of the three advanced studies would Calvin pursue— law, medicine, or theology? His father had always intended John for theology but apparently now thought differently, believing that law was the more stable and financially wise avenue. And so, in 1528, Calvin was sent by his father first to Orléans and then to Bourges to work on a law degree. He studied law between 1528 and 1532, and he received his license in civil law in 1532. While at Bourges, in 1532, Calvin learned Greek from the evangelical German scholar Melchior Wolman. During the same period, Calvin continued his humanist studies and in 1532 published a learned commentary on Seneca's essay *On Clemency*. Calvin saw himself in the tradition of Guillaume Budé, the giant of French humanism. Calvin's book was an academic success and financial failure.

The decisive political event in Calvin's life happened on All Saints' Day in 1533, when Nicholas Cop, a friend of Calvin and the rector of the University of Paris, preached a reforming sermon from the Beatitudes. Cop's sermon echoed ideas from Erasmus. Cop was forced to leave Paris, lest he be arrested, and he fled to Basel. Calvin was implicated—he may have had a hand in writing the sermon—and he was forced to flee also, probably to Noyon. Calvin's travels over the next year are hard to trace. In May 1534 he was in Noyon again, because that was when he renounced his church benefice.[27] In October came the affair of the placards, when posters attacking the mass were tacked up throughout France; arrests and executions followed. Calvin fled to Basel in January 1535.

In the summer of 1536, when the *Institutes* were first published, around the time of his twenty-seventh birthday, Calvin was traveling with his brother and half-sister from Paris to Strasbourg. Staying but a night in Geneva, he was interrupted by Guillaume Farel, the fiery reformer who had led the Genevans to embrace the new evangelical faith. He called down the wrath of God on Calvin should Calvin not stay and lead the city in its reformation. Calvin stayed as pastor and teacher. Soon both Calvin and Farel ran afoul of the Genevan magistrates over church discipline, and they were expelled in April 1538.

Calvin went to Strasbourg while his friend Farel continued to labor in the area around Geneva. In Strasbourg, Calvin found a father figure in Martin Bucer, who influenced him strongly. Calvin also married, and his public vocation found three areas for fulfillment. The first was as a pastor, because the French refugees in Strasbourg needed a minister for their church. Calvin preached and administered the sacraments. For worship Calvin used the Reformed worship services, which had long been available in Strasbourg, and he translated psalms into French meter to be sung. Second, Calvin became a teacher. The famous scholar John Sturm had founded a school at which Calvin was a lecturer in Scripture. Finally, Calvin was a writer for the Protestant church. He completely revised his *Institutes*, now on a completely different model. The 1539 form of the *Institutes* was to be the form that it would carry for the next twenty years.

During his three years in Strasbourg, Calvin was the happiest he would be for his entire life. Then Geneva decided it wanted him back. He refused to go back to that "great abyss," saying, "Rather would I submit to a hundred other deaths." Bucer and other friends prevailed on Calvin, and he returned to Geneva in September 1541. With his first return to the pulpit, Calvin opened the Scripture to the exact chapter and verse where he left off three years prior and began to preach again.

During this second ministry in Geneva, two main areas of conflict occurred in the city's life. First, the people continually objected to the discipline of the ministers. Notes were tacked on church doors. Letters were written to the Geneva councils. Sermons were interrupted by protests. Second was the influx of French refugees into Geneva, which taxed the economy. The Swiss, especially the Genevans, were not known for their political inclusiveness toward foreigners, and they viewed the French as political and economic burdens. Social turmoil continued for fourteen years in Geneva, until a series of events in 1555 led anti-Calvin forces to overestimate their strength and plan a political coup in the city. Calvin's power was too strong, and from that year onward his political life was eased.

Calvin's Theology of Baptism: Through 1536

In these reforming efforts during his ministries in Geneva, Strasbourg, and Geneva again, Calvin thought himself to be a follower of Luther, advancing the theological insights that Luther had seen at the dawn of the Reformation.[28] Not only did Calvin most likely model the 1536 *Institutes* on Luther's Small Catechism,[29] but his early sacramental and baptismal arguments reflected Luther's thought. As we have seen, when Luther wrote *The Babylonian Captivity of the Church* in 1520, he argued that the papacy had carried the Western church into exile through sacramental abuse. As a corrective, Luther emphasized the proper appropriation of the sacraments, which happened when faith grasped the divine promise that the sacramental sign represented.

Chapter 1 noted in detail that Luther's opponents changed during the decade of the 1520s. Whereas in 1520 he contended with Rome over faithful appropriation of the sacraments, by the end of the decade he defended the sacraments against any attempt to base the sacrament on human faith.[30] According to the Anabaptist view, without faith there was no sacrament, and infant baptism was no baptism whatsoever. Responding to this challenge, Luther wrote *Concerning Rebaptism*, in which he insisted that baptism was a *correct sacrament* not because of human faith but because it was a sign of God's promise. The promise of forgiveness stood fast, as did God's command to baptize, and our bad faith could not negate that promise any more than the bad faith of the Israelites negated the covenant that God made at Mount Sinai.[31]

In his 1536 *Institutes*, Calvin began his discussion of the sacraments by asserting:

> It is fitting to first consider what a sacrament is. And it is an external sign, by which the Lord represents and witnesses to us his good will towards us, in order to sustain the weakness of our faith. One can also define it another way by calling it a testimony of God's grace, declared to us by an external symbol. For which reason we also understand that *a sacrament is never without a preceding promise, but rather is joined to it as an appendix* for the purpose of sealing and confirming the promise itself, and, so to speak, for making it more of a witness.[32]

The similarity of this position to Luther's should not surprise us; but Calvin knew another definition of a sacrament, one he likely learned from Zwingli, the other giant of the first-generation Reformers. Calvin summarized this position as follows:

> A sacrament, they say, although it has many meanings among esteemed authors, has only one meaning that agrees with "signs": namely, it signifies that solemn oath which a soldier swears to his commander when he enters the military. Just as new soldiers pledge their faith to the commander by this military sign and publicly declare military service, so by our signs we publicly declare Christ as commander and witness that we serve under his sign.[33]

Calvin questioned this definition by pointing to a subtle distinction that he believed had been missed by those (Zwingli, for example) who put forward the argument.[34] Yet he acknowledged a limited role for this definition:

> The comparisons which they bring forward, we accept; but we do not allow that which is secondary in the sacraments to be established by them as the primary and indeed only meaning to the sacraments. Now this is what is primary—that they should serve our faith before God; after this, that they should witness our confession before others. As for this latter argument, their comparisons are valid.[35]

It is evident why Calvin began his discussion on the sacraments speaking, as did Luther, about God's promise. God's promise, which "serves our faith," was primary, and Calvin saw no need to mention the secondary, public confession of faith that was given when the sacrament was received.

Calvin introduced his section on *baptism* in the 1536 *Institutes* in a way that was quite different from his section on the sacraments: "Baptism was given us by God; first to serve our faith before him; and then to serve our confession before others."[36] That Calvin introduced the secondary meaning of a sacrament in the baptism discussion made sense in light of his overall position. Baptism, with its profession of faith, suited this secondary meaning; and baptism was the context in which Zwingli also applied the meaning. Yet Calvin gave the notion of public appropriation very little attention in 1536. Two of his references were titular in nature,[37] and where Calvin did discuss this idea he devoted little space to it.[38] His far greater concern was to establish baptism as the sign of God's immutable promise. This promise remained steadfast even though our faith might not grasp (*non tenuisse*) the promise God offered.[39] In such a case, even though God's promise was not truly received,

> [s]till we believe that the promise itself did not pass away. In fact, we reckon the other way: that God promises us forgiveness of sins through baptism, and without doubt he will fulfill his promise to all believers. As this promise was offered us in baptism, so let us appropriate it in faith.[40]

This definition corresponded to the needs of the young Calvin, who in 1536 attempted to distinguish the French evangelical party from both the Roman Catholic Church and the more radical reformers, such as the Anabaptists, whom monarchs such as Francis I thought to be seditious.[41] The sign-promise theology that Luther so successfully used in the *Babylonian Captivity* treated a sacrament as God's personal, visible promise of grace, appropriated only through faith. For Calvin, this definition pared away the superstitions, liturgical accretions, and sacramental theology of the late medieval church. At the same time, the sign-promise theology maintained the sacraments as primarily divine actions of grace instituted for the life of the church. Accordingly, Calvin opposed those who would "weaken the force of the sacraments and completely overthrow their use."[42]

The same concern to distinguish the French evangelical party from both Roman Catholicism and more radical movements can be seen in Calvin's ecclesial discussions.[43] In the 1536 *Institutes* the predominant idea of the church was that of the entire company of believers elected by God. In accord with Bucer and Luther, as well as Augustine, Calvin wrote in his dedicatory letter that the church existed from Christ's hand, transcending time and space, and was able to exist without visible appearance.[44] The true church thus was not coterminous with the historically evolved, late medieval church, despite Catholic claims as well as Calvin's sly invocation of the great forebears of the medieval church.[45] Furthermore, the outward marks of the true church were the sacraments properly administered and God's Word properly preached and heard.[46] In this way, Calvin's extended discussion of the sacraments and false sacraments (see chapters 3 and 4, below) further distinguished the French evangelical party from the Roman Church. At the same time, the concept of God's election and the 1536 exclusion of discipline as an ultimate mark of the church required Calvin to be modest when he identified the "elect and members of the church" as all those who have proper faith confession, lifestyle, and sacramental participation.[47] Here Calvin criticized the eagerness of those reformers (unidentified) who "overzealously" excluded those who were not truly Christian.[48]

Calvin's Theology of Baptism: 1536–1539

The years from 1536 through 1539 were eventful for Calvin.[49] On May 26, 1536, the citizens of Geneva voted to live "according to the gospel." In August that same year, Farel pressed Calvin into service for the sake of Geneva, as Calvin was detouring through Geneva on his travel from Paris to Strasbourg. Five months later, on January 16, 1537, Calvin and Farel presented to the city council their *Articles on the Organization of the Church and Its Worship at Geneva*. Discipline in morals and faith confession were important parts of the *Articles* because they were believed to be crucial to the life of the church. Those who were lax in morals and those who did not publicly subscribe to the Confession of Faith were to be excommunicated and thus deprived of the Lord's Supper. Calvin and Farel struggled to have this discipline enforced and were opposed by a united front of Libertines, who resented moral enforcement, and Anabaptists, who resented civil interference in church matters. The church discipline controversy, along with various other ecclesial-political struggles, resulted in the expulsion of Calvin and Farel from Geneva shortly after Easter 1538.

By September 1538, Calvin assented to Bucer's request to accept the call as pastor of a French refugee congregation in Strasbourg. Strasbourg had been a haven for Anabaptists, who called the city the "Refuge of Uprightness." Part of Calvin's work was to minister to the French Protestants, many of whom were converting to Anabaptism. In turn, Calvin seems to have had some influence among Anabaptists because they found the church discipline of his French congregation appealing.[50]

As Calvin began his Strasbourg ministry, Martin Bucer and the city of Strasbourg were finishing a decade of ecclesiastical struggle with various radical reformers such as Michael Servetus, Sebastian Franck, and Caspar Schwenckfeld.[51] Among the Anabaptists, the local activities of Pilgram Marpeck, Michael Sattler, and Melchior Hoffmann persistently challenged the Strasbourg church. These reformers modeled the true church on the New Testament notion of gathered believers who entered the church by adult confession and baptism. This true church was obedient to Christ alone, marked by love and mutual aid, and formally disestablished from civil rule.[52] Anabaptists criticized the Strasbourg church for its moral and spiritual laxity, as well as its allegiance to the civil magistrates instead of to Christ alone. Bucer responded by critically examining the external and internal organization of the church. The result was new ecclesiastical ordinances, several catechisms, a system for confirmation of children, and the influential *Von der waren Seelsorge* (1538), which linked doctrine, church discipline, and *diakonia* into a vision of pastoral care and oversight.

It is not surprising that when Calvin finished his revised edition of the *Institutes* in the summer of 1539, he emphasized the appropriation of baptism. He added four references to the sacraments and baptism as public declarations of one's faith before others. Three of these four additions occurred within what later became section 19 of the chapter on sacraments in general. After he argued that ceremonies not founded on God's Word or referring to God's truth deserved no further mention, Calvin went on to describe the nature of true sacraments. First, to the 1536 material that he here reworked Calvin added that sacraments "are marks of declaration by which we publicly swear allegiance to God's name, binding our faith to him in turn."[53] Next, Calvin included a quotation from John Chrysostom about the sacraments[54] and noted that "just as in them, God promises to erase any guilt and punishment incurred by doing wrong, so do we mutually pledge ourselves to piety and innocence by this declaration."[55] Finally, Calvin ended this sacramental section by expanding his 1536 summary, incorporating human response to the definition of a sacrament. Calvin thus acknowledged a Zwinglian idea that he had been critical of only three years earlier. Compare the concluding definitions of a sacrament from the two editions of the *Institutes*:

1536	1539
Thus you can define sacraments of this type to be ceremonies by which the Lord wishes to exercise and confirm the faith of his people.[56]	Thus you can define sacraments of this type to be ceremonies by which the Lord wishes to exercise his people, first, to encourage, inspire, and confirm faith within; *second, to attest to religion in the sight of others.*[57]

Additional evidence indicates that, by 1539, Calvin had become more interested in how we appropriate baptism. During this period, Calvin composed the French infant baptism tract, which became incorporated into the 1539 *Institutes* and later received a separate chapter (4.16) in the 1559 *Institutes*.[58] Infant baptism inherently raised the question of baptismal *appropriation*, with which, by 1539, Calvin was increasingly concerned. Consider also Calvin's *Order for Baptism*.[59] Immediately after questions to the parents and their profession to raise the child properly, the Strasbourg *Order* (1540) followed Farel's *La Maniere* and proclaimed the text from Matthew 19:13–15 ("Let the little children . . ."). Then followed the giving of the child's name and the baptism. This scriptural interlude was omitted when the *Order* appeared in Geneva (1542), appearing instead as a paraphrase within the baptism exhortation that had occurred earlier.[60] A scriptural warrant for infant baptism would be needed where there was strong Anabaptist pressure for adult baptism, but it could well be paraphrased as part of a larger exhortation where the Anabaptist pressure had diminished.[61]

With regard to Calvin's ecclesiology through 1539, it is evident that his sacramental theology contributed in two ways to his emerging ecclesiology. First, Calvin's increasing emphasis on the public appropriation of the sacraments and baptism supported an increasing emphasis on the visible church. In 1539, Calvin followed Augustine and distinguished "belief in the church" from "believing the church." He argued that the latter correctly showed the church to be the means for salvation, while the former attributed salvation to the church and not to God.[62] During this period, Calvin first used the expression "visible church" in a positive sense; he described the church as the "mother" of the faithful through whom one has rebirth and salvation.[63] Calvin also emphasized public ministry and church discipline.[64] Although the discussion of the visible church still lacked polity details, the shifting emphasis from invisible to visible church was clear.[65]

Within Calvin's discussion of baptism, a second, more subtle change in 1539 had implications for his 1543 sacramental theology and ecclesiology. Calvin had begun to argue that whatever benefits were ascribed to baptism—forgiveness, mortification and regeneration, engrafting into Christ—found their meaning in Christ:

> Thus we see that the fulfillment of baptism is in Christ, whom indeed for this reason we call the proper object of baptism. . . . For whatever of God's gifts is offered in baptism, it is obtained in Christ alone.[66]

Calvin now explicitly enclosed his sign-promise theology *within the framework* of God's offer of Christ. To be sure, this only extended the 1536 idea that engrafting in Christ comprehended the two other benefits of baptism, forgiveness and mortification with regeneration. And yet the move to enclose Luther's language of God's promise within the christological framework of God's offer of Christ helped connect more directly the visible church, with its offer of Christ, to the invisible church, comprised of those elected and engrafted in Christ and seen by God alone.

Calvin's Theology of Baptism: 1539–1545

Calvin's increasing emphasis on the public appropriation of baptism culminated with the 1543 *Institutes*. Notice, first, that the human appropriation aspect of the sacraments, which Calvin added to the concluding definition of a sacrament in the 1539 *Institutes*, is now part of the section that begins the entire sacramental discussion. Compare the introductory passages of this section in the earlier editions with that of the 1543 edition of the *Institutes*:

1536 and 1539 *Institutes*	1543 *Institutes*
It is appropriate to consider first what a sacrament is. And it is an external sign, by which the Lord represents and witnesses to us his good will towards us, in order to sustain the weakness of our faith. One can also define it another way by calling it a testimony of God's grace, declared to us by an external symbol. It is certainly acceptable to give another, briefer definition: that it is joined to it as an appendix for the purpose of sealing and confirming the	It is appropriate to consider first what a sacrament is. Now, it seems to me to be a simple and proper definition if we say that it is an external symbol by which the Lord stamps on our consciences the promises of his kindness towards us in order to sustain the feebleness of our faith; *and we, in turn, attest our devotion towards him before people.* For which reason we also understand that a sacrament is never without a preceding promise,

promise itself, and, so to speak, for making it more of a witness.[67]

but rather is to be called a testimony of divine grace towards us, confirmed by an external sign, *with a mutual attesting of our respect towards him.*[68]

As noted earlier, in 1536, Calvin criticized the view that a sacrament was a public declaration, considering this aspect to be secondary in importance. By 1539, Calvin began to place greater emphasis on the public appropriation of a sacrament, but he did not mention it in the introductory remarks on the sacraments. By 1543 he had added sacramental appropriation to the 1536 and 1539 opening definition of a sacrament. When Calvin turned to the opening definition of baptism, he not only emphasized this public appropriation aspect but did so in precisely the concrete terms that were lacking in the 1539 *Institutes*:

1536 and 1539 *Institutes*	1543 *Institutes*
Baptism was given us by God; first to serve our faith before him; and then to serve our confession before others.[69]	*Baptism is the sign of initiation by which we are received into the society of the church, that we might be engrafted in Christ and reckoned among the children of God.* Again, baptism was given us by God for this purpose (which I have taught to be common to all sacraments), first to serve our faith before him; and then to serve our confession before others.[70]

The definition of baptism in the 1536 and 1539 *Institutes* was where Calvin formally credited the idea of public appropriation, which he had borrowed from Zwingli. By 1543 this perspective on baptism had assumed such a prominent position that it was used to begin the baptism definition, thereby pointing to entrance into the visible church. But Calvin also *shifted the expression* of this appropriation aspect to the christological grounding present in 1536 and emphasized in 1539: the notion of engrafting in Christ. Before turning to this christological grounding, one final comment needs to be made concerning Calvin's increased emphasis on public sacramental appropriation.

As the public appropriation aspect of the sacraments increasingly came to the forefront, Calvin was careful not to emphasize this aspect of the sacramental event to the detriment of its fundamental nature as God's offer of Christ. To lose sight of the latter aspect would lead to the error that, as previously noted, Calvin believed Zwingli to have committed—that is, the error of removing the divine promise from its primary aspect in the sacrament. Furthermore, to overemphasize public appropriation might make his baptismal theology appear to be grounded in human response rather than God's offer. This understanding surely would have caused Calvin problems with Anabaptists over the issue of infant baptism.

During his stay in Strasbourg, therefore, Calvin reemphasized God's offer as the primary aspect of a sacrament that did not depend on human response for its validity. In the 1543 *Institutes*, which again reflected the patristic readings during his years in Strasbourg, Calvin distinguished the matter, substance (*substantia*), or nature (*natura*) of the sacrament from the appropriation of that nature by faith:

> Therefore you will ask: By their ingratitude, do the wicked make it that God's ordinance is invalid? I reply: What I said ought not be so understood as though the power and truth of the sacrament depended on the innate condition of the one who receives it. For what God has instituted remains fixed and retains its own *nature*, however people vary. But since it is one thing to offer and another to receive, nothing prevents the symbol, consecrated by the word of the Lord, from truly being the thing it is called and from keeping its power.[71]

So also in the Geneva Catechism (1545), Calvin addressed the issue of whether or not the grace of baptism was given indiscriminately to all. In response to the minister's question on this point, the child's response differentiated the nature of the baptism itself from its appropriation:

> Many do close the way by their perverseness and so make it worthless for themselves. Thus its fruit reaches only the faithful. Yet from that nothing of the *nature* of the sacrament disappears.[72]

As far as Calvin's ecclesiology was concerned, it was evident that by the 1543 *Institutes* Calvin had further developed the idea of the visible church,[73] which now was embodied and organized around a fourfold ministry, as found at Strasbourg.[74] From this church one must not separate:

> Therefore, just as it is necessary to believe that the church visible to God's eyes alone is invisible to us, so to this one, which is called church with respect to men, we are ordered to be reverent and observe communion.[75]

Calvin considered the invisible church a "true" church as the totality of the elect before God. Calvin also considered the visible church a "true" church because it was the authentic instrument that manifested and initiated those elected in Christ. Thus there were not two distinct churches, existing side by side, but rather one church that had two parts visible, one part visible only to God and the other part visible to humanity.[76] This basic structure had become clear to Calvin as early as his ministry in Strasbourg, when he wrote his commentary on Romans.[77] Commenting on election and God's covenant with Israel, Calvin had argued that

> the universal election of the Israelite people does not stop God from choosing for himself whomever by his secret plan he chooses. And in fact, this clearly mirrors free mercy because God has thought it worthwhile to make a covenant of life with one nation; but his hidden grace towers far higher in the second election which is restricted to a single part of the nation. . . .God's secret election rules over the external calling. And yet it by no means contradicts it, but tends rather to complete and confirm it.[78]

The double nature of the church, wherein visible and invisible were held as one but still distinguished, was reinforced by Calvin's sacramental and baptismal discussion. Sacramentally, Calvin reemphasized God's offer of Christ as the nature or substance of the sacraments. This offer always marked the one, true church: *explicitly* in the visible church through the sacraments, themselves a form of the Word that offered engrafting in Christ;[79] and *implicitly* in the invisible church, because the elect were those elected and engrafted in Christ.[80] The 1543 baptismal material likewise reveals this double structure. Baptism represented entrance into the visible church community, as Calvin's French edition of the *Institutes* makes clear, beginning with the 1545 edition.[81] Here God offered Christ, and baptism served as a mark of the church grounded in Christ. At the same time, for the elect baptism also meant being "engrafted into Christ" and being counted as "God's children."

Summary of Calvin's Development

We have seen that, in 1536, Calvin had already held together sacramental ideas learned from Luther and Zwingli. Discussing the nature of a sacrament, Calvin leaned toward the Lutheran idea of a sacrament as God's promise attached to an outward sign. With baptism, Calvin added the Zwinglian idea of sacrament as public pledge, though he made sure this aspect was secondary to the sign-promise theology. During the same period, Calvin's ecclesiology dwelled almost entirely on the invisible church and the divine activity of election. The sacramental theology and ecclesiology were consistent with the young Calvin, not yet the church leader in Geneva or Strasbourg and still concerned with distinguishing the new faith from Roman Catholic theology.

By 1539, Calvin's sacramental and baptismal theology began noticeably to develop the public pledge aspect of baptism. Calvin had played a crucial part in the Genevan conflict concerning church discipline and worthy admission to the Lord's Supper, and he entered his Strasbourg ministry at a key time in Bucer's efforts for church structure and discipline. The visible church aspect of Calvin's ecclesiology, though not yet concretely articulated, moved into full view.

When Calvin returned to Geneva in September 1541, only a few months prior to the completion of the 1543 *Institutes*, the human appropriation aspect of the sacraments, as well as the discussion of the visible church, gained increasing prominence in his thought. He also developed a more integrated sacramental, baptismal, and ecclesial view that brought together themes that had first appeared in the 1536 *Institutes*. Christ was offered to all through the visible church, and the offer, through Word and sacramental sign (*notae ecclesiae*), marked the presence of the one true church. The sacrament of baptism functioned as the visible vehicle for incorporation into that church. Only some people, however, truly accepted the offer of Christ; hence the elect known only to God. As early as 1536, Calvin had described these true believers as "the mystical body of Christ,"[82] and in the 1539 *Institutes*, he extensively referred to them as those elected in Christ.[83]

Finally, we have seen that an important aspect of Calvin's integrated baptismal and ecclesial view in the 1543 *Institutes* depended on the explicit christological terminology for his baptismal theology. By the 1539 *Institutes*, Calvin enclosed Luther's sign-promise baptismal theology within a christological framework; likewise, most of the passages in the *Institutes* on the christological grounding of election first appeared in the 1539 edition.[84] This christological development allowed Calvin, by the 1543 *Institutes*, to construct a baptismal theology and ecclesiology that work in tandem. The true church was visible only to God and was comprised of those who were elected in Christ. Those individuals were engrafted in Christ in accord with one of God's promises for baptism. The true church was also the visible church that offered Christ (through Word and sacrament) and then, through baptism, incorporated people into the society of the church.

3

CALVIN:
BAPTISM AND DIVINE POWER

Calvin was of the generation of evangelical Reformers who followed Luther and Zwingli. His 1536 *Institutes* appeared five years after Zwingli's death and only ten years prior to Luther's death. Calvin was disturbed by the fissures in the new evangelical faith, and he attempted a eucharistic theology that he hoped would bridge the gap between the great German reformer and his Swiss counterpart. The preceding chapter argued for a similar development in his baptismal theology.[1]

In the baptism controversies that they faced, Luther and Zwingli learned to distinguish the divine activity that grounded baptism from the human appropriation of the sacrament. Each reformer had a characteristic way of making this formal distinction (chapter 1). For Luther, God's word of promise was intimately attached to the sign, and the sacrament was to be appropriated by faithful trust in God's promise. For Zwingli, God had decreed a single covenant of grace, in response to which people gave their public pledge of allegiance.

Calvin began with a baptismal theology based on Luther's sign theology. A sacrament was always attached to its preceding divine promise for the sake of sealing and confirming the promise so that the promise might be witnessed all the better. Zwingli's idea that baptism was the public pledge by which Christians showed their loyalty to Christ, just as soldiers showed loyalty to their commander, was the secondary aspect to baptism. Calvin gave increasing emphasis to the public appropriation aspect of baptism as he served as pastor in Strasbourg and developed his ideas about the visible church under the influence of Martin Bucer.

While in Strasbourg, Calvin also composed a tract defending infant baptism that eventually became a chapter unto itself in the 1559 *Institutes* (4.16). Calvin elegantly grafted a covenant defense of infant baptism, likely learned from Bucer and Zwingli, onto the sign-promise theology learned from Luther (4.16.2–6). Both the old and the new covenant had the same divine promise grounded in Christ, and both covenants had an exterior sign attached to the promise. All that differed was the mode of the external sign. Calvin's ultimate christological orientation in baptism integrated into a whole his baptismal theology (sign theology, covenant pledge, and infant-baptism covenant defense) and his ecclesiology (invisible and visible church).

In sum, the decade from the 1536 *Institutes* through the 1545 Geneva Catechism saw a remarkable theological formation in Calvin's baptismal theology and ecclesiology (chapter 2). Around a christological center that connected a sacramental sign theology, a covenant theology, and election, Calvin integrated (1) influences from the first-generation reformers Zwingli, Bucer, and Luther; (2) pastoral experiences from Geneva and the three-year ministry in Strasbourg; and (3) ecumenical concerns over the splintered evangelical church. Two predictable results followed.

First, the years from 1545 through the last edition of the *Institutes* (1559) saw no substantial change in Calvin's baptismal theology. The power of the theological formation in the young Calvin and the complex synthesis that resulted would have been difficult to change substantially. This first part of this chapter looks at the increased emphasis on, and the increased nuance of, three key elements in Calvin's baptismal theology: (1) the sign as surety of God's divine promise of grace that evoked human faith; (2) human faith, however weak, as that which appropriated this divine promise; and (3) God's election in Christ of those within the divine covenant.

Second, Calvin's baptismal theology came under increasing scrutiny and criticism. With the deaths of Zwingli (1531), Johannes Oecolampadius (1531) and his successor Oswald Myconius (1552), Capito (1541), Luther (1546), Bucer (1551), and Cranmer (1556), and with the fragile health and impending death of Melanchthon (1560), Calvin stood all but alone as one of the early great Reformers. By 1560, only Bullinger also remained—Calvin's colleague, who would outlive him by eleven years though five years his elder. Critics of Protestantism and of its Reformed wing looked carefully at the baptismal theology and ecclesiology of the *de facto* leader of Protestantism. The second section of this chapter examines two principal areas of criticism leveled by Calvin's opponents—(1) the baptism of those who were predestined as reprobate and (2) the baptism of those infants already born into the covenant of grace. The final section appraises the principal difficulties in the complex synthesis that was Calvin's theology of baptism.

SIGN, FAITH, AND ELECTION

Between 1545 and 1559, Calvin increasingly emphasized and gave nuance to three key elements to his baptismal theology: the sacramental sign, human faith, and divine election.

The Sacramental Sign

The Genevan opposition to Calvin and the political intrigue both within Geneva and between Geneva and France continued to grow from 1547 through 1553.[2] Calvin's letters to friends such as Melanchthon, Bullinger, and Farel continually mentioned the political and personal turmoil that his opponents had inflicted on him. In response to a letter from Melanchthon written in October 1552, Calvin wrote:

> To be honest, in addition to the vast troubles which quite severely consume me, there is scarcely a day in which some new pain or worry is not added. And so, I would soon waste away beneath the heap of burdens which bear down on me, except that the Lord alleviates their harshness by his own remedies. Among these it was no small thing both to know that you are tolerably healthy, at least given your years and the delicate health of your body, and to have been assured by your own letter that your love for me had in no way changed.[3]

By the middle of the next year, the Libertines controlled the Little Council; ministers were forbidden to serve on the General Council; and Calvin had become so weary of the Geneva battle that on July 24, 1553, he asked the council for permission to retire.[4]

In this same period, Calvin was keen on strengthening the new evangelical faith in his homeland.[5] By the end of the 1550s, France had perhaps fifty Reformed congregations, many of which were influenced by literature Calvin had sent or by the one hundred or more ministers Geneva had sent.[6] When many of these newly started French churches met at the Synod of Paris in 1559, they composed a confession of faith based on Calvin's Geneva Confession. Early in this decade (May 1552), contemporaneous with Calvin's struggles with the Libertines, five young men, new ministers of the new evangelical faith and former students of Theodore Beza and Pierre Viret at Lausanne, were arrested at Lyon. In their year of imprisonment, prior to their death at the stake in May 1553, Calvin wrote a number of letters offering encouragement through the sustaining presence of God in Jesus Christ.[7]

During this period of conflict, Calvin had been working on his New Testament commentaries. From 1549 through 1554 he preached 189 sermons on Acts,[8] and the first of his two-volume commentary on Acts appeared in 1552, the second volume appearing two years later. In his commentary on Acts, when he discussed the first baptismal scene in the book, where Peter preaches at Pentecost, Calvin wrote about the need to be absolutely sure that God speaks to oneself about the surety of salvation divinely promised. In a passage perhaps more existentially indebted to the circumstances in Geneva and France during 1552 than to the historical context of the Pentecost baptism narrative, Calvin passionately asserted that

> it is necessarily required for a sure faith that each one is resolved in the soul that he or she is bound in the number of those whom God addresses. For this is the rule for truly believing, when I am thus persuaded that I am saved because the promise that offers salvation pertains to me.[9]

Throughout this decade, Calvin reemphasized that the sacraments in general and baptism in particular must convey the absolute surety that God spoke the word of promise to the heart of each believer. For instance, by the 1559 *Institutes*, Calvin had rethought the title for the section on the sacraments. From 1534 through 1554, the title to the chapter on the sacraments had remained "On the Understanding of the Sacraments" (*Nunc de sacramentorum ratione dicendum erit*). With the 1559 edition of the *Institutes*, Calvin more specifically titled this opening section on the sacraments "Another Aid to Our Faith in the Sacraments, Related to the Preaching of the Gospel" (*Praedicationi Evangelii aliud affine est fidei nostrae adiumentum in Sacramentis*).[10]

Likewise, when Calvin reached section 13, which discussed the Zwinglian idea that *sacramentum* refered to the public oath a soldier swore on entering the military—an idea that Calvin had acknowledged as early as 1536, giving it secondary place to the idea of *sacramentum* as God's promise—Calvin appended this ending in 1559:

> Meanwhile, let the first point endure; because otherwise, as we have seen, the mysteries become lifeless unless they are aids to our faith and supplements to our doctrine, appointed to the same use and end.[11]

As chapter 2 detailed, Calvin had allowed the secondary point to gain importance over the years. By the time of 1559 *Institutes*, however, Calvin saw the need to reassert the primary point that sacraments were promises from God to help our faith. The fifteen years between these two editions of the *Institutes* had reminded Calvin that human assurance comes not from human faith but from God's promise of grace.

When Calvin described the role of baptism, he likewise made changes to emphasize that baptism primarily aided faith. In the baptismal section that discussed the relationship between sign and reality, Calvin had asserted since 1536 that baptism was given to nourish and confirm faith. In 1559 he said that baptism was given to "arouse" faith as well as to nourish and confirm it. Calvin argued for a creative quality to baptism that evoked faith as well as nourishing it afterward.[12] So, too, when discussing infant baptism, Calvin had asserted from 1539 through

1554 that the enemies who were against infant baptism "assault our fortress" (*nostra praesidia impressionem faciant*). In 1559, Calvin declared that the assault was made on "the fortress of our faith" (*in fidei nostrae praesidia impressionem faciant*), whereby he defended the institution of infant baptism by appealing to its function of aiding faith.[13]

From his earliest days as a theologian of the evangelical faith, Calvin had argued that the sacramental sign was an important way by which God aided human faith. Recall the definition of a sacrament that Calvin gave in the 1536 *Institutes*:

> It is fitting to first consider what a sacrament is. And it is an external sign, by which the Lord represents and witnesses to us his good will towards us, *in order to sustain the weakness of our faith*. One can also define it another way by calling it a testimony of God's grace, declared to us by an external symbol. For which reason we also understand that a sacrament is never without a preceding promise, but rather is joined to it as an appendix *for the purpose of sealing and confirming the promise itself, and, so to speak, for making it more of a witness.*[14]

During the 1550s, when Calvin put more emphasis on the sacramental sign as an aid to human faith, he used various metaphors to do so. In the opening discussion of sacrament as word and sign, Calvin had asserted from 1536 through 1554 that God "makes us contemplate in the flesh itself the things which are of the spirit" (*atque in ipsa carne contemplari facit ea quae sunt spiritus*). In 1559, he amended this to read more strongly that God "sets before us in the flesh a mirror of spiritual blessings" (*atque ipsa carne proponere bonorum spiritualium speculum*).[15] The sacramental sign no longer merely helped humans contemplate the spiritual; humankind all but looked directly at God's grace offered us.

Or again, Calvin argued that the sacramental signs moved beyond any mere announcing of God's promised grace: They were visible guarantees of such grace. Note the phrase from the 1559 *Institutes* that Calvin inserted amid an argument made in 1536 and amended in 1539:

| They do not bestow any grace themselves but announce and tell us those things given us by divine bounty. (1536 and 1539 *Institutes*) | They do not bestow any grace themselves but announce and tell us *and, as they are guarantees and tokens, ratify among us* those things given us by divine bounty. (1559 *Institutes*)[16] |

We see later in the same section on the office of the sacraments that, in 1559, Calvin added that sacraments have a sure effect, according to their outward sign, which God truly executes:

> God therefore truly performs what he promises and represents in the signs; nor are the signs without their own effect to prove their author truthful and faithful.[17]

In the baptismal material, Calvin asserted the same importance of the sign itself. To his discussion of the sign and reality of baptism, written almost entirely in 1536 and having no major revisions until 1559, Calvin appended the following ending:

> Nor does he feed our eyes with only a bare spectacle, but he brings us to the present reality and that which it represents he effectively executes at the same time.[18]

And in the next section on baptism and faith, Calvin defended himself by saying:

> But it is not my purpose to drain the force of baptism—without reality and truth added to the sign—since God works through external means.[19]

It should not surprise us, then, that Calvin spoke about the special quality of baptismal water itself. From 1539 through 1554, he asserted in the infant baptism section that baptism benefits "the infants themselves who are baptized." With the 1559 *Institutes*, Calvin added that baptism benefits "the infants themselves who are baptized with the sacred water (*sacra aqua*)."[20]

Such talk about the sacramental sign and its sure guarantee of the divine promise risked a sacramental instrumentalism that Calvin wanted to avoid. The sacraments may well have been divine bearers and guarantors of God's grace, so much so that baptismal water was itself called "sacred," but they did not have such power in and of themselves. A sacrament drew all its power from the gracious God; or (the same thing for Calvin) baptism found its meaning in Christ alone.[21] Calvin had two means by which he clarified that God was the source of sacramental grace.

First, Calvin appended assertions that specifically denied he was handing over to the sacraments instrumental power *in se*. In the section of the *Institutes* on the office of the sacraments (4.14.17), we have just seen that Calvin twice added that sacraments not only announced the good news but were also guarantees (*pignora, arrhae*) or tokens (*tesserae*) of it. We also saw that Calvin asserted that the signs were not "without their own effect to prove their author truthful and faithful." After these remarks that strengthened the sacramental sign, in 1559, Calvin added an assertion that made clear that he wanted to avoid the error that would enclose the "cause of justification and power of the Holy Spirit" within the elements:

> We must note that what the minister represents and attests by outward action God accomplishes within, lest what God claims for himself alone should be turned over to the human person.[22]

Likewise, to the 1543 discussion that Christ was the substance of all sacraments and that there was no promise in them apart from Christ, Calvin in 1559 added a specific attack on Lombard:

The less tolerable, therefore, is the error of Peter Lombard who elo-
quently makes them the causes of righteousness and salvation of
which they are parts.[23]

Not surprisingly, therefore, when Calvin spoke about the virtue of
baptism, he once more reinforced the idea that the meaning to baptism
did not point Christians to the water itself but rather

pulls us away not only from that visible element, but from all other
intermediaries, so that it might bind fast to Christ alone.[24]

Human Faith

As Luther had so often argued, human faith had as its object the divine
promise to which the sacramental sign so intimately attested. Whenever faith accepted the promise of God, the sacrament had its effective
benefit. And thus a second way that Calvin made clear he was avoiding the error of sacramental instrumentalism was to reemphasize that
human faith was necessary in order to accept the promise of which the
sacrament was the sure sign.

In the section of the *Institutes* on the office of the sacraments (*Inst.*
4.14.17), Calvin had opened the discussion in 1536 by asserting:

Therefore, let it be regarded as a settled principle that the sacraments
have the same office as the Word of God: to offer and set forth Christ
to us, and in him the treasures of heavenly grace. But they avail nothing and profit nothing unless received in faith.[25]

Immediately after this opening portion of the section, Calvin appended
in 1559 the following metaphor, which elegantly used a materialistic
image of grace to prove his point and which implicitly reminded the
reader of baptism:

As with wine or oil or some liquid, no matter how much you pour
out, it will flow away and disappear unless the mouth of the vessel
to receive it is open; moreover, the vessel will be splashed on the outside, but will still remain void and empty.[26]

Furthermore, Calvin's insistence on the weakness of faith, which had
prompted his increased emphasis on the sacramental sign, itself provided a counterbalance to the view that the sacraments had effectiveness in and of themselves. Since sacraments profited only where they
were received in faith, and since faith itself was so weak, pastorally
speaking the sacraments could be effective only intermittently or occa-
sionally, but never automatically.

In the sacraments and baptism sections of the 1559 *Institutes*, Calvin
continually added discussions about the weakness of faith. (After

all, Calvin had had twenty years of ministry amid Genevan and international politics.) Where, in 1536, Calvin had described faith as "slight and feeble unless it is propped up on all sides" because (like a feeble person) it "trembles, wavers," and "totters," by 1559 he added—with his own physical health then a complete shambles—that such enfeebled human faith "trembles, wavers, totters, and *finally gives way.*"[27]

In a slightly different metaphor about faith, Calvin asserted in 1539 that faith is "born, grows and is completed" *(et nasci et augescere et consummari).* By 1559, however, Calvin came to express himself more cautiously when he amended this passage to read that faith is "born, grows and comes to maturity" *(et nasci et augescere et conscendere ad maturitatem).*[28] Faith may mature, but it does not become perfect. So, while Calvin had earlier argued that to reciprocate God's promises in the sacraments "we mutually bind ourselves by profession of piety and innocence" *(ita pietatis ac innocentiae professione illi nos mutuo obligamus),* by 1559 he more modestly argued that "in turn we bind ourselves by this profession to *eagerness for piety* and innocence" *(ita ad pietatis ac innocentiae studium hac professione illi nos vicissim obligamus).*[29] Calvin clarified what he meant by the word *profess.* One may strive after piety and eagerness, but one does not yet have them.[30]

Covenant Unity

The third key idea concerning baptism that Calvin had mentioned in prior editions of the *Institutes* and that received new emphasis in 1559 was the relationship between the old and new covenants. To his chapter on the sacraments, at the end of section 14, Calvin appended a comment that if his opponents (Aquinas)[31] had been more skilled in exegesis they would have seen that the sacraments of the old dispensation were not "representations devoid of truth" *(figuras veritate vacuas).* Rather, the ceremonial law had no effect apart from Christ.[32]

Calvin also appended a final paragraph to his discussion of the prototypes of baptism, which can be found in the story of the Red Sea (mortification) and cloud of Yahweh (cleansing). He added:

> Although the mystery was then shadowy and known to few, nevertheless, because there is no other way of obtaining salvation than in these two graces, God did not wish to deprive the ancient fathers, whom he had adopted as heirs, of the tokens of both.[33]

Given the continuity between the two covenants, it was then easy enough for Calvin to replace the old assertion (1539–54) that "the sign of circumcision is added to seal the promise *(obsignando promissio)*" with a stronger one: "the sign of circumcision is added to seal the grace *(gratiae obsignandae)."* As with baptism, circumcision has Christ as its foundation *(fundamentum)*.[34]

The next section of the *Institutes* (4.16.4), which deals with the purely external differences between the two covenant signs, again shows that, by 1559, Calvin had reinforced the idea that God's saving grace was present to those under the old covenant. Up to 1559, Calvin had ended this section by asserting that beyond question baptism had taken the place of circumcision. In 1559, to make sure that all saw the point, he added the phrase "in order to discharge the same offices among us."[35] Because baptism and circumcision shared the same mortification and regeneration in Christ, and because they fulfilled the same office, they both signaled salvation to those who received the sign. This was why Calvin said in the 1559 *Institutes* that by circumcision the Jews learned that "God is the guardian of their salvation" *(Deum sibi esse salutis praesidem)*, not merely a "guardian and protector to them" *(Deum sibi praesidium ac protectorem)* as he had said prior to 1559.[36] Here circumcision marked more than God's mere protection; it marked the "one and the same" *(una et eadem)*[37] salvation unto eternal life promised in Christ.[38]

THE REPROBATE AND INFANT BAPTISM

As Calvin increasingly asserted that sacraments "have their own effect," that God "effectively executes" what the signs represent, that the water of baptism is "sacred water," and that there is a unity of covenants whose foundation is the salvation realized in Christ, questions arose about the effect of the baptism toward those who were reprobate and toward those baptized as infants who were born into the covenant. Calvin had answers to such questions. To the situation of the reprobate, he spoke about the God who promised and the validity (or "nature") of the sacrament; to the situation of infants, he spoke about the covenant, to which he added a metaphor (the "seed" of future repentance) to try to explain what effect baptism might have for those already included in the covenant of grace.

Baptism and the Reprobate

Calvin engaged the issue of predestination primarily during two periods. Prior to 1539, Calvin's writings show no developed doctrine of predestination. In the 1536 *Institutes*, for instance, Calvin mentioned predestination twice: once in his exposition of the Apostles' Creed and once when he discussed the nature of the church.[39] One year later, in the French Catechism that he wrote in Geneva, and in the Latin translation of that catechism one year after that (1538), Calvin had devoted an entire section to the topic of "election and predestination."[40] The section appeared after the section on the law and prior to the discussion of redemption, amid sections that concerned faith.[41] Calvin spoke straightforwardly about God's predestination to both election and reprobation.[42] By the 1539 *Institutes*, however, Calvin had developed the ideas from the catechism into a longer discussion about predestination in the eighth chapter, "On Predestination and the Providence of God."[43] Calvin's commentary on Romans appeared one year later (1540), followed three years later by his first response to Albert Pighius (ca. 1490–1542), the Dutch humanist and Roman Catholic apologist who, in 1542, had published his work on human free will (*De libero hominis arbitrio*).[44]

Ten years later Calvin again debated predestination, this time coinciding with his second work against Pighius (1552), an essay that was signed by the pastors of Geneva,[45] and with his well-known controversy with Jérome Bolsec (ca.1524–84). Bolsec was an ex-Carmelite monk who left the Roman Church in 1545 and in 1550 became personal physician to Jacques de Bourgogne, lord of Falais and friend of Calvin.[46] Bolsec frequently attended the Friday gathering (*congrégation*) of the Genevan ministers (the Vénérable Compagnie) who, according to the instructions of the 1541 *Ordonnances*, met weekly to discuss Scripture. While Bolsec was in most ways Reformed in theology and in general agreement with Calvin, he disagreed with Calvin's doctrine of predestination. As early as May 15, 1551, Bolsec expressed criticism of this idea before the *congrégation*, and on October 16, 1551, he spoke more forcefully against the idea of predestination. Bolsec was arrested for saying that those who affirmed predestination made an idol of God. The case was tried before the civil magistrates, and the magistrates, needing help in this theological matter, wrote to various Swiss churches for advice. On December 23, 1551, the Genevan magistrates banned Bolsec from the city.

By the end of the decade Calvin had significantly revised and edited the 1539 material on providence and predestination. He reworked his discussion of providence, which now appeared without the discussion of predestination at the end of his discussion of God (1.16–17), and he moved the revised discussion of predestination to the end of book 3, which discussed the regenerative work of the Spirit (3.21–24).[47] These changes in the *Institutes* reflected the second round of theological debates about predestination that developed during 1551.[48]

Throughout all the editions of the *Institutes*, Calvin's steadfast response to the problem of the reprobate receiving the sacraments was that the substance of the sacrament was the word of promise from God. Thus baptism was itself absolutely effective, but only through the strictly *social* or *personal* power of God, the divine person, who offered promises to the human person. These promises, as analogously happens between human people, could be refused by the person to whom they were offered; yet the promises themselves were not without full divine power:

> But from this sacrament [i.e., baptism], as from all others, we obtain nothing except as much as we receive by faith. If we lack faith, it will be a witness of our ingratitude, by which we are convicted before God, because we have not believed the promises given there.[49]

Likewise, in the discussion of the sacraments having significance in Christ, we again can see that, by 1559, Calvin had clarified the issue of the wicked being offered the sacraments. When he originally wrote in 1543, Calvin argued that the sacraments were effective when received in true faith. He also replied to an objection:

> What I have said ought not thus be understood—as though the power and truth of the sacrament depended on the innate condition of the one who receives it.[50]

In 1559, to be certain that he described the activity between God and humanity to be social—the offering of a promise and its subsequent acceptance or rejection—Calvin changed his reply to read:

> What I have said ought not thus be understood—as though the power and truth of the sacrament depended on the condition *or choice* of the one who receives it.[51]

By 1559, Calvin had emended numerous sacramental and baptismal discussions to emphasize the *personal quality* to God's sacramental activity. Where Calvin had previously said that the Lord accommodated himself by giving us signs through which God would lead us to him (*nos ad se deducit*), in 1559, Calvin said that God, "according to his unending kindness" (*pro immensa sua indulgentia*), "did not regard it as a burden to lead us to him" (*nos ad se deducere non gravetur*).[52] And where Calvin in 1539 described the ordinary church sacraments and cited Chrysostom that they are called "covenants," in 1559, Calvin inserted the comment that they are covenants by which "God leagues himself with us."[53] In the next sentence, Calvin added the explanatory clause that we pledge ourselves in return to God "because here a mutual agreement is interposed between God and us."[54] And Calvin emphasized this personal quality to the covenant when he added:

> Here the astonishing kindness of God shows itself; that with familiarity he covenants with Abram, just as people usually do with their friends and equals. For this is the usual form of covenants between kings and others, in order to mutually promise that they have the

same friends and enemies. For this certainly is a priceless pledge of rare love; that God humbles himself for our sake.[55]

Finally, Calvin connected this strictly personal or social conception of divine power to the distinction, already seen in Zwingli, Luther, and Bucer, between valid or correct baptism and effective or beneficial baptism. For instance, from 1536 to 1559, Calvin had begun a discussion of sacramental reception by the reprobate by repeating arguments held against his position:

> Nor do they argue suitably enough when from this they contend that [the sacraments] are not testimonies of God's grace because they often *are received* by the wicked who, nevertheless, realize God is not more favorable to them but rather incur a more serious condemnation.[56]

By 1559, Calvin had rethought this assertion and realized that the issue is not that the wicked *received (accipio)* the sacraments—the wicked did not receive the sacraments at all, except superficially. The issue to be defended was that the sacraments were sure and powerful testimonies of God's grace even though they were *offered* to the wicked:

> Nor do they argue suitably enough when from this they contend that (the sacraments) are not testimonies of God's grace because they also *are offered* to the wicked who, nevertheless, . . .[57]

Calvin reemphasized this point in 1559 when he rhetorically replied:

> But they object that human ingratitude is not able to detract from or hinder anything of the trustworthiness of God's promises. Yes, of course, I agree; and I say that the power of the mystery remains unaffected however much the wicked are eager to enervate it, as far as it is *in se*. For all that, it is one thing to be offered, and another to be received.[58]

Calvin's increased insistence on the strictly personal activity of God and on the distinction between God's valid offer and beneficial human appropriation of that offer helped mitigate the challenge that baptism was not effective for the reprobate.[59] Baptism may pour forth the promise of God's forgiveness, and God's sure and unfailing promise can aid our faith; but a vessel must have an open mouth, otherwise nothing effectively enters in, and the only washing that occurs happens superficially to the outside of the vessel.[60]

The problem, however, was not merely one of the ineffectiveness of baptism for some particular person who *chose* not to trust God's promise. The problem was that the reprobate *in principle* could not have faith because faith was a gift of the Holy Spirit,[61] and God had chosen not to grant the reprobate the gift of faith. In a well-known study on Calvin and baptism, Egil Grislis aptly observed of this problem, "Although God indeed invites all men, he effectively calls only the elect."[62]

Grislis then commented, following the lead of Werner Krusche, that there remained for Calvin "the very real tension between election and the instrumentality of the sacraments."[63] Grislis seems, however, to misidentify the tension as that between election and the sacraments as "effective instruments." As we have seen, Calvin insisted that sacraments were effective (as compared to valid) only where human faith grasped the divine promises that inhere to the sign. Thus, while the sacraments could be *valid* instruments, they could never be *effective* instruments in and of themselves, no matter the condition of the sacramental recipient.

With this in mind, a more appropriate description of the problem that the baptism of the reprobate raises would be whether such baptism could ever be a *valid* baptism. Does it make sense to say that a promise is truly offered when the one who (putatively) offers already knows that the promise *in principle* could never be accepted? Such an argument suggests that the real tension exists between election and baptism as a "valid instrument," a tension that may actually be more problematic than one between election and baptism as an "effective instrument." After all, if the problem is whether baptism is a valid instrument in the case of the reprobate, and only God knows the reprobate, how would the church ever know that any baptism was valid?

Baptism and Christian Infants

In a letter dated June 24, 1556, Calvin wrote to the Frankfurt magistrate John Clauberger and discussed among other issues the charge brought against him that he taught that infants should be baptized at home, and even by women, lest they die without being baptized.[64] After an introductory discussion, Calvin insisted that

> this principle should always be held to: that baptism is not administered to infants that they might become sons and heirs of God; but, because they *already are reckoned* by God to that place and rank, the grace of adoption is sealed in their flesh by baptism. Otherwise the Anabaptists would correctly exclude them from baptism. For unless the truth of the external sign can belong to them, it will be mere profaneness to call them to participation in the sign itself. Nevertheless, if anyone would deny them baptism, we have an instant reply: they are already in Christ's flock and God's family, since the covenant of salvation which God contracts with the faithful, is also common to their children. Just as the words say, "I will be your God, and the God of your seed."[65]

Because infants, as the Anabaptists correctly pointed out, could not grasp the promise of God's forgiveness, which was the substance of the sacrament, Calvin did not believe that he could appeal to the offer of a promise for defending the practice of infant baptism.[66] The substance of the sacrament could in no way be theirs. Calvin's response to the practice of infant baptism was the same in 1556 as it was almost twenty years earlier, when the defended the practice in a separate French tract that he later incorporated into the *Institutes* as the chapter on infant baptism (4.16). Calvin argued for the continuity of the old covenant and the new and therefore for the continuity of the sacramental sign of the covenants. Just as circumcision was administered to infants in the old covenant because they were elected by God to this covenant, so baptism should be administered to infants in the new covenant. If Christian children were elected by God, we dare not deny them the sign of that election.[67] As we have seen, during the 1550s, Calvin reemphasized the unity of the two covenants and their foundation in Christ.

Calvin knew, however, that election into the visible covenant may not mean ultimate predestination to salvation by God's decree,[68] and by 1559, Calvin realized that he had to speak further about election into God's covenant because there were some who were born into the covenant who might not have received the second, secret election. When, in 1559, Calvin added to his 1539 discussion of election an entire section on God's second, secret election within the covenant, Calvin began this addition by asserting:

> A second, more restricted grade of election must be added, or one in which God's more special grace was discerned: when from the same race of Abraham God rejected some, while he revealed that he kept others among his sons by embracing them within the church.[69]

By extension, this argument about Israel would apply as well to the new covenant, since there is no material difference between the covenants. Just as some received the old sign of the covenant but were not elected into the church, so also for baptism and the new covenant:

> And indeed it is true what is written by Augustine: that there can be invisible sanctification without a visible sign, and, conversely a visible sign without true sanctification. For, as he writes elsewhere, people put on Christ sometimes as far as receiving the sacrament, sometimes as far as the sanctification of life. The former can be common to both the good and the bad; the latter is special to the good and godly.[70]

As early as 1539, Calvin had addressed this issue directly in his infant baptism tract. There he argued that " [i]t is perfectly clear that the Lord regenerates those infants whom he wishes to save, as it is certain that he saves some."[71] And then, to end this section, Calvin added that "[t]he Lord therefore completely sanctifies those whom he deems proper, as he has sanctified St. John, since his hand is not restrained."[72]

Calvin's insistence on God's sovereignty to predestine some infants to salvation and others to reprobation raised two difficulties with the argument that infants were to be baptized because they were born into the covenant and they deserved the sign of the covenant. First, since those so born into the covenant were not necessarily among those whom God saved—God "sanctifies those whom he deems proper"— under what possible condition could baptism be efficacious for any infant? Baptism could have no effect for infants predestined as reprobate, since they would never be gifted with the faith necessary for appropriation of the divine promise. But neither could baptism have any effect for infants born into God's second election, since these children already possessed the covenant of grace.

This problem naturally arose with any baptism, adult or infant, once the prior assertion of God's predestination was made.[73] With the baptism of adults we have seen Calvin argue (1) that the baptism was both valid and effective for those who were elect, since God's promise was a true promise and the recipient faithfully trusted that promise; and (2) that although the baptism of the reprobate was not effective, since the reprobate refused to trust the promise, yet the baptism remained valid with its saving power intact.[74]

In the case of infants who were elect, God's promise naturally remained steadfast, and so their baptism was valid. For these elected infants, baptism would *become effective* when they reached the age when they could be "taught the truth of baptism," and they took this truth to heart "at such time that God himself foresees."[75] But Calvin also knew there were infants born into the covenant, who were baptized, but who later turned out to be reprobate. At the time of the Bolsec controversy, he wrote in commentary on Acts 3:25:

> I grant, indeed, that many who are children of the faithful according to the flesh are counted bastards, and not legitimate, because they thrust themselves out of the holy lineage through their unbelief.[76]

When the time came for these children of the covenant to appropriate the truth of baptism, they did not. At that point, Calvin could apply to them the same arguments about the validity and efficacy of baptism that he applied to the baptism of the reprobate in general. Even though all the people of Israel were included in God's covenant through circumcision, yet the designation "children of the promise" belonged, strictly speaking, only "to those in whom its power and efficacy (*virtus et efficacia*) is found." Some members of the covenant, "by their *ingratitude*," do not "have the benefits" (*beneficio minime fruuntur*) of the promise.[77]

A second problem arose from Calvin's insistence on God's sovereign power to predestine and his insistence on a covenant defense for infant baptism. By the 1559 *Institutes*, Calvin had reemphasized (1) the importance of the sacramental sign ("sacred water") by which God effectively executed that which the sign signified; and this because (2) human faith was so very weak that it all but collapsed from its own frailty and needed such divine support as the sacrament offered. Here a valid sacrament had the power to awaken sacramental efficacy by arousing and nourishing faith, through the power of the Holy Spirit.[78] This was certainly the case for the elect adults.[79] Even for those adults who were reprobate, the sacraments were not without some effect at the time of administration, though not sacramental efficacy as such:

> But from this sacrament [i.e., baptism], as from all others, we obtain nothing except as much as we receive by faith. If we lack faith, it will be a witness of our ingratitude, by which we are convicted before God, because we have not believed the promises given there.[80]

The baptismal sign thus had the effect of showing forth the ingratitude of those without faith and thus it witnessed that they indeed "have thrust themselves out of the holy lineage through their unbelief."[81]

But the question remained what, if anything, baptism could do for infants *at the actual moment* of administration. As the letter to Clauberger shows, Calvin readily admitted the obvious: Infants could not understand and thus could not grasp God's promise of grace, which was the substance of the sacrament. The faith of the infant, therefore, could not be supported by the sacramental sign.[82] So Calvin could not speak about the office of the sacraments to awaken and nourish faith. What Calvin did was pen a curious assertion that answered the objection that since infants were capable of neither repentance nor faith, baptism did nothing for them at the moment of its administration. Prior to 1559, Calvin had asserted that it was not objectionable to give an infant the sign of its repentance and faith, since the infant would appropriate the sign in later years.[83] In 1559, Calvin appended a sentence to the same passage that said rather more:

> In short, this objection can be solved with no problem—they are baptized into future repentance and faith—which although they are not yet formed in them, the seed of both lies concealed in them through the secret operation of the Spirit.[84]

While it certainly is the case, as Grislis observes, that Calvin "does not say that the seed is given through the instrumentality of the administration of baptism,"[85] the context in which Calvin added this 1559 phrase implies that the planting of the seed occurred at baptism.[86] The "hidden planting" would then obviously occur at the administration of the sacrament. The "seed" would refer not to "a present possession of the child" but to something "held over the child transcendentally and eschatologically through the potentiality of Baptism and the Spirit."[87]

The "seed," then, functioned in a manner analogous to how the sacrament of baptism functioned for an adult at the time of administration of baptism. For those baptized as infants, the once and prior baptism would later awaken and nourish the faith of that person because of the trustworthy nature of the divine promise that the sign signified. Note what Calvin said when he replied to the argument that (any) baptism is void if the recipient comes to faith *after* the sacramental act (a case strictly analogous to infant baptism):

> Now our opponents ask us what faith came to us during some years after our baptism. . . . To this question we reply that we indeed, being blind and unbelieving, for a long time did not grasp the promise that had been given us in baptism; yet that promise, since it was of God, ever remained fixed and firm and trustworthy. . . . We therefore confess that for that time baptism benefitted us not at all, inasmuch as the promise offered us in it—without which baptism is nothing—lay neglected. Now when by God's grace we begin to repent, we accuse our blindness and hardness of heart—we who were for so long ungrateful toward his great goodness. But we believe that the promise itself did not vanish.[88]

Furthermore, the activity of the Holy Spirit in "planting the seed" would bring infant baptism into alignment with the rest of Calvin's sacramental theology, in which the instrumental effectiveness depended on the agency of the Holy Spirit.[89]

Two difficulties, however, arise with the "seed" metaphor. First, it is one thing to say that delay in repentance does not make baptism *invalid*, because God's promise remains steadfast and the baptism will become effective at such time that faith grasps the divine promise; true enough. The adult who was baptized as an adult could remember the baptism and that person could say, "I have been baptized." In this case, the valid baptismal act did do something for the one being baptized, even if the baptism was not yet effective: The divine promise was sealed to the person, and the person could always remember that seal and return to the promise. It is quite another thing to attempt the same argument for an infant, as Calvin did, since the infant itself could not remember what happened at baptism. Here the only way to argue that the valid baptismal act had effect for the child was to abstract the discussion by way of a metaphor—the Holy Spirit "plants the seed of future repentance and faith."

The second problem with the "seed" metaphor has to do with the language of the metaphor itself. Calvin's primary description of God's activity during baptism is social: God promises or makes an offer or offers forgiveness. During the 1550s, Calvin reemphasized just this point when he insisted that the sacrament became effective when a person trusted the promise or received the offer or accepted forgiveness. While Calvin in no way wanted to credit such human activity with any merit,[90] he did make it clear that the sacramental event was personal and that the divine offer must be personally *received*.[91] Yet the metaphorical language of the Spirit "hiding" a seed within the infant implies a *nonpersonal* divine activity that guarantees a result, such as planting a seed in the earth. When the gardener plants, the ground cannot refuse.

SUMMARY AND EVALUATION

To summarize, from 1550 through 1560, Calvin found himself the elder statesman for Reformed Protestantism. He struggled in Geneva with political intrigue and ever-deteriorating health. In this decade he produced most of his Old Testament commentaries and the remainder of his New Testament commentaries. He also revised the *Institutes* several times, finally editing and arranging it in an order he liked (1559), while sick with malaria and afraid he would die with the project unfinished.[92] During this period Calvin worked on his sacramental and baptismal thinking not just as a biblical theologian but also in the context of the ministry to which he believed God had called him.

Calvin's baptismal material shows that he reemphasized the sacramental sign as the sure bearer of God's promise; so much so that he could call the water of baptism "sacred water." He also reemphasized the need for human faith and added material to the *Institutes* about the weakness and frailty of human faith. The more sharply perceived weakness of human faith undoubtedly contributed to reemphasizing the sacramental sign. A third area that received renewed emphasis was the continuity of covenant between the old and new dispensations. Much of the covenant baptism material Calvin first wrote for the infant baptism tract that appeared in the 1539 *Institutes*. This material received little change until the 1559 *Institutes*, when Calvin strengthened the references to covenant and highlighted God's personal character in "leaguing himself" with humankind.

Difficulties arose for Calvin in two areas of his baptismal thought: the effectiveness of baptism for the reprobate and the effectiveness of baptism for those children already born into the covenant. Of these two areas, the question of the reprobate received more attention. The Bolsec controversy was personally hard for Calvin, occurring during a difficult period of Calvin's Genevan ministry. This conflict influenced the editing and arranging of the providence and election material for the 1559 *Institutes*. Also, the question of God's predestining to election or reprobation itself connected to the question of baptism for those children already included within the covenant of grace.

Calvin had a steadfast twofold answer to the question about the effectiveness of baptism for the reprobate. God's sacramental activity was personal or social in nature. The divine offer of grace required faithful human response in order to be effective. Calvin also made clear the distinction between a valid sacrament and an efficacious sacrament. As he so clearly put the matter in 1559,

> But they object that human ingratitude is not able to detract from or hinder anything of the trustworthiness of God's promises. Yes, of course, I agree; and I say that the power of the mystery remains unaffected however much the wicked are eager to enervate it, as far as it is *in se*. For all that, it is one thing to be offered, and another to be received.[93]

This raised the question of how the church would ever know that it possessed a valid sacrament at all. A valid sacrament depended on God's promise being offered, and the concept of promise assumes an agent who is capable of accepting or rejecting such an offer. But when faced with a divine offer of grace, the reprobates were *in principle* not such personal agents. When, therefore would the sacramental offer be a real, valid offer, and when not? No one could know. Does this not then question the marks of the church and the very existence of a true visible church?

The second difficulty in Calvin's baptismal theology specifically concerned what effect present baptism would have for children already in the covenant of grace. On the one hand, baptism could not offer them anything they did not already have. On the other hand, at the moment of administration, baptism could not provide the support for faith that Calvin wanted baptism to be for adults. For adults, baptism awakened and nourished faith so that the valid baptismal offer could be taken to heart and made effective. Calvin's answer was to abstract the discussion by means of a metaphor: The seed of future repentance and faith was concealed in the infants through the Holy Spirit. The seed metaphor, however, incorrectly made the baptism of an infant analogous to that of an adult who had heard God's promises at baptism and who later came to faith. The metaphor also described God's sacramental activity in a way contrary to the strictly personal activity that Calvin elsewhere ascribed to God.

PART TWO

THE TRAJECTORY OF
REFORMED BAPTISMAL THEOLOGY

4

FROM THE REFORMED CONFESSIONS
THROUGH THE TWENTIETH CENTURY

The modern liturgical renewal movement reenvisioned the sacrament of baptism according to a model of Christian initiation whose pattern dates to the patristic era. The Second Vatican Council embraced this model, and in 1972 the Roman Catholic Church issued the Rite of Christian Initiation of Adults. The scholarship that lay behind this liturgical change has influenced many old-line Protestant churches in America and the worship books that they use. A brief look at the theology operative in the liturgical renewal movement and the RCIA suggested that the theology may not necessarily be compatible with some of the traditions that adopted this rite. The final section of the Introduction suggested that the *Lutheran Book of Worship,* for example, may well contain such a baptismal rite. The challenge, then, was to do the detailed historical-theological work needed in order to evaluate the Reformed tradition.

Chapter 1 looked at the first-generation reformers Zwingli, Luther, and Bucer. Several lessons were gained. First, understanding the context in which various theological positions originally were taken is necessary to understand adequately the Reformers' sacramental and baptismal theology. Second, the distinction between valid and efficacious baptism is key to understanding correctly the issues surrounding baptism in its various contexts. Third, where Luther asserted the validity of baptism by referring to the divine promise of forgiveness that attached to the sign, Zwingli and Bucer made the same point by referring to the covenant of grace given to Abraham and his seed.

Chapter 2 turned to the principal Reformed theologians of the second generation, Bullinger and Calvin. Bullinger argued for a covenant of grace that extended from Adam onward. Human responsibility upon accepting this covenant was love of God and love of neighbor. Prior to Jesus Christ, circumcision was the sign of taking on the covenant, and baptism became the Christian sign of taking on the covenant. While Bullinger ultimately thought that God predestined the elect to this covenant of grace, he more practically thought that personal confession and right living out of the covenant were sufficient signs of being among the elect.

The Calvin study showed that Calvin's original sign-promise theology developed further as he spent time in Strasbourg, learning from Martin Bucer and serving for the first time as the minister of a local congregation. In Strasbourg, Calvin was confronted by the Anabaptist challenge to church order, discipline, and infant baptism. Calvin's ideas on the visible church expanded, as did his sacramental and baptismal theology. By the time of the 1545 Geneva Catechism, Calvin had established an integrated, christocentric theology of baptism that united Luther's sign-promise theology, Zwingli's interest in the public pledge aspect of baptism, a lengthy and articulate covenant defense of infant baptism developed during the Strasbourg ministry, and the question of election and initiation into the visible and invisible church.

Chapter 3 argued that Calvin's baptismal theology held together diverse elements that had inner tensions. Contrary to much of the secondary literature, Calvin's concept of election was not the sole source of these inner tensions. Rather, the difficulties lay (1) in the combination of election with the issue of the validity of the baptism and (2) with the combination of election, the baptism of infants, and the question of how baptism might be effective *at the moment of administration* for children already in the covenant.

Chapter 4 now traces the trajectory of Reformed baptismal thought after the second generation of the Reformation. The first section treats the Reformed confessions; the next section turns to Reformed orthodoxy; the third section studies the baptismal theology of Friedrich Schleiermacher; and the final section studies the Reformed baptismal debates from the twentieth century.

THE REFORMED CONFESSIONS

Without a central teaching office or an official document such as the *Book of Concord* (1580) to specify a unified body of doctrine, the Reformed tradition has relied instead on its dynamic tradition of confessions to supply both a heritage of confessed beliefs and an open-ended attitude toward the work of the Spirit in future Reformed communities.[1] Each confession is understood to be occasional to a particular time and place. These confessions represent the spectrum of Reformed traditions in several ways. Geography most naturally comes to mind, since the Reformed tradition took root outside Switzerland in diverse locations—from eastern Europe to the Americas and to Asia—finding exemplification in ways fitting to new contexts. The Reformed confessions are also varied in type of material.[2] We find confessions, as such, typically drawn up by national ecclesial bodies that expressed Reformed faith for that context (e.g., the Westminster Confession).

There are also catechisms that served as both instruction and confessional guide (e.g., the Heidelberg Catechism). And there are "pronouncements" that speak to particular issues in particular contexts (e.g., the Barmen Declaration). Theological diversity can also be seen, for example, when comparing the high Calvinism of Dort with the moderate and ecumenical Heidelberg Catechism.

Questions naturally arise about which confessions are to be construed as Reformed. Do we include Anglican confessions, as the Continental collections of Reformed confessions do? Or does the Anglican Church represent a different Protestant tradition? Or perhaps the Anglican confessions are not Protestant at all but truly "catholic." Anglican sacramental theology surely is Reformed, but Anglican polity surely is not. Does polity represent something essential to the Reformed tradition? What about Puritan confessions? The Savoy Declaration was taken from the Westminster Confession; but again, what about polity? And does the Anabaptist influence in Puritanism, with the emphasis on personal conversion and a saintly life, not lead to a view of baptism that is more Baptist than Reformed (the "Halfway Covenant")? And these questions about what constitutes a Reformed confession lead to the further difficulty of *which* Reformed confessions are to be examined or given priority.[3]

Since chapters 1 through 3 have looked at the baptismal theology of Zwingli and Calvin, with attention to chronological development, among the Swiss confessions this section will look at the First Helvetic Confession (1536), the Geneva Confession (1536), the Geneva Catechism (1545), and the Second Helvetic Confession (1561). Next will follow the Continental confessions: the French Confession (1559), the Belgic Confession (1561), and the Heidelberg Catechism (1563). Among the British Reformed confessions appear the Scots Confession (1560), the Articles of Religion (1563), the Anglican Catechism (1647), and the Westminster Confession and Westminster Catechisms (1647).

The Swiss Confessions

The First Helvetic Confession (1536) was drawn up by a team of Swiss theologians, including Heinrich Bullinger, Oswald Myconius, Leo Jud, Simon Grynaeus, and Caspar Megander, who were chosen from among the delegates sent by Zurich, Basel, Bern, Biel, Schaffhusen, St. Gall, and Mühlhasen to a conference in Basel. The hope was for a confession that would speak for the Reformed Swiss cantons. The Strasbourg theologians Bucer and Capito hoped for a document that would work toward reconciliation between the German and Swiss Reformations. The original confession was in Latin, and Leo Jud translated the confession into a somewhat longer German version.[4]

Article 21 (or 22) treats baptism with two distinct but connected assertions (made a bit clearer by the Latin text, which gives two sentences, a paragraph for each). The confession first says that baptism is the christologically instituted bath through which regeneration (*wydergebärliche, regenerationis*) is offered to the elect through the outward, visible sign. Then follows the assertion that children are to be baptized because they have been born into God's people and it may be presumed that they are among God's elect. Here several features appear that have already been noted in chapters 1 and 2.

First is the valid sacrament, instituted by Christ, that offers regeneration through the outward sign. Article 20 (19) on the "Power and Efficacy of the Sacraments" has just made it clear that the sacraments are not "bare signs" (*nudis signis*) but consist of both sign and reality (*signis simul et rebus*). As such, they are not merely outward signs signifying membership in the Christian community. Here the confession implicitly rejects Zwingli's purely social construction of baptism, which denied that baptism was a means of grace.

Second, the benefits of baptism come to the "elect," a term not defined in content, although infants are assumed to be elected. The prior discussion on the power of the sacraments aids the understanding of this baptism material. The German text of article 20, in an elaboration of the Latin, has just said that "the entire power, effect and fruit of the sacraments" lies in their spiritual reality that has been received in faith.[5] Here the efficacy of the sacrament is linked to faithful reception and distinguished from, though not separated from, the validity of the sacrament. This means, third, that the confession implies the pragmatic and pastoral meaning to "election" seen in Bucer and later in Bullinger. To change one's life and to profess one's faith or to be born into a Christian household and grow up to profess one's faith may be generally taken as a sign of God's election.[6]

The Geneva Confession (1536), along with the *Articles concerning the Organization of the Church and of Worship at Geneva* (1537) and the Geneva Catechism (1537), was offered by William Farel and John Calvin for guiding the Reformation in Geneva. The confession, most likely the work of Farel, was presented to the council in November 1536 (perhaps January 1537), and it was Calvin's desire that the council and then the citizens of Geneva subscribe to it.[7]

Article 15 treats baptism and essentially falls into two assertions. First, baptism is the sign by which God testifies to the divine desire to adopt humankind as God's children. This outer sign represents the washing from sin (*representee la purgation de nos pechez*) that is to be had in Jesus' blood and the mortification of the flesh that one has living in Christ through the Spirit (*vivre en luy par son espirit*).[8] Second, the baptismal article says that since Christian infants belong to such a divine covenant (*nos enfans appartiennent à une telle alliance de nostre Seigneur*), they ought not be denied the external sign.

Here we see (1) that baptism testifies to God's grace toward humankind (adoption); (2) that baptism portrays the cleansing from sin and the human regeneration that come through the blood of Jesus and the power of the Spirit; and (3) covenant appears as the reason for infant baptism. Taken as a whole, these themes represent an early and somewhat unintegrated Reformed position on baptism, displaying implicitly the distinction between validity and effect, yet not mentioning faith. The confession gives an abbreviated covenant defense for infant baptism.

This early Geneva Confession should be compared with Calvin's Geneva Catechism (1545),[9] in which we see much of Calvin's carefully evolved baptismal theology.[10] Beginning with the sacraments in general, Calvin makes clear that they are another medium (*moyen, medium*) by which God communicates with humankind (Q. 309). Quite simply, a sacrament is an exterior witness (*tesmoignage exterteur, externa testificatio*) by which God testifies divine grace to us and inwardly seals such grace in our hearts (Q. 310). The activity of sealing the grace to the human heart is the work of the Spirit independent of, but intimately connected to, the external sign, which itself has the function of witnessing (Qq. 311–13). Such sealing takes place only through faith, which is where the Spirit works and the sacrament has effect. The inherent nature and power (*vis et natura*) of the sacrament thus remain even if someone lacking in faith should reduce to nothing (*in nihilum*) the divine gifts offered in the sacrament (Qq. 316–17).[11]

The same distinction between the nature of the sacrament and the effect of the sacrament appears in the baptismal material. On the one hand, the water is not merely a symbol but a symbol to which reality is attached (*C'est tellement figure, que la verité est conioincte avec*). The sacrament is a form of God's Word. Since God does not deceive us when God speaks, the reality that God promises is attached to the sign (Q. 328). On the other hand, such divine grace has no effect for the wicked, since they lack the faith to appropriate the promise. Even with reception by the wicked, the sacrament has lost nothing of its own nature (*nihil sacramenti naturae decedit*) (Qq. 329, 331). Divine grace still has its effect for those who have faith and repentance (Qq. 330–32).[12]

These arguments are then reworked in the infant baptism material. The promises of God given to Israel now extend through the whole world (*per totum orbem publicatae, estendues par tout le monde*), so that the grace given to the Israelites is poured out on us all the more (*abundatius effudit*) (Qq. 335–36). If Christ thus broadened the covenant, then the sign of the old covenant can rightly be replaced by the sign of the new covenant. As Israelite children received circumcision, so Christian children ought to receive baptism (Qq. 335–38).[13] Infants need not have "faith and repentance" during infancy. They just need faith when they are grown, for then the effectiveness of their baptism can be present (Qq. 333, 339).

The Second Helvetic Confession (1561) was mentioned briefly in the discussion of Bullinger's baptismal and covenant theology, and the material in the confession needs to be understood in the context of Bullinger's thought.[14] Bullinger finished the Second Helvetic Confession in 1561 while gravely ill, intending the confession to be an inheritance received by the Zurich church from its chief pastor of some thirty years.[15] Bullinger's personal confession was then passed on to Frederick III, elector of the Palatinate, who was under attack from the Lutherans for publishing the Heidelberg Catechism. Frederick intended to use Bullinger's confession of faith to help defend the orthodoxy of his faith. By 1566 the Latin and German versions of this confession were published and accepted in the Swiss cantons, the Palatinate, and various Reformed territories on the Continent and in Scotland.

The confession begins the sections on the sacraments by describing them as signs, or "mystical symbols, or sacred rites, or sacred actions." They are God's Word plus the signs and the realities so signified (*verbo suo, signis, et rebus significatis*). The sacraments outwardly represent what God inwardly does through the Spirit, which seals the Word of God in the heart.[16] Said another way that reflects both Luther and Calvin, the sacraments are symbols to which God has attached divine promises, and promises require faithful hearing in order to have effect. The substance or preeminent reality (*substantia vel praecipuum*) of the promises is Christ himself.[17]

The signs themselves are taken from everyday life—water, bread, and wine—and consecrated by the Word of God for sacred use. As such, these signs take on themselves, by the divine will, the reality of that which they signify, becoming neither the reality itself (for then they would not be signs) nor "common signs" (for then they would be "neither sacred nor effective").[18]

When comparing the sacraments of the "old and new people," Bullinger asserts that the "preeminent reality and thing itself" remains the same—Christ, in whom the grace and promises of God are fulfilled. With regard to the outer signs themselves, there are differences that move from lesser to greater: from sign to reality signified (Christ), from laborious and grand to simpler, from a local dispensation to a global dispensation, from less effective in faith and Spirit to more effective.[19]

The confession then discusses baptism ("De Sancto Baptismo"). After a brief discussion of the dominical institution of baptism and the assertion of one baptism throughout the church and throughout one's life, the confession moves to discuss what it means *to be baptized*.[20] Bullinger's use of the passive here must not be overlooked, because this section treats not baptism as such but *what baptism does for one who receives it in faith.* For the faithful baptismal candidate, "to be baptized in Christ's name is to be enrolled, entered, and received into the covenant, and family, and thus into the inheritance, of the God's children."[21] Added to this description are cleansing from sin and the renewal, regeneration, and new life that come through the Spirit.[22] This inner renewal has corresponding outer obligations, which include obedience to the God whose property one now is. As for infants, they are to be baptized because they are members of the people of God and thus are entitled to the sign of the covenant of which they already are members.[23]

The Continental Confessions

The French Confession (1559) came from the first national synod held by French Protestants in Paris.[24] Although sometimes attributed to Calvin—and indeed, the confession represents a good summary of Calvin's teaching—the confession was a joint effort by Genevan theologians and was based on prior confessional material.[25] The sacramental sections (articles 34–38) are concise, to the point, and reminiscent of Calvin.

The sacraments are added to God's Word as "pledges and seals" and thus are outward signs through which God works. God does not work "in vain." The divine pledge is adoption by God and engrafting in Christ, with its cleansing from sin by Christ's blood and renewal of life. The Spirit is the effective agent.[26] Such inner effect happens only with faith, since baptism "is a sacrament of faith and repentance." Children, however, are also to be baptized since "into his church God receives small children along with their fathers."[27]

The Belgic Confession (1561) was written, or perhaps cowritten, by Guy de Brès, a Protestant reformer and martyr in the Netherlands who struggled to have the new faith find toleration in the Low Countries. Modeled on the French Confession, the Belgic Confession became the confessional standard in the Netherlands and linked the Reformed churches there with Reformed traditions elsewhere.[28]

Article 33 treats the sacraments in general and follows the argument of the French Confession: The sacraments are both pledges and seals. As pledges (*pignora*), they outwardly testify to the "good will and grace" of God. Since God's signs are neither empty nor useless and do not deceive, what the signs outwardly witness happens inwardly in the human heart through the power of the Spirit. As with the French Confession, the Belgic Confession clearly sets the goodwill and grace of God in a christological context by asserting that Christ is the sacraments' ultimate truth.[29]

The baptismal article (34) lengthens the French Confession by beginning with a christological statement on the sacrifice of Christ. The confession then details the effect that baptism has for the believer by adding a discussion, aimed at the Anabaptists, on the sufficiency of a person's one baptism, even if administered as a child. Water signifies the cleansing from sin accomplished by Christ's blood and the regenerated life that follows. Outwardly, the ministers administer the sacrament; inwardly, the effect is accomplished through the power of the Spirit.[30] The somewhat disjointed section against the Anabaptists argues that baptism bears fruits throughout a person's life, not just when administered. Furthermore, since children of the old covenant received the sign, so also children of the new covenant should receive the sign, since the promises given in the covenants are the same and are fulfilled in Christ.[31]

Nowhere in the sections on sacraments and baptism is the necessity of faith mentioned, nor the distinction between the validity and efficacy of a sacrament. The faith of the Reformed Christians that this confession described was simply assumed. For instance, Anabaptists are criticized because they "condemn the baptism of infants born to believing parents."[32] When we recall that the Belgic Confession came from a threatened minority, was written to defend the Reformed faith as orthodox and nonseditious, and was given to Philip II in the hope of toleration, the assumption that the Reformed Christians were faithful is easy to understand.

At the same time, the Anabaptist traditions themselves were vocal in their insistence on being converted, faithful communities, and Anabaptism had made its own inroads in the Low Countries. Given that the events surrounding Jan Matthijs, John of Leiden, and the Melchiorite presence in the Netherlands were not long in the past, it is also easy to understand why the Belgic Confession spent time distancing the Reformed faith from that of the Anabaptists.

The Heidelberg Catechism (1563) was a product of the ecclesial and civil politics of the Palatinate, a territory whose ruler was one of the seven electors of the Holy Roman Emperor. The Reformation in the Palatinate began in 1546 under Frederick II and continued during the short reign of Frederick's nephew and successor Elector Ottheinrich, who was Lutheran in his reforming efforts. With the accession of Frederick III a more Reformed direction was taken, and a catechism was drawn up that reflected both Lutheran and Reformed traditions.[33]

The baptism questions (Qq. 69–74) reflect themes that have appeared already. To the external sign Christ has affixed the promise (*unnd darbey verheissen hat*) of washing from sin.[34] The "divine pledge and sign" (*Göttlich pfand unnd warzeichen*) are thus assurances that God accomplishes inwardly what the outer sign signifies.[35] We have seen the sign-promise structure as it developed in Calvin's thought.[36] The language of inner/outer appeared not only in Zwingli's and Bucer's thought[37] but also in the Geneva Catechism (Qq. 310–13), the Second Helvetic Confession (chap. 19), and the Belgic Confession (art. 34).[38]

Wilhelm Neuser has carefully analyzed the Heidelberg Catechism and compared it with the *Catechesis minor* of Ursinus that preceded it. He argues that the central and prominent sign-promise emphasis came from Melanchthon—probably not from Calvin. So also was the baptismal theology from Melanchthon, at least as far as the issue of later faithful appropriation of the divine promise (sanctification).[39] In this regard, the baptismal theology is not a covenant theology as such but concentrates on the Word, on which the sign invariably depends and which continues to evoke the faith and spiritual growth of the one baptized.[40] The covenant description for baptism is made not to defend infant baptism but to distinguish the baptism of the children of believers from the children of nonbelievers. Nonbelievers will not raise the child in the church. This finds a parallel in Ursinus's *Catechesis minor*.[41]

Neuser shows that the Heidelberg Catechism places the sign-promise sacramental theology at the center of sacramental and baptismal theology. Furthermore, he shows that appropriation of the divine promise and growth in faith are a process of the Word, attached to the sign, through the Spirit. With these emphases, the catechism also pushes covenant into the background. It must be asked, however, whether covenant theology is as distant from the Heidelberg Catechism as Neuser argues. First, this study has already shown how Calvin integrated a sign-promise theology and covenant baptismal theology into a coherent whole. Also, Neuser's arguments about the covenant discussion in the infant baptism section (Q. 74) are not quite as convincing as the rest of his argument, especially considering that preceding the Heidelberg Catechism was a forty-year history of the Reformed tradition appealing to covenant for its practice of infant baptism. Just because a sign-promise theology has come to the foreground so clearly does not mean that covenant theology has to be explained away completely.

Finally, as with the French Confession, the Belgic Confession, and the Second Helvetic Confession, the baptism discussion existentially centers on the benefits that come to the one who is baptized when that person has faith. Neuser argues that such faith comes in response to the Word, not just at one's own baptism but at all baptisms in the community. Each time there is a baptism the baptismal sign, along with the Word and Spirit, continues to remind and confirm a person of God's promise.[42]

The British Reformed Confessions

The Scots Confession of Faith (1560) was composed in four days by a committee of six men, including John Knox, and was presented to the

Scottish parliament, which adopted it on August 24, 1560.[43] The confession shows itself to be the quick work of a committee,[44] and its confessional roots reach back to Calvin, the French Confession, the First Helvetic Confession, the First Confession of Basel, the Articles of Religion, and other sources.[45]

The three chapters on the sacraments are not arranged in the usual pattern of sacraments, baptism, and supper. Instead, the confession has chapters divided into "On the Sacraments" (21), "On the Right Administration of the Sacraments" (22), and "To Whom Sacraments Appertain" (23). Within each chapter, the confession treats both the Lord's Supper and baptism. The confession makes quite clear that Christ himself, not his benefits or power, is what God ultimately promises in the signs. So the sacraments are not "naked and bair signes." They are the means by which God has ordained that, "in richt use of the Sacraments," those who have faith may be "ingrafted in Christ" through baptism and in the Lord's Supper be "joined" with Christ or have "unioun and coniunction" with "the body and blude of Christe Jesus."[46]

By far the bulk of the discussion in chapter 21 ("On the Sacraments") pertains to the Lord's Supper, but it applies, *mutatis mutandis*, to baptism as well. The confession distinguishes between "Christ Jesus in his natural substance" and "the Elimentis in the Sacramentall signes." The signs are neither worshiped, since they can be distinguished from Christ, nor despised, since Christ is given through them.[47] Only true faith, however, can make effective use of the sacraments because faith "apprehendis Christ Jesus, who only makis this Sacrament effectuall unto us."[48] Three other times in this opening section the confession refers to the "richt use" of the sacrament (the Eucharist), and a fourth uses the plural "Sacraments."[49] Thus, while the confession asserts that "by Baptisme we ar ingraftid in Christe Jesus, to be maid partakaris of his Justice, by the quhilk our Synnis ar covered and remittit," strictly speaking this would be so only when baptism was "rychtlie usit," as is immediately asserted about the effectiveness of the Lord's Supper.[50]

The next chapter, on the right administration of the sacraments (chap. 22), asserts that they must by administered only by those who "ar apoyntit to the precheing of the worde."[51] The other demand for right administration is that the ritual itself be in accordance with what God has appointed: no "oyle, salt, spattle, and sicke lyke in Baptisme," for such are human invention. Ritual misuse (including emergence baptism by midwives) means the sacrament ceases "to be the richt Sacraments of Christ Jesus."[52] The distinction between lawful and valid sacramental administration does not hold here.

Chapter 23 concludes the sacramental portion of the Scots Confession by addressing who should receive the sacraments. Infants of the faithful are to be baptized, as are those who "bee of age and discritioun." Anabaptist errors are condemned. By contrast, no one is to be admitted to the Lord's Supper unless that person "can trye and examyne thaimn selfis, alsweill in thair faith as in thair dewtie towardis thair nychtbouris."[53]

The *Articles of Religion of the Church of England*, better known as the "Thirty-nine Articles," had an English heritage reaching back to the 1536 Ten Articles produced during the reign of Henry VIII.[54] With the growing influence of Reformed theology in England during the reign of Edward VI, in 1552, Thomas Cranmer produced the Forty-two Articles. These articles were later edited by Archbishop Matthew Parker and in the ratification process were reduced to thirty-nine. The Thirty-nine Articles of 1562, which in 1563 had been sanctioned by Elizabeth I and her council, underwent further revision in 1571 and were approved by Parliament. To what extent Anglican confessions as a whole may be considered within the corpus of Reformed confessions cannot be addressed here. The sacramental sections, however, are widely understood to reflect the Swiss Reformed traditions.

The very beginning of the article on the sacraments (25) echoes Calvin's assertion in the 1536 *Institutes* (which carried on steadfastly through all the editions of the *Institutes*): Sacraments are "not onely badges or tokens of Christian mens profession: rather they be certaine sure witnesses and effectuall signes of grace and Gods good wyll towardes vs, by the which he doth worke inuisiblie in vs." This was Calvin's point against Zwingli's sacramental theology, insofar as Calvin knew Zwingli's theology here. The sacraments are primarily effective signs that offer God's grace. They also are badges of human profession.

The next article on sacraments (26) takes up the long-standing assertion, dating back to Augustine, that the moral condition of the minister affects neither the hearing of the Word nor the receiving of the sacraments. Word and sacrament are done in Christ's name and ministry, and they offer God's grace to be received by human faith.

Article 27 discusses baptism and gives the twofold Calvin-like definition that baptism is both a sign of human profession and a sign to which God has appended divine promises of forgiveness of sin and adoption as children. Baptism is thus a sign of the regeneration that is ours when the sacrament is rightly received. Infant baptism, however, is defended not by reference to covenant but to "the institution of Christe."

The same sacramental theology of Calvin can be seen in the 1549 Anglican Catechism, whose sacramental sections were added in 1604 by Bishop Overall, dean of St. Paul's Cathedral.[55] In 1662 the catechism was printed in the *Book of Common Prayer* and placed between the rites for baptism and confirmation. The questions on sacraments and baptism (and the Lord's Supper also) are Calvin's position stated concisely. A sacrament is an outward and visible sign of an inward and spiritual grace given unto us, ordained by Christ himself, as a means whereby we receive the same, and a pledge to assure us thereof.[56]

The outward sign is both a pledge of God's grace toward us and the means, when received in faith,[57] by which such grace is inwardly given us. In baptism the outer sign is water, "wherein the person is baptized *In the Name of the Father, and of the Son, and of the Holy Ghost*." The "inward and spiritual grace" consists of "a death to sin, and a new birth unto righteousness," and "hereby we are made children of grace," no longer "children of wrath."[58] Repentance and faith are required for such regeneration. Even though infants cannot "stedfastly believe the promises of God made to them" in baptism, they are still to be baptized and are responsible for their faith and baptism "when they come to age."[59]

In 1643, the so-called Long Parliament called together 121 Puritan ministers, along with thirty members of Parliament (ten from the House of Lords, twenty from the House of Commons), and six Scottish Presbyterian advisers.[60] Their charge was to reform the worship, discipline, and government of the Church of England. Over the objections of Charles I, the assembly was convened July 1, 1643. Within three months the English and Scottish parliaments approved the *Solemn League and Covenant* by which they pledged to reform the churches of England, Scotland, and Ireland in matters of confession of faith, polity, worship, and catechism. For the English parliament it meant a military ally in the struggle with the king. For the Scottish parliament it meant securing the Reformed faith. For the Westminster Assembly, which subscribed to the covenant, it meant that work was to begin on issues of church government, worship, confession of faith, and catechism. With large agreement in theological matters (as compared to polity and worship), the assembly finished the Westminster Confession in November 1646. The two catechisms were presented to Parliament in their final form in April 1648. In 1648, Parliament approved the Westminster Confession and the Larger and Shorter Westminster Catechisms.[61]

Chapter 27 of the Westminster Confession treats the sacraments in general and begins with the simple assertion that "Sacraments are holy Signs and Seals of the Covenant of Grace, immediately instituted by God, to represent Christ and his Benefits." The sacraments were also instituted by God for strengthening our faith both inwardly and in outer service to God (sec. 1). In the sacrament there is "a spiritual Relation, or sacramental Union, between the Sign and the Thing signified," so that "the Names and Effects of the one, are attributed to the other" (sec. 2). So far this is a clear restatement of Calvin's sacramental theol-

ogy in a later context. The chapter on the sacraments then asserts that
the efficacy of the sacraments is dependent on the work of the Spirit
and their dominical institution, not on the sacraments themselves or
the condition of the minister (sec. 3). There are only two sacraments,
baptism and the Lord's Supper, which can be "dispensed" only by a
"Minister of the Word lawfully ordained" (sec. 4). The conclusion to
the chapter asserts that the spiritual things signified by sacraments in
the Old and New Testaments were same as to their substance (sec. 5).

The baptism chapter (28) begins by asserting that baptism was
ordained by Jesus Christ not just as a sign of entering the visible church
but as a "Sign and Seal of the Covenant of Grace," of engrafting into
Christ, regeneration, remission of sins, and renewal of life. On the one
hand, as a sign that has "sacramental union" with God's grace, baptism truly offers that grace to the one being baptized (sec. 1). On the
other hand, "the Efficacy of Baptism is not tied to that Moment of Time
wherein it is administered." One would then expect the usual claim
that only where there is faith can there be sacramental efficacy. The
Westminster divines would undoubtedly have agreed with that theological claim. However, the confession is thoroughly predestinarian,
and so faith as such comes only from the divine will. The confession
therefore makes the logical step in shunting human faith and directly
connecting baptismal efficacy with the mystery of the divine will:

> [T]he Grace promised is not only offered, but really exhibited and
> conferred by the Holy Ghost, to such (whether of Age or Infants) as
> that Grace belongeth unto according to the Counsel of God's own
> Will, in his appointed Time. (Sec. 6)

In trying to explain how baptism could be effective for an infant
already in the covenant, Calvin's metaphorical description of God
planting the "seed of future repentance and faith" may indeed merit
some criticism,[62] but compared to Westminster's predestinarian assertion, Calvin's metaphor seems welcome.[63]

Before moving to the catechisms, it should be noted that the
covenant defense for infant baptism had become so well known that
the Westminster Confession simply uses a shorthand, so to speak:
"[T]he Infants of one or both believing Parents, are to be baptized" (sec.
4). In other words, since one or both of the parents are within the
covenant of grace, the infant born into that covenant community ought
to receive the covenant sign, baptism, just as infants born into the old
covenant community received its sign, circumcision.

The Shorter Catechism begins with as clear and concise a definition
of a sacrament as one can find in the Reformed confessions: "A sacrament is a holy ordinance instituted by Christ, wherein, by sensible
signs, Christ and the benefits of the New Covenant are represented,

sealed, and applied to believers" (Q. 92). First, sacraments are signs that represent and seal Christ himself and thus the benefits of the New Covenant. Next, Christ and these benefits are themselves applied to the one receiving the sacrament. What is required for the sacraments to "become effectual means of salvation"?

> The sacraments become effectual means of salvation, not from any virtue in them, or in him that doth administer them, but only by the blessing of Christ, and the working of His Spirit *in them that by faith receive them.* (Q. 91, italics added)

Here we find exactly what was expected but was lacking in the Westminster Confession. On the issue of sacramental efficacy, human faith is required for the sacrament to become effective through the power of the Spirit. How fascinating, then, to find in the Larger Catechism this answer to sacramental efficacy:

> The sacraments become effective means of salvation not by any inward power in themselves, or by any virtue derived from the piety or intention of the one administering them, but in fact only through the power of the Holy Spirit and the blessing of Christ by whom they are instituted. (Q. 161)[64]

This precisely matches the assertion in the confession, and they both stand opposed to the answer given in the Shorter Catechism, where the necessity of faith is mentioned. The divines naturally would have answered that these two responses are perfectly compatible, since faith is the gift of the Spirit "given" only to those whom God had chosen.[65] We have seen Calvin use this very language. What causes wonder is the "double-ledger" bookkeeping here. A child learning from the Shorter Catechism would learn that faith was needed. But those who wrote and accepted the confession and Longer Catechism, including the minister who used the Shorter Catechism for children, would know that the public books really did not read the same as the private theological ledger.

In the Shorter Catechism, baptism is described as a sacrament that signifies and seals "our ingrafting into Christ and partaking of the benefits of the covenant of grace, and our engagement to be the Lord's" (Q. 94). Such baptism is not to be administered to anyone outside "of the visible church" unless that person professes faith in and obedience to Christ. However, "the infants of such as are members of the visible church" can be baptized (Q. 95). These assertions reflect the Westminster Confession, and they are paralleled by the Larger Catechism, which gives more detail. The Larger Catechism, for example, fills out the covenant details for the case in which an infant has one or both parents who are "believers" or "members of the visible church." The

Larger Catechism then adds a long section (Q. 167) on "how our baptism is cultivated by us in order that we accordingly harvest better fruit." Here the catechism describes the "necessary but much neglected duty" (*necessarium (at neglectum nimis) officium*) of "life long" cultivation of our baptism, especially at times of temptation but also when baptism is administered to others. We are to reflect earnestly and thankfully on the meaning and the blessings of baptism, our own baptismal vows, how far short we have fallen, and then to take strength from Christ in our work toward a regenerated life.[66]

REFORMED ORTHODOXY

As Protestantism moved from the last third of the sixteenth century into the seventeenth, and as the second generation of great Reformers died, classical Protestantism moved into the period of orthodox Protestantism.[67] When the Formula of Concord (1577) formalized the division between Lutheranism and the Reformed tradition, new challenges arose. The two traditions needed to be defined carefully; pastors needed to be trained in those traditions; and Protestantism needed to defend itself against Roman Catholicism. The task of formalizing the Reformation insights fell on the Lutheran side to men such as Johannes Gerhard, Abraham Calov, and Johannes Andreas Quenstedt. For the Reformed tradition, the work was carried on by Theodore Beza, Amandus Polanus, Johannes Wollebius, Johann Heinrich Heidegger, Francis Turretin, and others.

Using conceptual tools learned from Aristotle and carefully reasoning out the details of Christian doctrine, Protestantism produced highly organized, lengthy, and technical works of theology. It was Protestant scholasticism at its best, though not everyone has appreciated this development. The same year that Reformed orthodox theologians wrote the *Consensus helveticus* (1675), which defended the predestinarian and limited atonement teachings of Dort as well as the literal and verbal inspiration of Scripture, Philip Spener published his *Pia desideria*. Spener argued that being Christian concerned Christian life, not just correct doctrine. Bible study, prayer, charity in controversy, and training of pastors in devotional life and real preaching were the more crucial activities for the church.

Despite the criticism that has often been leveled at Protestant orthodoxy, the meticulous argument, the knowledge of Scripture, and the organizing of Protestant theology in carefully constructed *summas* have much to commend this period of Protestantism. Protestant theologians of the twentieth century as diverse as Paul Tillich and Karl Barth recommended the study of Protestant orthodoxy as a formative and learning experience, even should one not agree with the orthodox thinkers.[68] In the nineteenth century, the views of Lutheran and Reformed orthodox theologians were compiled in single books, organized around theological loci. Heinrich Schmid produced his well-known book *The Doctrinal Theology of the Evangelical Lutheran Church*, and Heinrich Heppe produced *Reformed Dogmatics*, a book influential on and commended by Karl Barth.[69]

Chapter 25 of Heppe's *Reformed Dogmatics* specifically treats baptism. Of the eighteen sections that subdivide the topic, sections 1, 5, 8–11, and 13–16 relate to the theological issues raised in this study; sections 2–4, 6–7, 12, and 17 treat issues of administration and their meaning; and section 18 connects Christian baptism to that of John the Baptist.

For Reformed orthodoxy, baptism outwardly consisted of the element to which was added the Word. Word meant not just the Trinitarian formula but Christ's institution of baptism (Matt. 28:19), within which the entire gospel was implicitly found.[70] This exterior action was the means by which God sealed on the hearts of the elect the divine promise that they were participants in the covenant of grace. As such, baptism (and the Eucharist) was instituted only for true believers—the elect, more generally named as those with whom God had covenanted.[71]

Baptism that was done with water and the proper Trinitarian formula was thus inherently valid, even when done by heretics. Heppe cites the distinction made by Leonhard Riissen between heresy that denied the substance of baptism (e.g., Arianism) and that which observed the substance but denied other doctrines (e.g., Donatists). The former had invalid baptism, but the latter had valid baptism.[72] Such valid baptism was to be done only once, and the orthodox views cited by Heppe differed slightly here. Johannes Cocceius referred to the engrafting in Christ, which obviously could be done only once. Polanus referred to covenant, asserting that God established the covenant with a person only once.[73]

Although all baptisms correctly done were absolutely valid, not all such baptisms had efficacy. The source of baptism's efficacy was ultimately the promise of God attached to the signs, not the signs themselves. Heidegger explicitly distinguished the Reformed position from that of Thomas (and the Dominicans) and Scotus (and the Franciscans), who he thought too closely allied the divine work and the earthly sign. Heidegger and Antonius Walaeus both explicitly distinguished the Reformed position from that of the Lutherans. Walaeus allowed that in ordinary circumstances Word and sign worked together, as long as one realized that the Spirit worked where it would.[74] Naturally, such efficacy was for the elect only, as followed from the understanding of sacraments and baptism.[75]

With the loosened connection between sign and efficacy, and within the larger context of election and double predestination, baptism as such was not a means of grace. Baptism sealed the salvation present through the divine promise and human faith, and baptism therefore was not strictly necessary for salvation. The necessity of baptism came rather from its divine institution.[76] To the question about who should be baptized according to the dominical mandate, the orthodox answered that all who belonged to the covenant were to be baptized. For adults this meant those who professed their faith, although it was acknowledged that they might be either truly faithful (i.e., elect) or merely reckoned faithful (i.e., by profession of faith, whether their inner state was election or reprobation).[77] Children of covenant parents (or parent) were to be baptized, and this even in the case where the outward behavior of the parents would have indicated them not to belong to the church.[78] Baptism was truly the sign of regeneration only for the children of the elect within the covenant community, even though love hoped for this to be the case with any particular child. Even with this, baptism could be conceived as bringing privilege to the nonelect children in the covenant, namely, "the outward privileges of God's covenant."[79]

To summarize the various orthodox theologians, as cited by Heppe, on the variety of issues concerning baptism, an appropriate description would be:

> Baptism was the divinely instituted activity which sealed the participation of the elected person in the covenant of grace. This covenant was also described as the death and resurrection of the person in Christ, as well as the forgiveness of all sins of the person's life, and including their regeneration (secs 1, 8, 13). As such, baptism did not impart salvation but rather sealed it as a means of strengthening the person (secs 1, 9–10, 12, 14, 16). Salvation itself came from the promise of God to impart grace in Jesus Christ (secs 9, 12). Such salvation as baptism sealed had efficacy only insofar as the person received the sacrament (and thus the divine promise) in faith (secs 10, 12). The validity of the sacrament, however, was dependent not on faithful reception but on its proper administration with water and the triune baptismal formula instituted by Christ as the word of grace (secs 4–5). All people were entitled to receive this sacrament who belonged to God's covenant of grace—both confessing adults and children of believers (secs 14–15).[80]

By way of comment, much of this definition echoed the position of Calvin as he had developed his baptismal theology by 1543. Baptism sealed the covenant that God had made with the elect. The covenant was ultimately christological in character, embracing the themes of mortification/vivification, forgiveness of sins, and sacrament as a divine promise of grace attached to an outward sign. Children born into the covenant were to be baptized since baptism is the sign of covenant membership. Finally, the validity of the sacrament was distinguished from its efficacy, the latter depending on the faithful reception of the sacrament by the person receiving it.

On the other hand, there were differences between the baptismal theology of Calvin, Bullinger, and much of the Reformed confessions and that of Reformed orthodoxy. First of all, the covenant theme has stepped further to the foreground. At the same time, the sign-promise theology that Calvin learned from Luther, which formed the backbone of Calvin's sacramental theology and appeared with varying strength in the confessions, has receded toward the background. This shift allowed two other changes to appear. Where Calvin was careful to insist that baptism actually did something at the time of administration—offer God's promise of grace attached to an outward sign—Reformed orthodoxy backed away from such sacramental language by insisting that baptism outwardly sealed what God internally did otherwise (secs. 9, 16).[81] This shift in emphasis toward baptism as the seal of a salvation otherwise imparted then helped Reformed orthodoxy deal with the problem that Calvin had to address so carefully: whether predestination to reprobation prohibited baptism from having sacramental efficacy, since the reprobate who received baptism could not have received the reality that the sign signified. Rather, the reprobate would have received the outward baptism, to be distinguished from the inner baptism that took place only where there was faithful reception (secs. 9–10) and thus not received by the reprobate.

FRIEDRICH SCHLEIERMACHER

One hundred years after orthodoxy ended the seventeenth century and the pietism of August Sebastian Francke, Philip Spener, and others had produced fruit within Lutheranism and Anglicanism, the forces of orthodoxy, pietism, and the Enlightenment coalesced in the life of the most influential Reformed theologian of the nineteenth century, Friedrich Daniel Schleiermacher.[82]

Schleiermacher was born in 1768, the second of two children for Katharina-Maria and Gottlieb Schleiermacher. Friedrich's father was a Reformed army chaplain who had found his spiritual life renewed through contact with the Moravians. As a boy, Schleiermacher attend Moravian schools and seminary, where he also was spiritually formed by this distinctive pietist tradition. His problem was that he found traditional Christian doctrines hard to believe. Schleiermacher went on to study at the University of Halle. From there he served as tutor for a noble family in East Prussia; he went on to serve as assistant pastor, then moved to Berlin in 1796, where he was a hospital chaplain.

While in Berlin (1796–1802), Schleiermacher became acquainted with Friedrich Schlegel and the German Romantic writers. With Schlegel, he began the translation of Plato into German, a project he would complete alone some years later. Schleiermacher's best-known work of the period was *On Religion: Speeches to Its Cultured Despisers* (1799). There he argued that to be interested in the human condition without being interested in religion was to end up with an insufficient view of the human person. Religion was at the heart of being human, and organized religion fundamentally concerned the religious association that people had, since human beings were fundamentally social.

After Berlin, Schleiermacher served another pastorate. He then spent a short term teaching at the University of Halle (1804–6). Eventually he became professor at the new University of Berlin in 1810, which he helped found and where he remained until his death in 1834. Among his many and wide-ranging writings, Schleiermacher's crowning work was his book *Christian Faith* (*Der Christliche Glaube*). Always the preacher and churchman as well as the scholar, Schleiermacher not only influenced the study of aesthetics, Plato, philosophy of religion, hermeneutics, ethics, and Christian theology but also was active and influential in the life of the German church under Frederick III.[83]

Before turning to Schleiermacher's view on baptism, a brief introduction to his theological system is needed. Upon self-reflection, asserted Schleiermacher, all people have a "feeling of absolute dependence." By this terminology Schleiermacher did not mean a particular emotion but rather an awareness, or sense, or consciousness, underlying all selfhood that the self and world were not only mutually related but also absolutely dependent. The "feeling of absolute dependence" was itself the awareness of being immediately related to God. This original revelation of God lay behind all religions, and in Christianity it was called forth, named, and shaped by the decisive revelation of God in the Redeemer, Jesus Christ:

> If it be the essence of redemption that the God-consciousness already present in human nature, though feeble and repressed, becomes stimulated and made dominant by the entrance of the living influence of Christ, the individual on whom this influence is exercised attains a religious personality not his before.[84]

Rejecting the classical formulation of Christ's two natures, Schleiermacher instead argued that Christ had perfect "God-consciousness." The power of this consciousness was mediated to others through his physical existence, exerting redeeming influence on them. The God-consciousness of Christ remained available through those whose lives he had redeemed and who proclaimed him as their redeemer.[85] The church, therefore, not only derived its existence from Christ, but the God-consciousness that was his was passed on to the church, which continued his activity:

> On the one hand, as the organism of Christ—which is what Scripture means by calling it [the Christian Church] His body—it is related to Christ as the outward to the inward, so that in its essential activities it must also be a reflection of the activities of Christ. And since the effects produced by it are simply the gradual realization of redemption in the world, its activities must likewise be a continuation of the activities of Christ Himself.[86]

Simply put, through the church Christ himself still evoked and shaped the "feeling of absolute dependence," which for Christians was known only in the experience of redemption through Christ. It should always be remembered that *Christian Faith* was a reflection on faith from within Christianity and addressing the Christian community.

For Schleiermacher, a person entered the Christian community through baptism, which was, at one and the same time, "the act of will by which the Church receives the individual into its fellowship" and "the channel of the divine justifying activity, through which the individual is received into the living fellowship of Christ (*Lebensgemein-schaft Christi*)."[87] The proclamation of the Word must have preceded baptism, and the one to be baptized must have acknowledged the Word.[88] It naturally followed that the faith of the person baptized was a precondition of the baptism;[89] and Schleiermacher said straightforwardly that "[b]aptism is received wrongly if it be received without faith, and it is wrongly given so."[90]

This raised the question of infant baptism, but before addressing that question Schleiermacher took up several other issues about baptism. First, Schleiermacher understood that faith must precede baptism. But this would mean that salvation also preceded baptism, since he had "explained faith as the appropriation of the perfection and blessedness of Christ." To this objection Schleiermacher replied that faith may indeed be that inward state that is such appropriation, but influence of Christ's perfection and the enjoyment of his blessedness "become real only within the fellowship of believers."[91]

Second, since baptism is "the channel of the divine justifying activity," and since justification and conversion occurred together as aspects of the activity that Schleiermacher called "regeneration,"[92] then regeneration occurred at baptism.[93] This would obviously be the case if the church baptized only those who were as ready and mature as those whom Christ called to be his disciples. In actual practice, however, both the church's act and the state of regeneration are less than

perfect. Baptism and regeneration thus happen without strict coinci-
dence. The result, as Schleiermacher observed, is that

> there will always be some regenerate persons who are not yet bap-
> tized but who might well have claimed to be received earlier into the
> Church; similarly there will be baptized persons who are not yet
> regenerate but in the most active way are being commended to
> divine grace for regeneration by the prayers of the Church.[94]

In the situation where someone has been baptized but not yet regenerated, Schleiermacher argued what we saw Luther and the first two
generation of Reformed theologians argue: Baptism "is ineffectual
only when it is imparted prematurely, before the work of preaching is
complete and has awakened faith."[95] The parallel to infant baptism
hardly escaped Schleiermacher, who simply said:

> Thus infant baptism is the same as any other baptism which has erro-
> neously been imparted prior to the full faith of the person baptized
> and yet is valid; only its proper efficacy is suspended until the per-
> son baptized has really become a believer.[96]

The issue for Schleiermacher was that these baptisms were themselves "imperfect" and reckoned as a "reproach" to the church. Was
there not some *positive reason* to baptize infants? It was not a matter of
apostolic practice, although sympathy could be had for why the early
church began the practice (*Christian Faith*, sec. 138.1). Schleiermacher
then found reason for infant baptism: The future of such infants was
entrusted to the church, whose duty then was "to bring them . . . into
direct relation to the Word of God, and to maintain them therein until
faith awakens."[97]

The Reformers could well have abolished infant baptism as not
appropriate to Christ's institution, said Schleiermacher. In fact, this still
might be done without causing any serious problems for raising children in the Christian community.[98] For the moment, however, infant
baptism, understood as raising children with the Word ever before
them, was still to be allowed, but only insofar as confirmation was still
seriously undertaken and demanded of the children at the appropriate
age. "For it is only as combined with confirmation," argued Schleiermacher, "that infant baptism answers to Christ's institution."[99]

THE TWENTIETH-CENTURY DEBATES

A little more than a century after Schleiermacher wrote his *Christian
Faith*, the very issue about infant baptism that Schleiermacher raised
was to be raised again in the Reformed tradition.[100] In 1937, on the

occasion of giving the Olavus Petri Lectures at the University of Uppsala, Emil Brunner began the modern Reformed debate about infant baptism.[101] Under the condition of a state church, in which many people were baptized as a matter of civil course and did not know or care about their baptism, infant baptism was problematic. The "objective" aspect of the sacrament was emphasized to the loss of the "subjective," the need for faith, so that the sacramental word had become merely a "sermon-word."[102]

In 1943, Karl Barth, at a lecture to Swiss theological students, picked up the theme broached earlier by Brunner and strenuously argued, as Brunner had not,[103] for complete rejection of infant baptism. When Barth's lecture was translated into English five years later, the controversy swirled.[104] Barth argued that baptism powerfully and effectively re-presented (*ein Abbild*) the death and resurrection of Jesus Christ and the renewal of the Holy Spirit. Baptism portrayed Golgotha with its threat of death and its deliverance unto life. In baptism was to be found the representation of our association with Christ and the covenant of grace realized and concluded in him.[105]

To the one being baptized, baptism was the "speaking likeness of that threat of death and deliverance unto life" in which one found oneself addressed and delivered, as one yielded to that threat and deliverance. Naturally, adult baptism alone was appropriate, since only an adult could know the threat and deliverance that was baptism's. Only an adult could have the faith whose ground was "in the objective reality of the divine covenant of grace."[106] Not surprisingly, Barth then carefully distinguished the cause of salvation (*causa salutis*), which was found only in the "word and work of Jesus Christ," from the knowledge of salvation (*cognitio salutis*), which came to us, and to the one being baptized, through the words of the sermon and sacrament.[107] Both the church and the one being baptized had their responsible roles, as obedient proclaimers and hearers, and in these roles infant baptism, though valid, was certainly not responsible.[108]

Did baptism then actually effect anything? Or (in Calvin's words) did God "mock us" by not performing inwardly what the signs signify outwardly? Barth, it seems, had a change of mind here. In *The Teaching of the Church regarding Baptism*, Barth began by arguing that baptism actually effected what it signified:

> Baptism is no dead or dumb representation, but a living and expressive one. Its potency lies in the fact that it comprehends the whole movement of sacred history (*Heilsgeschichte*) and that it is therefore *res potentissima et efficacissima*. All that it intends and actually effects is the result of this potency. It exercises its power as it shows to a man that objective reality to which he belongs in such a way that he can

only forget or miss it *per nefas*; in such a way, at all events, that he becomes by its marks a marked man, by its portraiture one who is himself portrayed.[109]

This theme later concluded the essay. Baptism was an effective sign that did what it signified because in baptism the one being baptized stood amid death, was convinced of the new beginnings of life that divine assurance brings, and willingly bound the self in obedience to this new life known in the death and resurrection of Jesus Christ.[110]

By the writing of the last section of the *Church Dogmatics* (IV/4),[111] Barth had changed his mind, not least because of the exegetical work done by his son, Markus Barth.[112] The elder Barth accepted his son's negative thesis that baptism in the New Testament was not sacramental. Barth divided IV/4 of the *Church Dogmatics* into two parts: baptism with the Spirit and baptism with water. Christian life had its foundation in God through God's free grace that changed us into what we otherwise could not be—faithful. God brought us this new life in Jesus Christ, who was outside us and effectively for us, and thus was "in us." Such renewal happened through the baptism of the Spirit.[113] In response to this Spirit baptism, we had the human response for obedience, whose *basis* was in Christ's commands and baptism,[114] whose *goal* was the reconciling activity of God unto our obedient life,[115] and whose *meaning* had no sacramental reality as such but could be found instead in faithful human response to the divine initiative.[116]

Karl Barth was soon answered by Oscar Cullmann, his Lutheran colleague at the University of Basel who was professor of New Testament and early church history there.[117] Of the numerous Reformed responses to Barth, three are helpful for this study. Two very different voices came from theologians within the French Reformed tradition. Franz Leenhardt's 1946 work on baptism worked carefully with the New Testament texts themselves.[118] Leenhardt, who was professor of New Testament at the University of Geneva, traced the history of baptism in the early church, from John the Baptist through the apostle Paul (chaps. 2–5). The early church, argued Leenhardt, correctly conformed to the divine plan when it conceived that baptism "expressed, concretized, and actualized the will of God to save all people by faith in the gospel of Jesus Christ."[119] This fundamental assertion naturally had consequences when Leenhardt turned to the issue of infant baptism (chap. 6). Here Leenhardt began by saying that even the defenders of infant baptism cannot find New Testament evidence explicit enough to decide the issue of whether the early church baptized infants. Further, it was clear that Calvin's own exegesis trying to prove divine institution of infant baptism would not bear scrutiny.[120] By contrast, since baptism was "the sign of the divine will to save," not the sign of an "accomplished, recognized, and sufficient regeneration," the believer was called to turn away from introspection and toward Jesus Christ, who embodied God's gracious will.[121] Thus, concluded Leenhardt, one can justify infant baptism in a way that does not contradict its apostolic meaning. A child is baptized into the promise of God, whose will is to save, and the duties of the parents are to raise the child with that promise ever present so that the child can appropriate its reality when he or she grows up. In this way the parents, and the community, make up for what is otherwise a defect in the rite of infant baptism. To neglect this responsibility is to abuse the sacrament.[122]

Pierre Marcel took up the challenge to Barth from the French Reformed churches and in so doing made direct appeal to Calvin and, through him, to Scripture.[123] Critical of Leenhardt for trying to settle a sacramental issue by doing exegesis while bracketing theology proper, Marcel avowedly did a "dogmatic" exegesis. By this phrase he meant that he would lean "upon the works of *Reformed* exegesis" and effect "a synthesis in accordance with the standards which characterize its discipline. That is to say, it is not bound either in order or in methods to the critical exegesis." Such study, argued Marcel, would show that infant baptism is *"biblical, Christian, and Reformed,"* despite what exegetes such as Leenhardt had argued.[124]

Central for Marcel, and, he believed, central to Calvin because it was scripturally central, was the unity of God's covenant of grace. The promise was given to Abraham and his seed and thus to the church of the New Testament. The church as such has always been one.[125] The promise was given corporately and so is a "legal relationship." In time, this communal and corporate meaning became balanced by the individual appropriation of the promise, when the "legal relationship" became a "living relationship."[126] Because this unity of covenant was by God's sovereign decree of the covenant of grace, covenant was the basis for baptism. Only an express scriptural prohibition against infant baptism should deter the church from baptizing infants.[127]

The Dutch Reformed Church responded to Barth and took up the defense of infant baptism by appealing not only to the covenant defense but to another aspect of Reformed theology—predestination.[128] As Dutch Reformed churches looked to the Heidelberg Catechism (1562), the Belgic Confession (1566), and the Canons of Dort (1619), they found what they believed was an insistence on God's unconditional election, which became the backbone of their position against Anabaptist believers' baptism. God's sovereign predestination, linked with God's covenant promises, formed the foundation for the practice of infant baptism. This position was not without difficulties, because the normative sequence for adults—depravity, election, regeneration by the Spirit, and then faith and the fruits of election, including baptism—could not be followed in the case of infant baptism. The idea of "inactive regeneration," or "sleeping regeneration," as well as the idea of the "potency of faith" within infants (as compared to actualized faith), was needed to overcome the problems inherent when predestination to election is linked with infant baptism and covenant theology.

Finally, Neuser's study on the Heidelberg Catechism deserves mention again. Neuser addressed Barth's challenge and, by using a specific historical document, showed how the sacramental and baptismal sections of the catechism were designed to answer the question of infant baptism.[129] Neuser showed that the Heidelberg Catechism quite consciously moved the discussion of faithful reception out of the opening question that defines the sacraments (Q. 66) and out of the infant baptism question (Q. 74). At the same time, the catechism moved into prominence the idea of the gospel promise as attached to, and having the same content as, the external sign.[130] In baptism as in preaching, of which baptism was the embodied sign, the Word came, addressed, and evoked faith through the Spirit. Faith was not demanded prior to the address of the Word. After baptism the Word, attached to the sign and through the Spirit, continued to evoke faith and the increasing sanctification of the person addressed.[131] The Heidelberg Catechism thus presented an integrated sacramental and baptismal theology of the Word (*pace* Barth), borrowing from Luther, Melanchthon, and Calvin while avoiding their errors.[132]

SUMMARY

Three short comments summarize this long post-Reformation trajectory of Reformed baptism. First, time and again the distinction between sacramental validity and efficacy was made. God's offer of Christ stood on its own, valid whether or not one had faith. Yet the demand for faithful appropriation was also there. Where there was seemingly too much emphasis on the objective offer, or where the valid act had too frequently been administered without concern for faith, Reformed theologians emphasized the appropriation of the baptismal offer (so Schleiermacher, Brunner, and Barth).

Second, from the Reformed confessions through Schleiermacher, what was offered ultimately was Christ himself, not merely his benefits or the covenant of grace. Here the Reformed trajectory continued what the first two generations of Reformers had also argued. Some of the Reformed confessions and theologians were more covenant oriented in their christological expression: for example, Bullinger, the Westminster Confession and catechisms, Reformed orthodoxy, Barth, the Dutch Reformed Church, and Marcel.

Third, where infant baptism was defended such defense always appealed to the divine initiative, usually appealing to the divinely initiated covenant that embraced infants but also appealing to the promises or will of God attached to the sign.

5

QUO VADIS?
THE *BOOK OF COMMON WORSHIP*

With this chapter, the book comes full circle. The Introduction discussed the modern liturgical renewal movement and the history and
structure of the Rite of Christian Initiation of Adults. A brief look at the
issue of ecclesiology suggested that the liturgical theology operative
in the RCIA may not be compatible with that of Luther and Calvin. To
answer the objection that one might borrow forms without borrowing
theology, the last section of the Introduction took a brief look at the
first Protestant worship book to be influenced by the liturgical renewal
movement, the praised and much-used *Lutheran Book of Worship*. At
the end of the chapter, I suggested that something of Luther had been
lost when one compares Luther's rite and Flood Prayer with that of
the *LBW*. Might there be an analogous problem with Reformed baptismal theology and the rite of baptism in the *Book of Common Worship*?

The next four chapters examined Reformed baptismal theology.
Chapter 1 looked at the foundations by studying the first-generation
reformers Zwingli, Luther, and Bucer. Chapter 2 turned to the second-
generation reformers Bullinger and Calvin. Chapter 3 continued the
Calvin study into issues of predestination and infant baptism. Chapter 4
then traced a trajectory of Reformed baptismal theology through the
Reformed confessions, Reformed orthodoxy, Schleiermacher, and the
twentieth-century baptismal debates. With this historical-theological
task completed, this chapter returns to the task of practical theology.

Does the current baptismal rite in the *Book of Common Worship*
(*BCW*) show a Reformed baptismal theology? If not, can it be emended
to make it more adequately Reformed? The first section of this chapter reflects on the Reformed baptismal material from the previous four
chapters. The next section moves to the liturgical material itself. The
final section summarizes the discussion and suggests appropriate
emendations to the baptismal rite in the *BCW*.

REFLECTIONS ON REFORMED BAPTISMAL THEOLOGY

Divine Gracious Sovereignty and Covenant

Some comments can be made about Reformed theology as it pertains
to baptism. First, baptism proclaims God's sovereign grace. This

means, negatively, that the emphasis on God's predestining election to salvation or reprobation is itself not the *central* aspect to the divine activity proclaimed in baptism. In the first place, a primacy of sovereign predestining power misses the christological center of classical Reformed Protestantism in the sixteenth century.[1] It also misses the christological emphasis in the Reformed confessions, Schleiermacher's "christo-morphic" theology,[2] and Barth's christocentric approach to theology.

God's sovereign grace refers to the insistence in Reformed theology on the primary and prevenient activity of God, as God self-discloses as the one who is with us and for us and to whom we are called to loyalty out of thankfulness. A strong case has been made that this is so for Calvin, both as an overarching theological theme and in terms of his sacramental theology more specifically.[3] Detailed work on the Reformed baptismal rites of the sixteenth century has shown just this emphasis on the priority of God's gracious activity.[4] In slightly varying ways, we have seen throughout the Reformed trajectory the same insistence on grace as God's self-disclosing as the one with us and for us. In the twentieth-century Reformed baptismal debates, this formal point stood out among all the key theologians: from Barth's idea of divine election into the covenant of grace, to Leenhardt's assertion of God's gracious will to save, to Marcel's covenant of grace. All are agreed that God's gracious and sovereign initiative, made known through Christ, forms the basis of the sacrament of baptism.

Second, covenant thinking has typically characterized the way that Reformed baptismal theology has expressed God's gracious initiative toward humanity. Zwingli's development of covenant baptismal theology moved through stages to an emphasis on covenant unity and the grace of God offered in the sign of the covenant. Bucer likewise emphasized the unity of the covenant, linking the eternal covenant of grace in Genesis 17 with the (deutero-)Pauline connection of baptism and circumcision (Colossians 2). Bullinger developed his covenant ideas apart from Zwingli, uniquely conceiving a single covenant of grace from Adam onward. Calvin likely learned his covenant ideas from Bucer and from the Latin works of Zwingli: Calvin had ecumenical interests, and he blended sacramental ideas from Luther and Zwingli. Calvin was also influenced by Bucer during his Strasbourg ministry.[5]

Reformed theology, through the work of Zwingli, Calvin, Bullinger, and later sixteenth- and seventeenth-century federal theologians, retained the idea of the divine covenant of grace and the idea of baptism as the new sign that replaced the old sign of circumcision.[6] Twentieth-century Reformed baptismal theology continued this trajectory. Barth argued that baptism comprised a union with Christ and thus participation in the one eternal covenant of grace realized in him. And Marcel defended infant baptism through insistence on the covenant of grace and its unity between old and new covenants.

It must also be said that covenant was not prominent in the baptismal theology of the French Confession, the Belgic Confession, the Heidelberg Catechism, and Schleiermacher.[7] Instead, the christocentric orientation stood out. Finally, Calvin, the Heidelberg Catechism, and to some extent Reformed orthodoxy gave significant voice to a sign-promise baptismal theology.

Two Types of Covenant Theology

Chapter 2 showed that Bullinger viewed covenant as God's call of all people into the one covenant that began with Adam and found its telos in Jesus Christ. While Bullinger indeed thought of this eternal, gracious call as made to the elect only, he pragmatically concentrated on God's universal gracious call rather than on single predestination. Karl Barth represented a twentieth-century variation on this covenant theology. Barth discussed divine election in sections 32 through 35 of his *Church Dogmatics.* The details of his thinking are well known, and this essay can hardly treat them in depth. There are, however, similarities to Bullinger's ideas that suggest the Reformed tradition has two general covenant ideas with which to work when considering baptism.

After an introductory section in the *Church Dogmatics* in which Barth oriented himself to Scripture (sec. 32), he asserted the christological basis of election (Jesus as both electing God and elected human). He argued for placing election within the doctrine of God proper, and he discussed the election of Jesus Christ (sec. 33). As the Son of God, Jesus Christ was the electing God; as the Son of Man, he was the elected human. Thus, Jesus Christ inclusively displayed the sum of the gospel—the unmerited, gracious acceptance of all people. This was God's eternal predestining will, whose content was not obscure in the traditional sense. Not only was the individual elected into God's covenant of grace, but the community was also (sec. 34). When Barth turned to the individual (sec. 35), he made clear that each person was already elected in Jesus Christ. The person could accept this election and live by receiving its promise, or the individual could reject the election, which rejection itself was overturned and rejected in Jesus Christ. Not everyone knew the salvation of being elected and the service demanded, nor did the Spirit move to carry out the divine will. All people lived confronted by the divine offer and their own decision. God's gracious and eternal election remained.[8]

The differences between Bullinger and Barth should not be overlooked, particularly with respect to eschatology. Will there be some future eschatological event in which God's elect are saved and the reprobate are damned? What would this mean for universalism, as Bullinger and Barth might see the issue? Yet, when the issue at hand is *the work of the church in the world,* the covenant theologies of Bullinger and Barth are strikingly similar. God covenants with all humanity, regardless of human acceptance or rejection of that covenant. All people have the opportunity to accept that covenant and live according to its gifts and demands. Whoever takes the covenant on him- or herself as one of the elected ones enters the church. And the church is thus comprised of those who acknowledge God's gracious activity and promise to live accordingly.

A second type of elect covenant community in Reformed theology and baptismal theology can be found in part of Calvin's theology. Calvin posited a double covenant: a general election given to Abraham and his seed and a secret election to those who were among the company of the elect according to God's predestination to salvation.[9] Through the mid-1550s, and exemplary in the 1545 *Institutes,* Calvin was able to hold together his sacramental theology, Christology, and this double-covenant community—the visible and the invisible church. But difficulties arose for Calvin as he tried to defend his baptismal theology against the charges that baptism had no effect for either the reprobate or children already born into the covenant. In short, by allowing predestination to enter the covenant discussion, Calvin conceived of the community of the elect differently from Bullinger, and this introduction of predestination also produced difficulties in his sacramental theology that Bullinger's position did not entail.

The Dutch Reformed Church, responding in the twentieth century to Barth's challenge to infant baptism, represented a contemporary variation of this covenant baptismal theology. Recall that the Dutch Reform Church looked back to the Synod of Dort and God's unconditional election and thus predestination. Part of the historical heritage drawn on by modern Dutch theologians, as they discussed baptism, was the high Calvinism that became popular in part of the Calvinist wing of the Reformed tradition. This form of Calvinism gained prominence through the response of Franciscus Gomarus and the Synod of Dort to the theology of Arminius. In this tradition a double covenant was posited: the covenant of works made with all humankind, which was unable to be fulfilled, and the covenant of grace made with the elect through God's sovereign predestination.[10]

Problems for this position arose because infant baptism disturbed the usual sequence of depravity, regeneration, faith, and fruits of election. To deal with this issue, Dutch Reformed theologians argued for such doctrines as sleeping regeneration and potency of faith. Further, there was the problem that some children never seemed to achieve active regeneration and true faith. Problems also occurred for Calvin's baptismal theology in accounting for the baptism of children who were among the elect.[11]

And so two types of elect covenant communities can be identified in Reformed baptismal theology. One posits a single, gracious covenant made to all and working through divine power that calls for but does not guarantee acceptance. The other posits a double covenant: the visible and general covenant made to all and the invisible covenant with those divinely predestined to election, working ultimately through divine power that guarantees its results. Might Reformed theology prefer one type to the other for its baptismal theology?

Both Calvin's baptismal theology and that of the Dutch Reformed Church showed internal problems. Calvin's integration of covenant theology and predestination led to the serious problem of whether the church would ever know a baptism to be valid. It also led to assertions about infant baptism that showed confusion about the how the child was viewed and how divine activity occurred. The Dutch Reformed Church kept infant baptism and predestination together only by making claims about inactive or sleeping regeneration and about potency of faith. Can these claims ever be meaningfully redeemed? By contrast, if the Calvinist-type covenant is to be rejected for baptismal theology, is there a *constructive* reason for choosing the Bullinger-Barth-type covenant?

A case has recently been made, in a discussion of God's sovereignty, that were one to take Barth's christocentric approach with complete exegetical seriousness, the matter of divine predestination to salvation or reprobation would never arise as a subject.[12] The matter can be summed up like this.

First, the language typically employed by the earliest Christian witnesses, all of it diverse but having the same character, speaks of God's *personal* agency: forgiveness, justification, reconciliation, redemption, healing, love, and so on. These words testify to an encounter with God in which God does not work by a force that guarantees its results. God works in a manner analogous to how personal agents work when they witness. Second, we see primary New Testament authors exactly holding to this apostolic witness while trying to correct *culturally conditioned views* of God as one who does have a guarantee-type power. Mark attempted to correct a *theios aner* Christology. Paul proclaimed the word of the cross that was a stumbling block to those who wanted signs and wonders. John recast the Signs Source in the context of faith. Thus, if Jesus is taken as the starting point for thinking about God, then divine power is construed in the manner typified by the Bullinger-Barth-type covenant. God proclaims a gracious covenant and humanity must respond.

Simply put, historical-theological considerations in the Reformed tradition and in the norm to which the tradition itself looks—Scripture—suggest a greater adequacy for the baptismal covenant theology typified by Bullinger and Barth.

Infant Baptism

One final issue needs to be addressed: What about infant baptism? Once again, historical-theological observations can help the discussion. First, chapter 1 showed that sacramental theology cannot be grasped properly unless sacramental validity is distinguished from sacramental efficacy. This point was decisively put by Augustine during the Donatist controversy and made clear by Luther time and again, especially in his conversation with the Anabaptists.[13] Calvin, as well as several of the Reformed confessions, made the same point:

> But they object that human ingratitude is not able to detract from or hinder anything of the trustworthiness of God's promises. Yes, of course, I agree; and I say that the power of the mystery remains unaffected however much the wicked are eager to enervate it, as far as it is *in se*. For all that, it is one thing to be offered, and another to be received.[14]

Second, recall that in early 1528, Martin Luther wrote a letter to two pastors who had sought his help combating arguments put forth by Anabaptists.[15] Among the more telling arguments that Luther put forth was this reflection on human faith:

> They want to take this [Mark 16:16] to mean that no one should be baptized before he believes. I say they have ventured a very great presumption. For if they want to follow such a belief they must not baptize before they know for certain that the one to be baptized believes. How and when do they always intend to know this? Have they now become gods that they can see in people's hearts whether they believe or not? If they do not know whether they believe, then why do they baptize since they fight so hard that faith must be before baptism? Are they not going against themselves that they baptize when they do not know whether faith is there or not?[16]

As long as the word *faith* is taken to mean what it primarily means throughout the New Testament—trusting God in a concrete context—Luther's point seems incontrovertible. An irony is that Barth's theological enterprise was concerned to build Christian doctrine and community on God's Word rather than on human ideas and words—on theology rather than on anthropology. Yet how could one ever know whether another person was *faithfully* obedient? Not that faithful obedience is not expected. It is expected, but at the moment of baptism, no one could ever know for certain that another person has faith. And so, finally, the church baptizes on the basis of God's election to grace, urging that such baptism be taken to heart by the one being baptized.[17]

In this regard the baptism of children stands *much closer* to adult baptism than most theologians have seen. The principal difference is that the infant *will have to be told* about the baptism and helped to appropriate the promise of God that baptism proclaimed. The adult *is told* about the baptism and helped to appropriate the promise of God that baptism proclaims.[18] In neither case can we say for certain that the person being baptized has faith.

In short, the church is built on the Word of God, not on human response. When a sacrament rightly proclaims the Word and signifies this divine promise with an outward and visible sign, the sacrament is validly administered. However much we understand the contexts of Schleiermacher and Barth, both of whom were critical of infant baptism; however much we also object to casual and indiscriminate baptisms; and even should we think adult baptism to be preferable to infant baptism, infant baptism can hardly be ruled out as a practice of the church.[19]

BAPTISM IN THE *BOOK OF COMMON WORSHIP*

This reflection on Reformed baptismal theology provides sufficient background to evaluate the baptism rite in the 1993 *Book of Common Worship*.[20] While every element of the baptismal material cannot be analyzed, the material divides into two general areas for discussion: the structure of the rite and the liturgical material itself.

The Structure of the Rite

To its credit, the *Book of Common Worship* places the baptism rite in Sunday worship immediately after the proclamation of the Word through Scripture and sermon. Preaching with the sacrament fulfills the insight common to both Calvin and Luther, to both Reformed and Lutheran traditions, that the life of the church is proclamation. The audible sacrament that speaks God's promise is joined with the visible Word that simultaneously attests to the promise and is dependent on the promise.[21] Whatever else might be said about this baptism rite, its structural place during the service indicates that it is intended to be *primarily divine proclamation*. Does the rite itself indicate this purpose, and does it do so in a way that is fitting for Reformed theology and congregations? In outline, the structure of the rite goes like this:

Presentation
Profession of Faith
Thanksgiving over the Water
The Baptism
Laying on of Hands
Welcome
The Peace

An examination of the Presentation shows that the rite does not begin with God's gracious activity despite the theological assertion, repeated by the placement of the rite in the service order, that baptism is primarily divine proclamation. Instead, the liturgical dialogue in the Presentation concerns the presentation of baptismal candidates to the congregation on behalf of the session, followed by a congregational response to that presentation. This is *liturgical dialogue about baptism*, and in this regard the *Book of Common Worship* baptism rite fares no better than the one in the *Lutheran Book of Worship*.[22]

The second element of the *Book of Common Worship* baptism rite is the Profession of Faith, which comprises renunciation, profession, the Apostles' Creed, and profession to the local church. Once again, the activity of the rite consists of liturgical conversation, individual and corporate, directed to other members of the gathered community. One might argue that these words are said in the presence of God, but the third-person language makes clear that *this dialogue happens primarily amid and for the gathered congregation.*

After these professions, the Thanksgiving Prayer is said over the water. Here, for the first time, the congregation addresses God. The Thanksgiving Prayer and its options are discussed at some length in the next subsection. Baptism follows the Thanksgiving Prayer; and the baptism dovetails into the Laying on of Hands, in which divine preservation is invoked and announcement of entrance into God's covenant is spoken (at least with option 1). Sections of congregational Welcome and the sharing of The Peace conclude the rite.

The baptism rite in the *Book of Common Worship* has fundamentally the same structure that appeared for the baptism rite in the *LBW*: a liturgical dialogue within the community, explaining what baptism is, followed by renunciation, profession, baptism, and communal greetings. This structure has become the *de facto* normative structure for current worship books, Roman Catholic and Protestant alike. Why should this basic structure be used? Three comments are in order.

First, this structure derives from the patristic period of the church, certainly by the year 200 C.E. and partly by the middle of the second century. This represents not the apostolic beginnings of baptism but a stage in which the contextual diversity of the early church was gradually moving to uniformity in worship, doctrine, canon, and ecclesial structure. Ecumenicity might be given as an answer to why this rite was used in the *BCW*. But then one must ask why ecumenicity must occur through uniformity of rite?

Second, this patristic initiation structure is by no means the only baptismal rite structure that could be used. By way of comparison, recall that Luther's 1526 rite (and thanksgiving prayer) had a basic structure of God's gracious activity calling forth a turn from the old, a turn to the new, and then prayer.[23]

Third, the *structure* of the *BCW* baptism rite shows that it *primarily concerns human response*, both individual and congregational, to the initiating gracious activity of God. In the *BCW*, however, the *position* of the rite in Sunday service indicates *it primarily concerns divine proclamation*. There would seem to be a misfit between the structure of the rite and its role in the service.

The issue here is not divine initiative *or* human response but rather which is primary. Luther's rite and prayer show the priority of divine proclamation over human response, but both are necessary. One could also talk about the asymmetrical relationship between the human and divine: God initiates with grace and we respond. Recall, from chapter 2, Calvin's clear insistence that what is primary in baptism remain so— God's gracious activity—and that human response to that grace always remain necessary but secondary.

Liturgical Material

Moving from formal structure to material content, do the ritual elements of this rite fit Reformed baptismal theology? While not every liturgical element can be discussed, some key elements stand out. The Presentation begins with this scriptural passage:

> Hear the words of our Lord Jesus Christ:
> All authority in heaven and on earth
> has been given to me.
> Go therefore and make disciples of all nations,
> baptizing them in the name of the Father,
> and of the Son,
> and of the Holy Spirit,
> and teaching them to obey everything that I have commanded you.
> And remember, I am with you always,
> to the end of the age.

This seems at first to be a sensible starting place for a baptism rite, since it begins by citing the so-called dominical institution of baptism. Also, Reformed orthodoxy urged this passage be used in the baptism rite both as warrant and as proclaiming the gospel. This passage also seems to begin the Presentation with divine initiative, to which people then have their liturgical dialogue. Several reasons, however, argue for rethinking this start.

First, Scripture scholars concur that Matthew 28 is an ecclesial composition that indicates Matthew's own first-century missionary and confrontational place within Judaism. This is hardly a dominical warrant for baptism. The one certain scriptural passage that could suggest dominical institution of baptism—Jesus' baptism by John—might be used here, but there is a better place for this narrative, as is seen when the Profession of Faith is discussed.

Second, the Bullinger-Barth type of covenant theology expresses God's gracious sovereignty through the idea of God's eternal covenant of grace offered to *all human beings* from Adam and Eve onward. This sense of universal covenant, concretely embodied for the one to be baptized, seems lacking in the Matthean passage, which is more a command to the Matthean community than a proclamation of the divine, sovereign grace that already has claimed all people.

If the Presentation were to begin with Scripture, presumably reflecting a Reformed commitment to the Word first addressing the community, then Scripture option 5 (Acts 2:39) more adequately speaks the Reformed concern for the divine sovereignty that graciously covenants with all:

> The promise is for you, for your children,
> and for all who are far away,
> everyone whom the Lord our God calls.

The Thanksgiving Prayer over the water also lacks the elements of Reformed baptismal theology that we have seen. We would do well to compare this prayer with that in the *LBW* and with Luther's original prayer in his 1526 rite.[24] The Thanksgiving Prayer (option 1) in the *Book of Common Worship* is strikingly similar to that in the *LBW*:

Lutheran Book of Worship	*Book of Common Worship*
Holy God, mighty Lord, gracious Father:	We give you thanks, Eternal God, for you nourish and sustain all things by the gift of water. In
We give thanks, for in the beginning your Spirit moved over the waters and you created the heaven and earth. By the gift of water you nourish and sustain us	the beginning of time, your Spirit moved over the watery chaos, calling forth order and life.
	In the time of Noah, you destroyed evil by the waters of

and all living things. By the waters of the flood you condemned the wicked and saved those whom you had chosen, Noah and his family. You led Israel by the pillar of cloud and fire through the sea, out of slavery into the freedom of the promised land. In the waters of the Jordan your Son was baptized by John and anointed with the Spirit. By the baptism of his own death and resurrection your beloved Son has set us free from the bondage to sin and death, and has opened the way to the joy and freedom of everlasting life. He made water a sign of the kingdom and of cleansing and rebirth. In obedience to his command, we make disciples of all nations, baptizing them in the name of the Father, and of the Son, and of the Holy Spirit.

Pour out your Holy Spirit, so that those who are here baptized may be given new life. Wash away the sin of all those who are cleansed by this water and bring them forth as inheritors of your glorious kingdom.

To you be given praise and honor and worship through your Son, Jesus Christ our Lord, in the unity of the Holy Spirit, now and forever.

the flood, giving righteousness a new beginning.

You led Israel out of slavery, through the waters of the sea, into the promised land.

In the waters of Jordan Jesus was baptized by John and anointed by your Spirit. By the baptism of his own death and resurrection, Christ set us free from sin and death, and opened the way to eternal life.

We thank you, O God, for the water of baptism. In it we are buried with Christ in his death. From it we are raised to share in his resurrection. Through it we are reborn by the power of the Holy Spirit.

Send your Spirit to move over this water that it may be a fountain of deliverance and rebirth. Wash away the sin of all who are cleansed by it. Raise them to new life, and graft them to the body of Christ. Pour out your Holy Spirit upon them, that they may have power to do your will, and continue forever in the risen life of Christ. To you, Father, Son, and Holy Spirit, one God, be all praise, honor, and glory, now and forever.

The prayer from the *Book of Common Worship* shows several changes from the Lutheran prayer. There is effort to be more gender inclusive with regard to language about God and Christ. The prayer in the *Book of Common Worship* also seeks to be more explicitly Trinitarian. Ironically, the *Lutheran Book of Worship* tried also to be Trinitarian because some people perceived lack of Trinitarian language to be a problem in Luther's prayer. A wide range of scriptural images for baptism are used, with some emphasis on dying and rising with Christ, perhaps influenced by Barth. Also, there is the hint of an image from the medieval font prayer found in the Gelasian sacramentary (*Reginensis Vaticanus* 316), in which the Holy Spirit is invoked on the font that it may be womblike and give forth life from its waters. Beyond these differences the prayers are quite similar. The *LBW*'s Flood Prayer has become so popular that one can think of a genre of baptismal prayer now existing.

The Thanksgiving Prayer in the *Book of Common Worship* conveys a strong sense of God's sovereignty. From its beginning section, where God's "Spirit moved over the waters of chaos," to the ending section, where God's Spirit is invoked "to move over this water" at the moment of baptism, the prayer passes through various scenes in salvation history in which God continually brought forth life out of water. The opening assertion grounds all this divine activity in God's eternal self, who always "nourishes and sustains all living things through the gift of water." Covenant is nowhere mentioned in this prayer.

The second option for a Thanksgiving Prayer also begins with a proclamation about the eternal God graciously self-revealing throughout the ages. This prayer does not follow Luther's prayer so closely, and its single Old Testament event, the freeing of Israel from bondage, is balanced by its single New Testament event, the baptism of Jesus by which we are freed from bondage. Again covenant is not mentioned.

There is a third option for a Thanksgiving Prayer, in rubric only. Using her or his own words, the minister can prayer according to certain guidelines, the first of which is "praising God for God's faithfulness in the covenant." Placing covenant language only in this third option subordinates the covenant theme to the theme of God's grace working through the gift of water, and it separates the theme of God's gracious sovereignty from its connection to covenant.

This raises the question of whether the central baptismal prayer in a Reformed baptism rite needs a covenant theme. To the extent that Reformed covenant theology yielded a material content of Jesus Christ, which then yielded the further material content of God's eternal offer of grace to humankind, there is no reason that the same *ultimate point* of God's grace cannot be made using different *proximate language*. For example, if Calvin learned from Luther's sign-promise theology and then expressed his point differently by using covenant ideas, can Reformed traditions not be similarly faithful to the meaning of covenant without actually invoking the covenant idea?

The key question is whether anything crucial would be lost in the change from covenant language to water imagery. Barth makes a point about the fundamental difference between Roman Catholic and Reformation views on grace that can help this discussion:

The Reformers, however, did not see themselves as in a position to construe the grace of Jesus Christ in this [material] way. They thought it should be understood, not as cause and effect, but as Word and faith. For this reason, they regarded the representative event at the centre of the Church's life as proclamation, as an act concerned with speaking and hearing, indicative of the fact that what is at issue in the thing proclaimed too is not a material connexion but a *personal encounter*.[25]

By its very nature, covenant language concerns communication between two personal realities, the one speaking the eternal Word of grace, the other hearing and responding. Historically speaking, covenant language shared this strictly personal characteristic with Luther's sign-promise sacramental theology and thus was capable of standing on its own as an appropriate restatement of Luther's point. The same cannot be said of the two Thanksgiving Prayers in the *Book of Common Worship*. These prayers may convey the ultimate meaning to the covenant theology of the Bullinger and Barth type discussed above: God eternally offers grace to all people, and everyone continually has the choice to accept such grace and live by its gift and demand. The language of these prayers, however, diffuses the personal divine address and human response by referring to divine activity with matter (water), which we must then interpret. In other words, covenant language in principle conveys a personal address and encounter that the poetic water imagery cannot convey so well.

There is another issue to discuss about covenant as it appears in the *Book of Common Worship*: whether baptism enters one into the covenant, or whether baptism is the seal of the covenant already established with the person being baptized. Answering the question is sometimes complicated by the ambiguous ways in which the terms are used. Purchase on this question can be gained by sorting through the various but limited possibilities.

When the person to be baptized is a child who has at least one parent who is Christian, then the Reformed tradition usually has viewed such baptism as sealing the covenant in which the child *already* had membership. As we have seen, from the very start the covenant defense of infant baptism was a hallmark of Reformed theologians, and this held true whether the covenant was viewed as essentially the same through history (e.g., Bullinger); or whether the covenant was viewed as having movement from the lesser to the greater (e.g., Calvin); or whether two covenants were conceived, one of works and one of law (e.g., High Calvinism). Israelite children were sealed with the sign of the covenant into which they were born; so Christian children are sealed with the new covenant sign.

When the person to be baptized is an adult and *divine predestination is asserted*, whether single or double, then the person baptized is either elect or reprobate. If the confessing adult is among the elect, then baptism can hardly enter that person in a covenant in which he or she already is a member. Baptism *seals* the covenant membership that already exists. If the confessing adult is reprobate, then that person receives the outward sign of baptism only, and baptism obviously does not enter him or her into the covenant. Reformed orthodoxy was clear here.

When the person baptized is an adult and *divine predestination is not asserted*, from the divine side baptism does not enter the person into the covenant, since God already has graciously included everyone within the scope of the covenant. All baptism could do would be to seal what God already had graciously decided. From the human side, however, one could speak of baptism as entering the covenant. Here "entering the covenant" means that the person baptized takes God's covenant, already established with the person, as determinative for his or her ultimate orientation. The person pledges to live according to the gift and demand of the covenant. Such a person never fell outside God's covenant and so had no need to enter it. But the covenant has *effect* only when the person already included in the covenant assents and accepts the offer. A similar pattern was seen not only in Bullinger and Barth but also in the baptismal theology of Zwingli and Bucer (see chapter 1). Recall that by the 1520s, Zwingli had shifted his covenant discussion to embrace the one eternal covenant made by God; and during the 1530s, Bucer likewise discussed the one divine covenant of grace within which humanity fell.

Simply put, Reformed covenant theology can talk about baptism entering a person into the covenant only insofar as this means appropriating for oneself the divine covenant in which a person already is embraced. One might think, as a parallel, of how the coronation of a regent does not make the individual king or queen—that happened on the death of the prior regent—but orients all people to this new reality so that it becomes their new world.

What does the *Book of Common Worship* mean by its covenant language? The concept of covenant appears only once as a mandated part of the baptism rite. The beginning of the Profession of Faith section has the following proclamation by the minister:

> Through baptism we enter the covenant God has established.
> Within this covenant God gives us new life,
> guards us from evil,
> and nurtures us in love.
> In embracing this covenant, we choose whom we will serve,
> by turning from evil and turning to Jesus Christ.

The minister then asks the following questions of the baptism candidate or of the parents or guardians if the candidates are children:

> As God embraces you within this covenant, I ask you
> to reject sin, to profess your faith in Christ Jesus,
> and to confess the faith of the church,
> the faith in which we baptize.

These passages seem ambiguous. The first passage (the proclamation) could be read along the lines of the Bullinger and Barth covenant language, *viewed from the human side*. God has already established an eternal covenant of grace that includes us, and by our baptism *we accept this covenant* as our ultimate orientation in life. The phrase "has established" could imply this interpretation. Likewise, the second passage (the interrogation) proclaims that God embraces the baptized one within the covenant. This does not mean that God's covenant has not already embraced the person with the offer of grace.

One must also say, however, that these passages can just as easily be interpreted in a different way. These two parts of the pastoral address may mean that baptism actually enters us into a graced relationship with God that previously did not include us. Might there be other evidence to help here?

Covenant language appears in the signation aspect of the Laying on of Hands (option 1), but this covenant language is neutral and offers no help in deciding the perspective of the *Book of Common Worship* ("N., child of the covenant, you have been sealed by the Holy Spirit in baptism, and marked as Christ's own forever"). The opening declaration in the Welcome section of the rite, however, suggests that this other meaning of "entering the covenant" is intended (italics added here):

> N. and N. *have been received into the one holy catholic and apostolic church* through baptism.
> God *has made them members* of the household of God,
> to share with us in the priesthood of Christ.
> Let us welcome the newly baptized.

At best, the covenant language in the *Book of Common Worship* is ambiguous; at worst, it fails to see that Reformed covenant theology has, no matter the variation, viewed baptism as sealing the covenant relationship *already established* with the person, rather than viewing baptism as entering the person into the covenant. Only insofar as the person takes up his or her part of the covenant could one speak of entering the covenant, and this meaning is not made clear in the *Book of Common Worship*.

SUMMARY AND SUGGESTIONS

Summary

If the marks of Reformed baptismal theology are (1) gracious divine sovereignty and (2) expressing this sovereignty through covenant theology, then the success of the baptismal rite in the *Book of Common Worship* can be partial at best. First, the scriptural introductions that begin the Presentation, presumably intended to be the Word addressing the gathered assembly, generally fail to communicate God's all-encompassing, gracious sovereignty. The Presentation and the Profession of Faith are primarily conversations about God done inwardly by the community. The Thanksgiving Prayer has a strong sense of God's sovereign work within a salvation history narrative, but this appears linked to God's activity through water rather than through covenant. And finally, analysis suggests that the structure of the baptism rite, which consists primarily of human response (adapted as it was from patristic initiation patterns), stands at cross-purposes with its Reformed position in the Sunday service, where it is intended to be primarily divine proclamation.

Second, the covenant theme fares no better. Covenant rarely appears in the rite, occurring only once in a mandated section—the pastoral proclamation and interrogation that begins the Profession of Faith section of the rite. When covenant language does appear, its meaning seems at best ambiguous and at worst confused.

The source of these structural and thematic problems seems relatively straightforward. A major liturgical element from the current liturgical renewal movement was grafted into a particular theological and liturgical tradition with which there are significant differences.

Suggested Emendations

Despite the differences between the theology and rites of the current liturgical renewal movement and Reformed liturgical and baptismal theology, some simple changes can be made that gently reshape the current baptism rite.

The Presentation

As strange as this may sound, *baptism is not about baptism but about God's gracious activity*. Baptism is the proximate sign, pointing beyond itself to its ultimate reality. The opening Scripture passage that begins the Presentation section ought to proclaim God's prevenient covenant grace, rather than didactically pointing us toward baptism itself. Of the

Scripture options presently available, option 5 would be the preferred one (Acts 2:39). Better yet, Genesis 17:1–8 could be used in some form. The universal covenant given to Abraham and his seed has long been linked to covenant theology in the Reformed tradition. Bucer and Bullinger both used Genesis 17 in their baptismal theology. Calvin, who was himself a wandering exile all his life and who served an exiled congregation in Strasbourg and lived as a foreigner in Geneva, found Genesis 17 to be a central motif for Christian existence. More generally, this call to Abraham connected the entire Reformed tradition, which, unlike the other traditions of the magisterial Reformation, had no country for its refuge. The Reformed traditions were connected not by earthly ruler but by divine covenant. What better passage, historically and theologically, to begin a Reformed baptism rite?

Passages other than Acts 2:39 or Genesis 17:1–8 could obviously be found and chosen as well. The point here is that the Presentation needs to begin strongly with a proclamation about God's sovereign, gracious activity, thus making the actual presentations come as *responses* to this proclamation of grace. Which particular passage is chosen for this task would depend on what is most fitting for the local congregation.

This suggestion warrants a historical observation about sixteenth-century Reformed baptism rites. Most of the rites contained didactic material about baptism, usually in the baptismal exhortation section. The Reformers were often aware of the catechetical aspects of the patristic rites, which had dwindled by the time of the late medieval period. For the Reformers, the catechetical material helped educate people about baptism so that they could be more responsible for their own baptism as well as toward the one being baptized.[26] When this pedagogical need is met liturgically within the baptism rite itself, however, the resulting ritual stands in some tension with the Protestant insistence that the sacraments are primarily visible forms of God's gracious Word. Just because the Reformers structured their rites with baptismal exhortations in order to educate does not mean that practice should continue. Other ways can be found for proper baptism education. There is no more reason to repeat the Reformation liturgical pattern than to repeat the patristic pattern. The theological insights that the Reformers had about baptism can and should be exemplified in new ways.

Profession of Faith

This section of the baptism rite begins with the pastor didactically explaining what baptism means, much as the *LBW* rite begins with an in-house dialogue about baptism. Let me suggest an alternative. Read from Mark 1:9–11 and then proclaim, "N, You are my Beloved Daughter [Son], with you I am well pleased." Here the Profession of Faith would open with divine proclamation claiming that the one to be baptized is *already* a beloved child, *prior to* the baptism. The baptism then becomes the embrace of the covenant reality already true, and it existentially orients the baptism candidate, the family, and the community to the preexisting covenant, making their world a new world indeed. Use of this Scripture passage would also ground the present moment of baptism in its actual dominical institution (John's baptism of Jesus), thus reinforcing the christological *telos* of baptism.

One might object that such an opening would be "too priestly" because the minister stands as the divine presence, much like the medieval priests who stood at the altar and once again offered Christ's sacrifice. In its own way, however, the Reformed tradition has a strong priestly theme and a high sacramental character to its worship life. The Reformed idea that the sermon and the sacrament can be the means through which the Word of God addresses the people means that both preaching and liturgical language are "priestly." God becomes present through human words and encounters God's people as the presence of Christ. Even the brief look at the sacramental and baptismal theology of the Reformed confessions indicated that Word and sacrament had the same office, namely, to present the people with Christ himself. Careful study of Calvin and Schleiermacher on preaching has shown this same point.[27] What Calvin said clearly about the eucharistic elements applies, *mutatis mutandis,* to the act of proclamation in preaching and sacrament. Our words can be the medium for God's Word, and we ought not "divorce" the two from each other. At the same time, neither are we to elevate the proclaimer so much that she or he becomes thought of as the divine reality incarnate. We are to distinguish without separating; hold together without identifying.

There is a sad irony here. Reformed worship has undoubtedly become far too didactic and glum,[28] and the *BCW* has tried to renew the worship life of the churches in the Presbyterian Church (U.S.A.) by renewing their sacramental life. For baptism, the *BCW* drew on the rite of Christian initiation that (supposedly) enlivened the patristic churches and that the Second Vatican Council hoped would renew the worship life of Roman Catholic churches. But the Reformed tradition contains within it a vital liturgical theology. The sacraments, and the words proclaimed by the worship leader in preaching and sacrament, are the very means through which Christ actually encounters us and sets free our joyous gratitude.

Thanksgiving over the Water

For reasons mentioned above, neither prayer 1 nor prayer 2 seems particularly appropriate for a Reformed baptism rite, though they are good examples of prayers from the liturgical movement. The third option, composing a prayer, would seem the best alternative here. The *BCW* gives rubrics for such a prayer, including the "praising God for God's faithfulness in the covenant."

In general, the traditional structure for any prayer is fairly simple. First, begin by addressing God with language that describes the enduring characteristics of God. The *BCW* uses "Eternal God" and "Eternal and gracious God" in Thanksgiving Prayers 1 and 2. The address to God should be fitting to the local context, perhaps even to the liturgy or hymns of the day. For example, should the congregation sing Harry E. Fosdick's great hymn "God of Grace and God of Glory," the baptismal prayer might begin, "God of grace and God of glory, we thank you . . ."

This opening address can also begin with a "who clause" that names the principal characteristics of God's grace; for instance, "Gracious God, who called forth Abraham into that covenant of grace that embraces us all . . ." Here the "who clause" can be tailored to particular covenant themes or theology.

The second part of a prayer typically gives thanks to God for the divine work on our behalf over the generations up to the present. For a baptismal prayer, this could include the redeeming work of God that has occurred in connection to water, and the emphasis could be on covenant. If Noah and the flood are mentioned, then the covenant and its sign ought to be mentioned; if the redemption of God's chosen people through the sea is mentioned; then the covenant to Abraham ought to be mentioned; and so on. Which themes are used would depend on the particular worshiping context, perhaps on the Scripture passage for the day. The key is to focus on the personal proclamation by God that addresses us when covenant language is used.

Finally, a baptism prayer ends with the invocation of God's presence now, during baptism, and in the life of the one being baptized. For example, note Luther's invocation of divine presence:

> [W]e pray through your same groundless mercy that you will look on this N. and bless him with right faith in the spirit so that everything may be drowned and go under which was born in him from Adam and to which he himself contributed; and that he may be torn from the number of the untrusting and kept dry and safe in the holy ark of Christendom, at all times burning in spirit and cheerful in hope serving your name.

While one would not want to repeat Luther's prayer verbatim, note the poetic use of imagery and the power of invoking God's gracious and merciful presence today on behalf of the one being baptized.

With these simple suggestions in place, or changes similar to them, the current rite would be nudged into line with Reformed baptismal theology. First, the Presentation and the Profession of Faith would begin with divine proclamation of grace, not liturgical conversation about baptism. The divine initiatory activity would then evoke the human response. The ritual structure of the baptism rite would then correlate to its place and function in Sunday worship as primarily divine proclamation that evokes response.

Second, with the covenant language of Genesis 17 beginning the Presentation, and with covenant language in the Thanksgiving Prayer, covenant as the expression of God's gracious sovereignty would be more adequately present in the liturgy. There would also be more clarity about baptism sealing the covenant already in place, and more clarity that "entering the covenant" means appropriation of what God already has graciously done.

Finally, it should be said that the intent of these changes is not to keep Reformed worship "pure" and unsullied by other traditions. Rather, two other intentions guide this chapter. First, Reformed worship has a rich and often lost heritage that insisted that God's very presence encounters us at worship. At a time when congregations are seeking to renew their worship life, this heritage needs to be remembered. The divine presence, of course, can come as challenge as well as joy and comfort. Second, the more a community's worship life reflects its often unconscious piety and theology, the less disjointed communal life can become. The ongoing process of growth to Christian adulthood may be helped with better harmony between the parts of the religious environment.

CONCLUSION:

THE SHAPE OF REFORMED BAPTISMAL AND SACRAMENTAL THEOLOGY

Some general comments can be offered about Reformed baptismal and sacramental theology. The comments are necessarily brief and naturally need more detailed treatment.

1. Baptism is *primarily* the promise, or offer, or pledge, of God's grace. It is not primarily initiation into the church, whether "church" be considered a local congregation or the mystical body of Christ. This seemingly bold assertion can be supported several ways.

First, Reformed theology has always maintained that baptism, as well as the Lord's Supper, is means by which God proclaims grace to us. In 1536 the young Calvin wrote that "the sacraments have no office other than the Word of God: they offer and put forth Christ for us, and in him the treasures of heavenly grace."[1] Calvin never wavered from this idea. The Reformers of the first two generations, most of the Reformed confessions, and Reformed orthodoxy all began the understanding of the sacraments here.[2]

Furthermore, as God's means of grace the sacraments, just like the Word, retain their character even should they not be received by faith. The "substance" or "nature"of the sacraments, to use words Calvin used when referring to the sacraments or baptism, remain even should the wicked receive them. Bullinger said this clearly in his Second Helvetic Confession:

> For just as the Word of God remains the true Word of God—when it is preached not merely bare words are recited but simultaneously the realities signified or announced by the words are offered by God—even if those who are ungodly and unbelieving hear the words, and understand them, but do not enjoy the realities signified because they do not receive them by true faith; so also the sacraments, composed of the Word, the signs, and the realities signified, remain true and uncorrupted sacraments, not merely because they signify holy realities, but because God offers the realities so signified, even if unbelievers do not receive the realities which are offered.[3]

Finally, we have seen that whether covenant was conceived as a single covenant from Adam onward or the double covenant (of works and of grace), and whether God did or did not predestine those who were within the covenant, baptism could not initiate anyone into the covenant, as far as God's grace was concerned. On God's side, the covenant already embraced those whom it included. Only from the human side could one call baptism initiation into the covenant. Then, insofar as a person took on the covenant promises offered through baptism, he or she personally took up the gift and demand of the covenant that *already included* that person.

2. Baptism as initiation is the *secondary* aspect of baptism. The promise, or Christ, and the initiation into the covenant through initiation into the visible church are aspects of baptism to be distinguished from each other. Most of the theologians and confessions we have seen made just this distinction. It was particularly clear among the first-generation Reformers who had the so-called double-front issue: Faithful appropriation was stressed to late medieval piety, but the primary validity of baptism was stressed to the Reformation's radicals.

Even where a theologian or confession said, as did the Second Helvetic Confession, that the one baptized is "enrolled, entered, and received into the covenant," care must be paid to the passage, to its context, and to the historical context of the author. So, for example, although Bullinger made this claim about baptism in the Second Helvetic Confession, he made this claim concerning "what it means to be baptized." Bullinger was describing what baptism meant to those of faith who have been baptized, not what baptism was as such. As the passage quoted previously clearly shows, Bullinger also asserted that baptism itself remained true and uncorrupted even though it may have been offered to someone who did not receive it in faith.

3. Historically speaking, while Reformed theologians or confessions typically held the divine offer as the primary aspect and initiation through human response as the secondary aspect, these aspects received different emphasis depending on context. For instance, Calvin in the *Institutes* and in the 1545 catechism, Bullinger in his Second Helvetic Confession, and the Westminster Confession all saw this arrangement with particular clarity. Their theological contexts were relatively stable, and their voices were not minority theological voices in their settings. In other contexts, however, faithful Christianity seemed to be imperiled, and there was the need to stress the faithful appropriation of baptism. The Belgic Confession, Schleiermacher, Brunner, and Barth, all found themselves in such a context. For Schleiermacher, Brunner, and Barth, this included the symbiosis of church and state, in which perfunctory infant baptism all but amounted to citizenship. Schleiermacher and Barth severely critiqued infant baptism. Both groups of Reformed voices need to be remembered and heard. The Reformed tradition, as Jack Stotts put it, is "itself

a wide river with many currents."[4] Differing parts of the tradition may need to be heard or emphasized in different contexts, and alternative voices are helpful.

Constructively speaking, the ultimate theological point is the one the young Calvin first taught in his 1536 *Institutes*: What is needed is to hold to both aspects together—the validity of baptism as offering God's grace and the witness of faith by the recipient—but to understand that there is a priority to the aspects.[5] We ought not tolerate what is secondary, the human response to grace, replacing what is primary, the initiating offer of grace that evokes our dependent response. This leaves the nature of the sacrament fundamentally grounded in the only reality that remains constant and cannot waver: the character of God as grace offered to humankind, to which we (secondarily or derivatively) make our response.

Is this not exactly the point that Luther and Calvin had in mind when they insisted, in the strict sense, that the two marks of the church were the Word proclaimed and the sacraments rightly administered? Both offered Christ. And was this not what lay behind the christocentric character of the Reformed confessions, in which one focused on God's grace through Jesus Christ, not on the faith of the believer?[6] Does this approach not also echo the primacy of grace over human response in theological systems as different as those of Schleiermacher and Barth? Grace and gratitude, in that priority, are a hallmark of Reformed sacramental theology as well as Reformed theology more broadly conducted.[7]

4. When baptism is conceived as having two aspects that together form a single event, then Christ is offered, faith clings to Christ, and God's presence is realized by the one who so trusts. In this way, baptism effects regeneration, as almost the entire Reformed tradition has insisted. By virtue of holding to divine election to reprobation or salvation, Reformed orthodoxy stood apart here. So did Barth in his last writings on baptism. At the same time, the Reformed theologians also insisted that baptism effected regeneration because God had entrusted that office to baptism.

Furthermore, the assertion that baptism effected regeneration would hold true for those baptized as infants as well as those baptized as adults. This was said precisely and clearly by one of the Reformed tradition's strongest critics of infant baptism. Schleiermacher argued that even where there was no faith at the time of baptism, of which infant baptism was a special instance, baptism still effected the needed saving faith:

> On the other hand, it may be said that even if faith is not yet present at the time of baptism, yet it will arise not merely *after* baptism but—

baptism being the first item in the whole series of influences which the Church brings to bear on the baptized—*through* baptism.[8]

5. Reformed theologians and confessions usually, but not always, have used covenant language to express the character of baptism as primarily divine offer and secondarily human response. In this asymmetrical structure, God has initiated the relationship by an act of grace, extending the covenant to include those whom God has included. Humankind then responds. Even should the response be ingratitude for the grace, human activity cannot abrogate the covenant. Other ways of exemplifying this relationship between God and humankind are found in the Reformed baptismal tradition, most notably the sign-promise theology that appears predominantly in Calvin and the Heidelberg Catechism. Covenant language and sign-promise language are not inherently incompatible, as the Calvin material has made clear, although one theme may be dominant given a particular theological construction.

From a historical perspective, the Reformed use of covenant to interpret Christian baptism first arose, almost always, when arguing for infant baptism. In other words, its origin was not in theological or exegetical reflection on baptism as such but as a specific response to the challenge to a long-held practice of infant baptism. From a theological perspective, although covenant language may have had a prominent position in some Reformed theologies of baptism—for example, Bullinger, the Westminster Confession, Reformed orthodoxy, Barth, and Marcel—such language was strictly proximate and in service of baptism's ultimate orientation, offering Christ in the sacrament and engrafting those with faith into Christ himself. The christocentric and near-mystical character to baptism was most observable in Calvin, the Reformed confessions, and especially Schleiermacher.

6. The end of chapter 5 offered emendations to the baptism rite in the *Book of Common Worship* so that the rite might reflect Reformed theology on (*a*) sacraments as a form of God's Word, (*b*) the distinction between the primary and secondary aspects of baptism, and (*c*) what being "initiated" into the covenant might mean. This calls for a further comment.

So far, the principal claim has been that in the *Book of Common Worship* a different tradition has been grafted onto the Reformed tradition. This is merely *descriptive*. One could agree with this observation and think such grafting was an improvement. While having lunch one day with an internationally known Protestant liturgical scholar, I commented that the baptism rite in the *Lutheran Book of Worship* "had sold Luther down the river." The liturgical scholar replied, "It did and it should have." Along the way I have suggested a *normative* point in addition to the descriptive point: Not only has another tradition been grafted onto the Reformed tradition, but the Reformed tradition already had a liturgical theology more adequate than that which was grafted. Given the scope of this study, only some basic differences can be suggested.

First, the Reformed tradition usually has insisted that sign and reality must be carefully distinguished in the following way: They must not be so closely identified that the sign loses its function as *sign* and the reality becomes identified with the external sign. This was one of the causes of medieval eucharistic idolatry, when the elements themselves were adored, if not worshiped. On the other hand, sign and reality are not to be so distinguished as to tear them apart in such a way that the reality itself does not participate with or through the sign. This was the sacramental mistake of the Reformation's radicals.[9] There was a fine line that the Reformers tried to walk, which Calvin put succinctly:

> Now here we ought to guard against two faults. First, we should not, by too little regard for the signs, divorce them from their mysteries. Secondly, we should not, by extolling them immoderately, seem to obscure somewhat the mysteries themselves.[10]

In a more recent period, careful analysis of the sign theology of Theodore Beza and Edward Schillebeeckx has shown the remarkable similarities between Reformed sign theology in the Lord's Supper and the sign theory present in Schillebeeckx's idea of the transignification of the eucharistic elements.[11] One of the differences between the two sign theologians, however, is whether the sign function happens *in* the elements (Schillebeeckx) or *through or because of* the elements (Beza). The Reformed tradition again carefully distinguished sign and reality while still asserting their intimate connection. This has implications for how Word and sacrament, or liturgy, are conceived.

In the Reformed tradition, Word and sacrament are means of grace because *through* them the divine reality ("the real presence of Christ") can encounter us with the comfort and the challenge that come from God's gracious presence. Reformed worship is inherently "sacramental" and "epiphanic." Here Reformed sacramental theology agrees with the liturgical renewal movement.[12] By contrast, the Reformed tradition has always held that the Christ who is offered through Word and sacrament does not happen *in* the Word and sacrament. To make that claim would be to identify sign and reality too closely, mistaking the means of grace for the grace itself. The Reformed tradition would resist claims such as that the liturgy *is* "revelation-in-motion," or that the liturgy *is* epiphanic, or that the liturgy *is* the ontology of the church.

Second, the difference over sign and reality points to another difference between Reformed sacramental theology and that of the liturgical renewal movement. The New Testament meaning to revelation is that the God already revealed in and to human existence as such no longer remains hidden but through Jesus Christ becomes revealed for the individual now.[13] This has an analogue in Christian worship.

Most Reformed theologians have understood that when the Word is proclaimed and the sacraments are rightly administered, *Christ himself* is offered, not merely his power or benefits.[14] Christ himself encounters the worshiper, so that what happened when Jesus encountered someone in Palestine can happen analogously during worship.[15] God can self-reveal through Christ in Word and sacrament. But again analogous to the New Testament texts, the faith of the one encountered is needed for such encounter. Where such faith exists, the believers are "engrafted into Christ," and this mystically happens for the Word as well as for the sacrament. By contrast, without faith, Word and sacrament remain mere events of social intercourse—they are, so to speak, "merely the carpenter's boy."

Reformed sacramental theology would therefore resist the claim that the liturgy *is* "epiphanic" or *is* "revelation-in-motion," because that would be so only where faith was present. The liturgy *can be* epiphanic when and where there is faith, but "church" in that sense is the church that comprises true believers. It is the invisible or hidden church, seen only by God's eyes, since only God can see who has faith.

In sum, the differences in liturgical and baptismal theology between the liturgical renewal movement and the Reformed tradition, so far as this study can pursue, indicate long-standing differences concerning the relationship between sign and reality and concerning ecclesiology. Further, to the extent that the Reformed tradition more adequately distinguishes the relationship between sign and reality and more adequately names the nature of faith and the nature of the invisible and visible church, Reformed sacramental theology is not just different from the theology operative in the liturgical renewal movement; it would seem more adequate.

7. In no way does this discussion intend to criticize either the reforms of the Second Vatican Council or the ecumenical movement. The Introduction discussed the way in which the RCIA creatively reenvisioned both the ecclesiology and the baptismal theology of the Roman Catholic Church. The foundation of the church was conceived as building upward from the ministry of all the members, each taking up her or his Christian ministry through the bestowal of the Spirit. At the same time, the old Augustinianism, with its baptismal emphasis on cleansing infants from original sin as a necessity for their salvation, has been superceded by a new vision of Christian initiation.

Further, the ecumenical movement understands that ecumenism begins with an honest appraisal of what the differing Christian traditions believe and where there is real difference. This approach avoids consensus made too easily and allows for traditions to learn about themselves as well as to learn from other traditions. To argue that the Reformed tradition has had more adequate insights about sacramental theology is to claim there are contributions the Reformed tradition can make to the wider church. Perhaps these are contributions the Reformed tradition itself has not always recognized.

8. Christian worship is certainly more than ritual informed by correct doctrine. To employ the language taken up by the liturgical renewal movement, worship is more than secondary theology. At the same time, secondary theology is more than mere reflective discourse derived from worship as primary theology. Secondary theology is itself normative for worship. Why? The answer can be sketched here only briefly.

First, the claim made by many in the current liturgical renewal movement (so David Fagerberg and Aidan Kavanagh) that secondary theology ought not be normative for the liturgy makes a theological mistake about the structure of religious authority. When Christian worship becomes the means through which the presence of God encounters a worshiper, then worship indeed has a normative relationship to the worshiper's experience of the divine presence.

But consider the very concept of authority. That which has authority and that which is governed by the authority stand on equal ground with each other relative to *that which authorizes* the authority. Consider two examples. The judge has authority over the defendant because she or he is authorized by the law to have such authority. But relative to the law, the defendant stands on equal ground with the judge. All defendants can appeal the judge's decision according to the law itself. This is the function of judicial appeals. Or again, the professor has authority over the student because she or he is authorized by the canons of scholarship to have such authority. But relative to the canons of scholarship appropriate to the discipline, the student and the professor stand on equal ground. The student can always appeal the judgment of the professor according to the standards of scholarship.[16]

So too with worship and revelation. While a given liturgy may have authority over the worshiper by virtue of being the means of God encountering him or her, relative to the divine presence revealed the worshiper and the worship forms stand on equal ground. And so all liturgical forms must be credible to us, simply as human beings, according to those features of human existence that make us recipients of divine revelation. Secondary theology reflects on such features and their implications, and it has something normative to say to worship.

Secondary theology has another role in shaping worship, and it comes from the discipline of New Testament studies. All liturgical forms are handed down from generation to generation. But the worship forms as we have them are distinct evolutions from basic patterns found roughly in the mid–second century. Before this time, New Testament communities were immensely varied in their worship life.[17] Three simple examples: Pauline word services included mystical visions and the dead speaking through the mouths of the living ("tongues"),[18] and the church at Corinth practiced vicarious baptism on behalf of the dead (1 Cor. 15:29); Johannine communities engaged in the "praxis of inclusive wholeness," with footwashing central to their worship life;[19] Christians around Jerusalem connected themselves to the rhythms of the Temple and its prayer hours. Yet standing chronologically behind this plurality of worship forms was the apostolic testimony to Jesus that began the church.

The earliest apostolic testimony witnessed to the real presence of God known through Jesus. To the meaning of these apostolic testimonies all later generations of Christians turn for guidance in naming and shaping the revelation of God present in and to human experience as such. This is not the old Protestant claim of Scripture over and against the living Christian community and its tradition. Rather, this claim recognizes that Scripture itself is tradition, and that within the early Christian Scriptures there is a tradition that itself guides later traditions.[20] We all want to "hand down" that which we "have received," and to do that appropriately we must make recourse to the meaning of the earliest apostolic testimonies to Jesus. In this sense, Christianity is built "upon the foundation of the apostles and prophets, with Christ Jesus himself as the cornerstone," as the author of Ephesians put the matter (2:20). And this goes for Christian worship as well, insofar as we want worship to stand in apostolic tradition with those whose faith was evoked and shaped by the one who was, and is, our Christ.

NOTES

INTRODUCTION

1. James F. White, *Protestant Worship: Traditions in Transition* (Louisville, Ky.: Westminster John Knox Press, 1989), 13.

2. For instance, in scriptural hermeneutics, we find Barth's comment that one must have "fidelity in all circumstances to the object reflected in the words of the prophets and apostles" (*Church Dogmatics* I/2, trans. G. W. Bromiley [Edinburgh: T. & T. Clark, 1975], 725, §21.2.) This approach applies, *mutatis mutandis*, to the current study. Also compare Luther's comment in the *Heidelberg Disputation* (secs. 29–30) that if one wants to use Aristotle, one must first "be a fool for Christ."

3. For summaries of the liturgical renewal movement, as well as bibliographies, see H. Ellsworth Chandlee, "The Liturgical Movement," in *The New Westminster Dictionary of Liturgy and Worship*, ed. J. G. Davies (Philadelphia: Westminster Press, 1986), 307–14; Virgil C. Funk, "The Liturgical Movement (1830–1969)," in *The New Dictionary of Sacramental Worship*, ed. Peter E. Fink, S.J. (Collegeville, Minn.: Liturgical Press, 1990), 695–715; and, for a detailed chronology in the twentieth century, see L. Brinkoff, O.F.M., "Chronicle of the Liturgical Movement," in *Liturgy in Development* (New York: Sheed and Ward, 1965), 40–67.

4. For an overview of and bibliographies on the topic, see Paul Bradshaw, "Christian Initiation," in Fink, ed., *New Dictionary*, 601–12; J. D. C. Fischer and E. J. Yarnold, S. J., "The West from about AD 500 to the Reformation," in *The Liturgy of the Church*, 2d ed., ed. Cheslyn Jones, Geoffrey Wainwright, Edward Yarnold, and Paul Bradshaw (London: Oxford University Press, 1992), 144–52; J. D. C. Fischer, *Christian Initiation in the Medieval West* (London: SPCK, 1965); Georg Kretschmar, "Die Geschichte des Taufgottesdienstes in der alten Kirche," in *Leiturgia: Handbuch des evangelischen Gottesdienstes*, vol. 5: *Taufgottesdienstes*, ed. Karl Ferdinand Müller and Walter Blankenburg (Kassel: Johannes Stauda Verlag, 1970), 59–273; *Made Not Born: New Perspectives on Christian Initiation and the Catechumenate* (Notre Dame: University of Notre Dame Press, 1976); Mark Searle, O.F.M., *Christening: The Making of Christians* (Essex: Kevin Mayhew Ltd., 1977), 16–39; Aidan Kavanagh, *The Shape of Baptism: The Rite of Christian Initiation* (New York: Pueblo Publishing Company, 1978). Also see the important discussion by Maxwell E. Johnson in "The Role of *Worship* in the Contemporary Study of Christian Initiation: A Select Review of the Literature" *Worship* 75 (2001): 20–35, esp. 21–4. Johnson summarizes the emergent consensus on the diversity of initiation rites from the second through the fourth centuries.

5. Elsewhere I have argued that the rite of Christian initiation began during the second century, developed during the second through fourth centuries, and flowered in the post-Constantinian period as a way of dealing with the massive numbers of so-called converts that the dubious means of conversion were producing. At the year 100 there were about fifty thousand Christians; by the year 300 there were 5 million (25,000 converts per year); and by the year 400 the church had grown to 30 million (250,000 converts per year). See John W. Riggs, "The Sacred Food of *Didache* 9 and 10 and Second-Century Ecclesiologies," in *The Didache in Context*, ed. Clayton Jefford (Leiden: E. J. Brill, 1995), 256–83.

6. See the summary in Kavanagh, *Shape*, 93–97.

7. Kavanagh, *Shape*, 89.

8. For a practical theological description of the initiation process, as it reenacts today the patristic pattern, see Searle, *Christening*, 43–233.

9. Lambert Beauduin, *La Piété de l'église* (Brussels: Vromant & Co., 1914), 5–44.

10. The literature on liturgical theology is extensive just within Roman Catholicism, not to mention the variations of liturgical theology present within Protestantism and the Orthodox Church. For entry to the literature, see Kevin Irwin, "Liturgical Theology," in Fink, ed., *New Dictionary*, 721–33; J. D. Crichton, "A Theology of Worship," in Jones et al., eds., *Liturgy*, 3–31; and, for a useful categorization of approaches to liturgical theology, see David W. Fagerberg, *What Is Liturgical Theology?* (New York: Pueblo Publishing Company, 1992), 23–179.

11. Fagerberg, *Liturgical Theology*; Aidan Kavanagh, *Confirmation: Origins and Reform* (New York: Pueblo Publishing Company, 1988); idem, "Initiation: Baptism and Confirmation," *Worship* 46 (1972): 262–76; idem, *On Liturgical Theology* (New York: Pueblo Publishing Company, 1984); idem, *Shape*.

12. Fagerberg, *Liturgical Theology*, 220.

13. Ibid., 201; Kavanagh, *Liturgical Theology*, 75–76, 87–88, 120, 146–47.

14. Kavanagh, *Liturgical Theology*, 97.

15. Fagerberg, *Liturgical Theology*, 290; cf. 15–22. The phrase "liturgy is the ontological condition for theology" repeats throughout Fagerberg's book and is borrowed from Alexander Schmemann. See Kavanagh, *Liturgical Theology*, 75–76.

16. Fagerberg, *Liturgical Theology*, 194–96, 287–91.

17. Kavanagh, *Liturgical Theology*, 79–87, 96–102; Fagerberg, *Liturgical Theology*, 200–227, 294–303. The close similarity between this position on liturgical theology and the so-called Yale school of theology is hardly accidental. What Kavanagh and Fagerberg assert about divine revelation, liturgy as the ontology of theology, and grammar as the way of ordering and shaping echoes, *mutatis mutandis*, the work of Hans Frei (biblical hermeneutics), Brevard Childs (canonical hermeneutics), George Lindbeck (historical theology), and Paul Holmer (philosophical theology). In this regard, Kavanagh rounded out the Yale School by bringing to liturgical studies a hermeneutic comparable to that already present in other disciplines. Note Fagerberg's use of the work by Lindbeck and Holmer.

18. Kavanagh, *Shape*, 53.

19. Fagerberg, *Liturgical Theology*, 200.

20. Kavanagh, *Liturgical Theology*, 146–47; cf. Fagerberg, *Liturgical Theology*, 200–212, 287–98; also 152–61. From a different approach, compare the work by Edward J. Kilmartin, S.J., *Christian Liturgy: Theology and Practice*, vol. 1: *Systematic Theology of Liturgy* (Kansas City, Mo.: Sheed and Ward, 1988), esp. 158–79, 217–34.

21. In fact, Kavanagh and Fagerberg understand this perspective to be decidedly un-Protestant, exactly to the degree that the Reformers, as *misguided* children of their *misguided* era, *misunderstood* liturgy and its ritual structures. See Kavanagh, *Liturgical Theology*, 103–11, 117–18; Fagerberg, *Liturgical Theology*, 184–85.

22. Martin Luther, *The Bondage of the Will* (De servo arbitrio), in *D. Martin Luthers Werke: Kritische Gesamtausgabe* (Weimar: Hermann Böhlaus, 1888), 18.651.24–30 (hereafter cited as W.A. with volume and page number); English translation in *Luther's Works*, ed. Jaroslav Pelikan and Helmut T. Lehmann, 55 vols. (St. Louis: Concordia Publishing House; Philadelphia: Fortress Press, 1955-1986), 33.88 (hereafter cited as L.W. with volume and page number). Also, from *The Bondage of the Will*, see W.A. 18.649.26–650.35; L.W. 33.85–86. From Luther's *Psalm 90*, see W.A. 40^3.504.11–505.12; L.W. 13.88–89.

23. From *On the Papacy in Rome* (Von dem Papstum zu Rome widder den hochberumpten Romanisten zu Leipzig), see W.A. 6.293; L.W. 39.65–66. From *Concerning Rebaptism* (Von der Widdertauffe an zween Pfarherrn), see W.A. 26.154.1–155.28; L.W. 40.239–41.

24. W.A. 18.650.23–35, 651.24–30; L.W. 33.86, 88. See also W.A. 40^3.505; L.W. 13.89.

25. W.A. 18.650.22–652.11; L.W. 33.86–88. Also see his 1546 (1530) *Preface to the Revelation of St. John*, in *D. Martin Luthers Werke: Kritische Gesamtausgabe. Die Deutsche Bibel*, vol. 7 (Weimar: Hermann Böhlaus, 1931), 421.6–17; L.W. 35.411.

26. See Luther's comments in *Concerning Rebaptism*, W.A. 26.154.1–155.28; L.W. 40.239–41. The comment here does not gainsay that Luther spoke more broadly that the church was visibly marked by personal confession, saintly lives, and other outward acts. For example, in his 1522 *Personal Prayer Book*, Luther wrote: "I believe that no one can be saved who is not in this community, peacefully holding with it the same faith, word, sacraments, and love" (W.A. 10^2.394; L.W. 43.28). At the same time, as the citations in nn. 22–25, above, show, it cannot be denied that Luther also asserted that another's faith cannot be seen and that the only true outward mark of the church *strictly speaking* was the Word given in preaching and the sacraments (cf. Augsburg Confession, article 7). Also compare Luther's comments on the "priestly offices," which he named as the ministry of the Word, baptism, eucharistic consecration, binding and loosing from sin, sacrifice, prayer, and judging doctrines. These duties properly belonged to all Christians, although, for the sake of order, one or more people could be chosen to perform them (W.A. 12.179.38–189.27; L.W. 40.21–34). The ultimate point to all these duties was to be Christ for one another; thus the "priestly offices," which were the common ministry of all within the church, echoed the marks of the church.

27. W.A. 40^1.131f.; L.W. 26.66. See also W.A. 17^1.232; L.W. 12.187. Also see B. A. Gerrish's useful summary and notes in *Saving Faith and Secular Faith* (Minneapolis: Fortress Press, 1992), 9–11.

28. John Calvin, *Calvin: Institutes of the Christian Religion*, ed. John T. McNeill, trans. and indexed by Ford Lewis Battles, 2 vols. Library of Christian Classics 20–21 (Philadelphia: Westminster Press, 1960), 2.21.3 (hereafter cited as *Inst.*, followed by book, chapter, and section number); idem, *Institution of the Christian Religion (1536)*, trans. Ford Lewis Battles (Atlanta: John Knox Press, 1975), 1.21, 23, 58, 59 (hereafter referred to as *Inst.*, followed by book and section number, then followed by page number for Battles's translation of the 1536 *Institutes*).

29. *Inst.* 1.24; Battles, 1536 *Institutes*, 59–60.

30. *Inst.* 2.24; Battles, 1536 *Institutes*, 81.

31. *Inst.* 1.24–25; Battles, 1536 *Institutes*, 59–61.

32. *Inst.* 1.29; Battles, 1536 *Institutes*, 62–63.

33. E.g., Fagerberg, *Liturgical Theology*, 294–98.

34. Note Fagerberg's autobiographical comment in the introduction to *Liturgical Theology*, 8: "This book was written when the author was a Lutheran pastor; as it is being published the author is Roman Catholic. Does the reader remember the optical illusions in which if one looks at black on white one sees a vase, but if one blinks and looks at white on black one sees two faces staring at each other? The basis of this book was my dissertation at Yale in which I tried to outline the perimeters of liturgical theology; then I blinked and saw an ecclesiology, one which drew me into the Roman Catholic liturgical tradition."

35. See White's brief discussion of the relationship between Protestant and Roman Catholic worship, including their recent convergence, in *Protestant Worship*, 25–35, esp. 32–35.

36. Aidan Kavanagh, "The Role of Ritual in Personal Development," in *The Roots of Ritual*, ed. James D. Shaughnessy (Grand Rapids: Wm. B. Eerdmans Publishing Co., 1973), 148–49.

37. Or see the more pastoral way I put this in John W. Riggs, "Normative Shape for Christian Worship," *Prism* 3, 2 (1988): 34–36.

38. Compare the classic essay by the cultural anthropologist Clifford Geertz, "Ethos, World View, and the Analysis of Sacred Symbols," in *The Interpretation of Culture: Selected Essays* (New York: Basic Books, 1973). Geertz argues that religion is a fundamental feature of human existence that has two aspects, ethos and world view. These aspects work together so that "the ethos is made intellectually reasonable by being shown to represent a way of life implied by the actual state of affairs which the world view describes, and the world view is made emotionally acceptable by being presented as an image of an actual state of affairs of which such a way of life is an authentic expression" (126 f.).

39. L.W. 40.239.

40. For a good, short introduction to Luther's 1523 baptism rite and to the Flood Prayer, see Hughes Oliphant Old, *The Shaping of the Reformed Baptismal Rite in the Sixteenth Century* (Grand Rapids: Wm. B. Eerdmans Publishing Co., 1992), 33–40, 227–30. Luther's 1523 rite was essentially a German translation of a Latin rite, which itself showed local variations. These rites also show the long-standing medieval history of revising initiation rites, which once were designed for adults, when these rites were used to baptize infants. See Gustav Kawerau, "Liturgische Studien zu Luthers Taufbüchlein von 1523," *Zeitschrift für kirchliche Wissenschaft und kirchliches Leben* 10 (1898): 407–31, 466–77, 519–47, 578–99, 625–43; K. Nümann, "Zur enstehung des lutherischen Taufbüchleins von Jahre 1523," *Monatsschrift für Gottesdienst und kirchliche Kunst* 33 (1928): 214–19; and Bruno Jordahn, "Der Taufgottesdienst im Mittelalter bis zum Gegenwart," in Müller and Blankenburg, eds., *Leiturgia*, 350–425. See Jordahn, "Der Taufgottesdienst," 380–83, esp. n. 150, for the Flood Prayer.

41. The influence of Luther's prayer on current worship books is well known; for the influence on early Reformed rites, see Old, *Reformed Baptismal Rite*, 33–43, 63–64, 230–34, 247.

42. W.A. 19.531–32; L.W. 53.106–9.

43. W.A. 19.531.

44. Lorenz Grönvik, *Die Taufe in der Theologie Martin Luthers* (Göttingen and Zurich: Vandenhoeck & Ruprecht, 1968), 22–34, 181–87.

45. Compare the German: *nach deinem gestrengen gericht die unglewbige welt verdampt / den glewbigen Noe selb acht nach deiner grossen barmhertzigkeit erhalten.*

46. Compare the German: *und den verstrockten Pharao mit allen seinem im roten Meer erseufft / und dein volck Israel trocken durch byn gefurt.*

47. Grönvik, *Taufe*, 15–16, 132–33, 174–79, 199–200.

48. Eugene Brand, "New Rites of Initiation and Their Implications in the Lutheran Churches," *Studia Liturgica* 12, 2–3 (1977): 151–65; Philip H. Pfatteicher and Carlos R. Messerli, *Manual on the Liturgy—Lutheran Book of Worship* (Minneapolis: Augsburg Publishing House, 1979), 167–98; Frank Senn, "The Shape and Content of Christian Initiation: An Exposition of the New Lutheran Liturgy of Holy Baptism," *Dialog* 14 (1975): 97–107; Lawrence Stookey, "Three New Initiation Rites," *Worship* 51 (1977): 33–49.

49. Pfatteicher and Messerli, *Manual*, 177. For a pastoral-theological explanation of how we "find our story in the story of the community," see Mark Searle, "The Journey of Conversion," *Worship* 54 (1980): 35–55; see also Senn, "Christian Initiation," 105.

50. For a brief summary, see Old, *Reformed Baptismal Rite*, 228–30. Although Old rejects the possibility that Luther revised the baptismal font consecration prayer, except in a most general way, the font prayer of the so-called Gelasian sacramentary does come to mind (*Vaticanus Reginensis*, 316). In this font prayer, not only is water connected to God's gracious activity through history, but the baptismal water itself has christological consecration. Perhaps we should recall that Luther still lived in an oral culture in which the great scholars, especially those trained in religious orders, had prodigious powers of memory for texts and liturgies. A prayer such as the font prayer might easily, and literally, come to mind, ready for creative adaptation, thus producing, as Old rightly notes, as many dissimilarities as similarities.

51. See chapter 7 for further remarks here.

52. See my discussion in John W. Riggs, "Emerging Ecclesiology in Calvin's Baptismal Thought, 1536–1543," *Church History* 64, 1 (1995): 29–30.

CHAPTER 1

1. The standard Zwingli biography is the four-volume work by Oskar Farner, who was the longtime pastor of the Grossmünster and lecturer and professor at the University of Zurich. The final volume was completed and edited by Rudolf Pfister: see *Huldrych Zwingli*, 4 vols. (Zurich: Zwingli-Verlag, 1946–60). In English, the fullest biography of Zwingli remains that by G. R. Potter, *Zwingli* (Cambridge: Cambridge University Press, 1976). Less extensive than the biography by Potter is that by Ulrich Gäbler, *Huldrych Zwingli: His Life and Work*, trans. Ruth L. C. Gritsch (Philadelphia: Fortress Press, 1986). Also see the shorter biography by Oskar Farner, *Zwingli the Reformer: His Life and Work*, trans. D. G. Sear (Hamden, Conn.: Archon Books, 1968). The collection of essays by Gottfried Locher is an important contribution to understanding various aspects of Zwingli's theology; see Locher, *Zwingli's Thought: New Perspectives* (Leiden: E. J. Brill, 1981). A good summary of Zwingli's theology and of secondary scholarship can be found in W. P. Stephens, *The Theology of Huldrych Zwingli* (Oxford: Clarendon Press, 1986).

2. See Stephens, *Theology*, 5–50.

3. Had Zwingli made his decisive Reformation turn? Scholars have all too

often looked for the "Damascus road" moment for Luther, Zwingli, and Calvin. What seems to have happened for Zwingli is that intellectual insights he appropriated became more influential over time in a variety of theological areas. These influences became crucial in times of crisis. When Zwingli moved to Zurich in 1519, much of his Reformation theology was in place; but during that year Zwingli suffered from the plague and almost died. He also became aware of Luther's courageous stand at Leipzig. Finally, during the appointment process to the Grossmünster, he was confronted with his sexual relationship with a local woman. Zwingli ultimately received the call in part because the other leading candidate, Laurenz Mär, lived with a woman with whom he had had six children; long-term concubinage was apparently deemed the greater offense. At the same time as these personal events occurred, Zwingli began his preaching duties by following a *lectio continua*—preaching through a book of the Bible chapter by chapter—rather than using the standard lectionary system. He also studied more intently the Gospel of John, the letters of Paul, and the works of Augustine. The end result was taking to heart the Word found in scripture, with its christocentric gospel message that all depended on the one source of all good, the gracious God revealed through Christ. For a good summary see Stephens, *Theology*, 21–34.

4. Secondary scholarship on Zwingli's theological formation was highly influenced by the work of Walter Köhler, who (especially early on) emphasized the influence of humanism on Zwingli; more recent scholarship has seen the influence of humanism mitigated by Zwingli's fuller embrace of a christocentric and scriptural approach when he began his Zurich ministry. See the historiographic essay by Locher in *Zwingli's Thought*, 42–71. Also see Stephens, *Theology*, 9–28. Liberal Protestant and neo-orthodox theologians have tended to line up along these perspectives: for example, compare the summaries of Zwingli's thought by Paul Tillich, *A History of Christian Thought* (New York: Simon & Schuster, 1968), 256–62, and Geoffrey W. Bromiley, *Historical Theology: An Introduction* (Grand Rapids: Wm. B. Eerdman's Publishing Co., 1978), 213–17 and passim. More recent discussions of humanism may soften such divisions. First, much scholarship suggests that humanism signifies not material agreement on philosophical concepts of humankind and world but rather the formal shift to original languages, texts, and conceptual tools such as rhetoric and grammar. Second, most if not all the Reformers, including the Zurich Anabaptists, were influenced by humanism. Steven Ozment aptly comments, "While the reformers set the humanist curriculum in place of the scholastic, doctrine was always the rider and the humanities the horse. The humanities became for the Protestant theologians what Aristotelian philosophy had been for late medieval theologians—the favored handmaiden of theology; the rhetorical arts served the more basic task of communicating true doctrine" (*The Age of Reform* [New Haven, Conn.: Yale University Press, 1980], 315; also see 290–317 for a suggestive overview of "Humanism and the Reformation"). For a larger view with extensive bibliography, see James D. Tracy, "Humanism and the Reformation," in *Reformation Europe: A Guide to Research*, ed. Steven Ozment (St. Louis: Center for Reformation Research, 1982), 33–57.

5. For the following, see Potter, *Zwingli*, 126–97.

6. For studies on Zwingli's view of baptism, see Martin Brecht, "Herkunft und Eigenart der Täuferanschauung der Züricher Täufer," *Archiv für Reformationsgeschichte* 64 (1973): 147–65; Jack Warren Cottrell, "Covenant and Baptism in the Theology of Huldreich Zwingli" (unpublished Th.D. diss., Princeton Theological Seminary, 1971); J.-V.-M. Pollet, "Zwinglianisme," in *Dictionnaire de Theologie*

Catholique (Paris: Librairie Letouzey et Ané, 1950), 15.3745–3982; Georg Finsler, *Zwingli-Bibliographie: Verzeichnis der Gedruckten Schriften von und über Ulrich Zwingli* (Nieuwkoop: B. de Graaf, 1968); Ulrich Gäbler, "Die Zwingli-Forschung seit 1960," *Theologische Literaturzeitung* 96, 7 (1971): 481–90; idem, *Huldrych Zwingli im 20. Jahrhundert: Forschungsbericht und annotierte Bibliographie, 1897–1972* (Zurich: Theologischer Verlag, 1975); Carl Hemmann, "Zwingli's Stellung zur Tauffrage im literarischen Kampf mit den Anabaptisten," *Schweizerische Theologische Zeitschrift* 36 (1919): 29–33, 79–85; Hans J. Hillerbrand, "The Origin of Sixteenth Century Anabaptism: Another Look," *Archiv für Reformationsgeschichte* 53 (1962): 152–80; Edwin Künzli, "Aus der Zwingli-Forschung," *Theologische Rundschau* n.s. 37, 4 (1972): 361–69; Locher, *Zwingli's Thought*, 218–19; H. Wayne Pipkin, *A Zwingli Bibliography*, Bibliographia Tripotamopolitana no. 7 (Pittsburgh: The Clifford E. Barbour Library, Pittsburgh Theological Seminary, 1972); Fritz Schmidt-Clausing, *Zwingli als Liturgiker* (Göttingen: Vandenhoeck & Ruprecht, 1952); idem, "Zwingli und die Kindertaufe," *Berliner Kirchen-Briefe* 6 (1962): 4–8; Johann Martin Usteri, "Darstellung der Tauflehre Zwinglis," *Theologische Studien und Kritiken* 3 (1884): 205–84; John Howard Yoder, "The Turning Point in the Zwinglian Revolution," *Mennonite Quarterly Review* 32 (1958): 128–40. Especially see the bibliographical essays by Finsler, *Zwingli-Bibliographie*; Gäbler, *Huldrych Zwingli*; idem, "Zwingli-Forschung"; Künzli, "Zwingli-Forschung"; Pipkin, *Zwingli Bibliography*. The majority of these essays are summaries that cluster Zwingli's baptismal teaching around a theme: Zwingli's avoidance of sacramentalism and legalism (Locher, *Zwingli's Thought*, 218–19) or Zwingli's struggle with the Anabaptists, which produced poor exegesis but a good theological description of baptism (Pollet, "Zwinglianisme," cols. 3819–24). The two best essays are those by Usteri and Cottrell, which trace the development of Zwingli's thought in the historical context of Zurich, particularly the controversies with the Zurich radicals. Usteri's older and classic essay finds careful support by Cottrell's scholarship, and the discussion below is indebted to these two studies.

7. See Cottrell, "Covenant and Baptism," 17–66.

8. *Proposal concerning Images and the Mass* (Vorschlag wegen der Bilder und der Messe) (May 1524), in *Huldreich Zwinglis sämtliche Werke*, ed. Emil Egli, Georg Finsler, Walther Köhler, Oskar Farner, Fritz Blanke, Leonard von Muralt, Edwin Künzli, Rudolf Pfister, vols. 88–101 of *Corpus Reformatorum*, vol. 1 (Berlin: C. A. Schwetschke und Sohn, 1905), vols. 2–5, 7–12 (Leipzig: M. Heinsius Nachfolger, 1908–), vols. 6/1, 6/2, 13–14 (Zurich: Verlag Berichthaus, 1944–), 3.120–31 (hereafter cited as Z.W., followed by volume, page, and line number); see Z.W. 3.124.32–125.25. Unless otherwise specified, all translations of this source in this chapter are the author's.

9. *Commentary on the True and False Religion* (*De vera et falsa religione commentarius*) (*March 1525*), Z.W. 3.628–912; *Baptism, Rebaptism, and the Baptism of Infants* (Von der Taufe, von der Wiedertaufe und von der Kindertaufe) (May 27, 1525), Z.W. 4.206–337. Translation of *Commentary on the True and False Religion* in *The Latin Works of Huldreich Zwingli*, ed. Clarence Nevin Heller (Philadelphia: Heidelberg Press, 1929), 43–343.

10. From *Commentary on the True and False Religion* (Z.W. 3.761.22–24): "The sacraments are therefore signs or ceremonies . . . by which someone demonstrates to the church that they are zealous for, or a soldier of, Christ" ("Sunt ergo sacramenta signa vel ceremoniae . . . quibus se homo ecclesiae probat aut candidatum aut militem esse Christi"). On the same theme, see, from *On Baptism, Rebaptism, and Infant Baptism*, Z.W. 4.206–337, esp. 4.217.24–218.24. For instance

(4.218.191–20): "Baptism is a sign that pledges us to the Lord Jesus Christ" ("Also ist der touff ein zeichen, das in den herren Jhesum Christum verpflicht").

11. Z.W. 4.294–95.

12. "Est ergo Christus certitudo et pignus gratiae dei"; Z.W. 3.676.12.

13. Usteri, "Darstellung," 214–20; cf. Hemmann, "Zwingli's Stellung," 29–31.

14. Cottrell, "Covenant and Baptism," 173–249.

15. *Commentary on Genesis* (Farrago annotationam in Genesis) (March 1527), Z.W. 13.5–288.

16. In June 1525, the *Prophezei* were begun to help train pastors and teachers for the Zurich church. Every morning but Friday and Sunday, a group of young men and local pastors gathered to hear exegesis from the Hebrew Old Testament, the Greek New Testament, and the Latin Vulgate, although most of the study was of the Old Testament. Careful attention was paid to grammar, language, and translation. Jud and Pellican, among others, helped conduct the Greek and Hebrew lectures. Zwingli conducted the Latin lectures. The result of these *Prophezei* were far reaching: scholars and pastors were trained; the Zurich Bible was produced; the "prophets" (pastors) that the lectures produced became guiding voices for the Zurich Reformation; and Zwingli's Old Testament commentaries had roots here. The Genesis commentary, for example, was put together from notes taken by those present and edited by Jud and Megander. See Oskar Farner, "Nachwort zu den Erläuterungen zur Genesis," Z.W. 13.289–90; Edwin Künzli, Z.W. 14.872. Literary critical work by Künzli has shown the Genesis commentary to be Zwingli's work and not the work of the compilers; see Edwin Künzli, Z.W. 14.876.

17. *Essay on the Eucharist* (*Subsidium sive coronis de eucharistia*), (August 1525), Z.W. 4.458–504: the one true covenant was with Abraham (499.9–24); circumcision is the sign of the covenant (499.24–555.9); and, as circumcision was the covenant sign, so now baptism is the covenant sign (500.11–39). Also see Cottrell, "Covenant and Baptism," 185–93. Translation of this essay can be found in *Huldrych Zwingli Writings*, trans. and ed. H. Wayne Pipkin (Allison Park, Pa.: Pickwick Press, 1984), 187–231.

18. *Reply to Balthasar Hubmaier's Baptism Book* (Antwort über Balthasar Hubmaiers Taufbüchlein) (November 1525), Z.W. 4.585–647. See Cottrell, "Covenant and Baptism," 194–204.

19. Z.W. 4.629.1–638.20.

20. Z.W. 4.638.21–639.11.

21. Z.W. 4.637.27–30.

22. *Refutation of the Tricks of the Anabaptists* (In catabaptistarum strophas elenchus) (July 1527), Z.W. 6/1.21–196. See Cottrell, "Covenant and Baptism," 236–47; Hemmann, "Zwingli's Stellung," 79–83, 84–85. English translation in *Selected Works of Huldreich Zwingli*, ed. Samuel Macauley Jackson (Philadelphia: University of Pennsylvania Press, 1901), 123–258.

23. Z.W. 6/1.48.5–15. Cf. *Reply to Hubmaier*, Z.W. 4.629.1–7: "Now, as it [circumcision] was given to children, so also baptism should be given to children" ("Wie nun die den kinden ggeben ist, also sol ouch der touf den kinden ggeben werden," 4.629.6–7).

24. Z.W. 6/1.155.27–156.34.

25. Z.W. 6/1.156.34–42; 156.41–157.34.

26. Z.W. 6/1.162.21–24.

27. "Ut unus essemus cum eis populos, una ecclesia, et unum foedus quoque haberemus," Z.W. 6/1.163.8–10.

28. Cottrell, "Covenant and Baptism," 83–172; cf. Usteri, "Darstellung," 217–20; Hemmann, "Zwingli's Stellung," 29–31.

29. Cf. Schmidt-Clausing, "Kindertaufe," who observes that if baptism is a pledge sign and, strictly speaking, baptism is not necessary for salvation, since the true spiritual baptism is a gift of God, then infant baptism is a "quasi adiaphoron", 7.

30. Cottrell, "Covenant and Baptism," 173–249; Schmidt-Clausing, "Kindertaufe," 8.

31. Alting von Geusau, *Die Lehre von der Kindertaufe bei Calvin* (Bilthoven: Uitgenerij H. Nelissen, 1963), 49–60.

32. Pollet describes Zwingli's 1525–27 shift as "the passage from a purely moral conception of the baptismal sign (*Pflichtzeichen*) to a properly theological notion (*Bundeszeichen*)" ("Zwinglianisme," col. 3822).

33. The current biographical standard for Luther has become Martin Brecht's three-volume study, now fully translated into English, *Martin Luther: His Road to Reformation, 1483–1521*, trans. James L. Schaaf (Philadelphia: Fortress Press, 1985); *Martin Luther: Shaping and Defining the Reformation, 1521–1532*, trans. James L. Schaaf (Minneapolis: Fortress Press, 1990); *Martin Luther: The Preservation of the Church, 1532–1546*, trans. James L. Schaaf (Minneapolis: Fortress Press, 1993). Among the many biographies that are useful, that by James Kittleson, *Luther: The Story of the Man and His Career* (Minneapolis: Augsburg Publishing House, 1986), is lively and an easy read for beginning students. Heiko Oberman's *Luther: Man between God and the Devil* (New Haven, Conn.: Yale University Press, 1989) is the standout single-volume biography that describes Luther in the complexity of his historical setting. Roland Bainton's *Here I Stand!* (New York: Abingdon-Cokesbury Press, 1950) remains an enjoyable classic. Bernard Lohse's *Martin Luther: An Introduction to His Life and Work*, trans. Robert C. Schultz (Philadelphia: Fortress Press, 1986), is an excellent entrance to Luther and the scholarly discussions that surround his life. For a detailed biographical essay with extensive bibliography, see Mark U. Edwards Jr., "Luther's Biography," in *Reformation Europe: A Guide to Research II*, ed. William S. Maltby (St. Louis: Center for Reformation Research, 1992), 5–20.

34. Does one date Luther's reformation change "early" (pre-1517) or "late" (post-1517)? The secondary scholarship here, substantial in both volume and quality and interwoven with modern Protestant–Roman Catholic debates, can hardly be reviewed. For entrance to the material, see Edwards, "Luther's Biography," 10–12. In particular, note the two collections by Bernard Lohse, ed., *Der Durchbruch der reformatischen Erkenntnis bei Luther* (Darmstadt: Wissentschaftliche Buchgesellschaft, 1968) and *Der Durchbruch der reformatischen Erkenntnis bei Luther—Neuere Untersuchungen* (Stuttgart: F. Steiner Verlag Wiesbaden, 1988).

35. For a summary of changes and entrance to the secondary scholarship, see Ozment, *Age of Reform*, 309–14.

36. For entrance to the discussion of grace and sacraments in the medieval church and for Luther's reaction the medieval sacramental system, see Ozment, *Age of Reform*, 22–42, 231–39. Also see Steven Ozment, *The Reformation in the Cities* (New Haven, Conn.: Yale University Press, 1975), 1–120.

37. *The Babylonian Captivity of the Church* (De captivate Bablyonica ecclesiae praeludium), in W.A. 6.497–573; 521.20–25; L.W. 36.49

38. W.A. 6.535.8–11; L.W. 36.69

39. "Omnia sacramenta ad fidem alendam instituta," W.A. 6.529.36; L.W. 36.61.

40. In the second section of his 1519 essay *The Holy and Blessed Sacrament of Baptism* (Eyn Sermon von dem heyligen hochwirdigen Sacrament der Tauffe), Luther asserted: "Therefore one must look at three things in the holy sacrament: the sign, the significance and the faith" (W.A. 2.727.23–25; L.W. 35.29–30). Notice the triad of significance–sign–faith. The significance was that which a person was to believe, and Luther described that significance as "a blessed dying to sin and a resurrection in the grace of God, so that the old self, conceived and born in sin, is drowned there, and a new self comes forth and rises up, born in grace" (W.A. 2.727.30–33; L.W. 35.30). This was a stage of Luther's baptismal theology a year prior to that of the *Babylonian Captivity*. The object of faith, strictly speaking, was a complex of ideas that described the effects of God's grace. By the time of the *Babylonian Captivity*, Luther saw that the object of faith was the present offer of divine grace itself.

For essays on Luther's baptismal theology, see Ernst Bizer, "Die Entdeckung des Sakraments durch Luther," *Evangelische Theologie* 17 (1957): 64–90; idem, *Fides ex auditu: Eine Untersuchung über die Entdeckung der Gerichtigkeit Gottes durch Martin Luther*, 2d ed. (Neukirchen Kreis Moers: Verlag der Buchhandlung des Erziehungsvereins, 1961); Martin Ferel, *Gepredigte Taufe: Eine homilitische Untersuchung zur Taufpredigt bei Luther* (Tübingen: J. C. B. Mohr [Paul Siebeck], 1969); Grönvik, *Taufe*; Werner Jetter, *Die Taufe beim Jungen Luther* (Tübingen: J. C. B. Mohr [Paul Siebeck], 1954); idem, review of *Die Taufe in der Theologie Martin Luthers*, by Lorenz Grönvik, in *Lutherische Rundschau* 19 (1969): 249.

For Luther and infant baptism, see Rudolf Lutterjohann, "Die Stellung Luthers zur Kindertaufe," *Zeitschrift für systematische Theologie* 11 (1934): 188–224. For a discussion of secondary writers prior to Lutterjohann, see Karl Brinkel, *Die Lehre Luthers von der fides infantium bei der Kindertaufe* (Berlin: Evangelische Verlagsanstalt, 1958), 9–14. Also see Paul Althaus, "Martin Luther über die Kindertaufe," *Theologische Literaturzeitung* 3 (1948): 705–14; P. Molwitz, "Luther's Lehre von der Kindertaufe," *Neue Kirchliche Zeitschrift* 38 (1917): 359–72; Jaroslav J. Pelikan, "Luther's Defense of Infant Baptism," in *Luther for an Ecumenical Age*, ed. Carl S. Meyer (St. Louis: Concordia Publishing House, 1967), 200–218; von Geusau, *Lehre von der Kindertaufe*, 23–27, 39–49.

41. Small Catechism (*Der kleine Catechismus*, W.A. 30¹.239–425); location and translation as given in Theodore G. Tappert, ed., *The Book of Concord: The Confessions of the Evangelical Lutheran Church*, (Philadelphia: Fortress Press, 1959), 4.9–14 (349).

42. "Accedat verbum ad elementum et fit sacramentum," Large Catechism (*Deudsch Catechismus* [Der Große Catechismus], W.A. 30¹.123–238); Tappert, *Book of Concord*, 4.17–18 (438).

43. Tappert, *Book of Concord*, 4.23–34 (439–41).

44. Oberman, *Luther*, 151.

45. For Luther's developing position on infant baptism, see Brinkel, *Lehre Luthers*. My discussion follows Brinkel.

46. *Concerning Rebaptism* (Von der Widdertauffe an zween Pfarherrn), W.A. 26.144–74; L.W. 40.229–62.

47. W.A. 26.159.25–166.8; L.W. 40:246–54.

48. "Abusus non tollit substantiam, imo confirmat substantiam," W.A. 26.159.36–37; L.W. 40:246.

49. W.A. 26.154.17–25; L.W. 40.239–40.

50. Grönvik, *Taufe*, 94–102.

51. Ibid., 101–31, esp. 101–6, 130–31, 127–29, 240.

52. Ibid., 102: "In the year 1520, the main question of the discussion for Luther was how one should make right use of the sacrament. In 1525 and later, the appearance of the enthusiasts caused him to take as the most important point of the discussion the question of what the sacrament is." The same point is made by Ferel, who studied baptism in Luther's preaching. Ferel shows that Luther spoke comprehensively against various opponents, and the task is to understand the whole in terms of the particular situation. Luther fundamentally distinguished between God's work and our work: God's work, which was central, lay in the sacraments and the Word, which daily brought resurrection to new life, whereas our work must follow God's work as a daily response. Concerning baptism, one had to distinguish the necessity of faith as an element that should come to baptism and the inappropriateness of faith as a constitutive element for correct baptism. Without faith there is "correct baptism" but "no benefits of baptism." In this regard, the mistake the Anabaptists made was to ground baptism in the mistaken surety of human faith, which was an act of "works righteousness." See Ferel, *Gepredigle Taufe*, 218–41.

53. For Bucer's biography, see Martin Greschat, *Martin Bucer: Ein Reformator und seine Zeit* (Munich: Verlag C. H. Beck, 1990), as well as the older but not always reliable work by Hasting Eells, *Martin Bucer* (New Haven, Conn.: Yale University Press, 1931). For an introduction to the bibliographical material, see Brian G. Armstrong, "Calvin and Calvinism," in Maltby, ed., *Reformation Europe*, 92–93. For a short introduction to Bucer, see Martin Greschat, "Das Profil Martin Bucers," 9–17 in *Martin Bucer and Sixteenth Century Europe*, 2 vols. ed. Christian Krieger and Marc Lienhard (Leiden: E. J. Brill, 1993), 9–16. For Bucer's work in Strasbourg, see Miriam Usher Chrisman, *Strasbourg and the Reform: A Study in the Process of Change* (New Haven, Conn.: Yale University Press, 1967). For his work in England, see Constantin Hopf, *Martin Bucer and the English Reformation* (Oxford: Basil Blackwell, 1946). Also see the collection of wide-ranging essays in Krieger and Lienhard, eds., *Martin Bucer*, especially the essays concerning Bucer's relationship with other Reformers (1:343–470).

54. So, for example, Eells, *Martin Bucer*, 415–22; W. P. Stephens, *The Holy Spirit in the Theology of Martin Bucer* (London: Cambridge University Press, 1970), 5–10; Chrisman, *Strasbourg*, 85–88. Compare the balanced appraisal by Reinhold Friedrich, "Martin Bucer—Ökumene im 16.257.68. Jahrhundert," in Krieger and Lienhard, eds., *Martin Bucer*, 257–68, who notes Bucer's scriptural boundary for ecumenism. Also see the essay by Gottfried Hamman that sets this pragmatic and ecumenical interest of Bucer's within the context of the work of the Holy Spirit, "La Démarche théologique de Bucer," in Krieger and Lienhard, eds., *Martin Bucer*, 71–81.

55. Greschat, *Martin Bucer*, 257–60.

56. For the Strasbourg story from 1520 through 1534, see Chrisman, *Strasbourg*, 81–232.

57. As has been long recognized, Bucer here sharply distinguished water baptism from Spirit baptism, much like Zwingli. See Johann Martin Usteri, "Die Stellung der Strassburger Reformatoren Bucer und Capito zur Tauffrage," *Theologische Studien und Kritiken* 3 (1884): 456–63, 487–90, 517, 521. Also see René Bornert, *La Réforme protestante du culte a Strasbourg au XVI*siècle (1523–1598) (Leiden: E. J. Brill, 1981), 339–49, who gives a fine analysis of Bucer's movement from Zwingi's dualism to a unified sign-reality baptismal theology. So also Stephens in *Holy Spirit*, 221–37.

58. Martin Bucer, *Martin Bucers Deutsche Schriften* (Gütershloh: Gütershloher

Verlaghaus Gerd Mohn, 1960), 1.254.16–20, 1.256.39–257.31 (hereafter, reference is made to *BDS*, followed by volume, page, and line citation).

59. *BDS* 1.254.23–30.

60. *BDS* 1.259.30–38.

61. *BDS* 1.260.31–39.

62. The critical German and Latin texts of the Tetrapolitan Confession can be found in *BDS* 3.13–185. Bucer's *Apology* for the confession (Apologie der Confessio Tetrapolitana) can be found in *BDS* 3.186–318, following the critical editions of the text.

63. *BDS* 3.121.6–8.

64. *BDS* 3.120–23.

65. *BDS* 3.272.38–273.3; also see his comments on baptism in 3.273.26–274.10.

66. *Quid de baptismate infantium iuxta scripturas Dei Sentiendum* (Strasbourg: Matthias Apiarius, 1533). This text was unfortunately not available to me. The work is cited, and Latin sections given, in Stephens, *Holy Spirit*, 229–30; Old, *Reformed Baptismal Rite*, 128–29; and Bornert, *Réforme protestante*, 346–47.

67. See the introductory essay in *BDS* 5.111–17.

68. See Bornert, *Réforme protestante*, 346, who gives the Latin text in n. 19; also see Stephens, *Holy Spirit*, 229.

69. "Esse signum promissionis diuinae benevolentiae . . ." See Old, *Reformed Baptismal Rite*, 128n50.

70. *Bericht auß der heyligen geschrift von der recht gottseligen anstellung und haußhaltung Christlicher gemeyn, Eynsatzung der diener des worts, Haltung und brauch der heyligen Sacramenten* (Strasbourg: Matthias Apiarius, 1534). Critical text in *BDS* 5.109–258. For background, see the introductory essay in *BDS* 5.111–17.

71. *BDS* 5.173.29–34.

72. *BDS* 6/3.19–22. For Bucer's efforts at church discipline during this period, see Amy Nelson Burnett, *The Yoke of Christ: Martin Bucer and Christian Discipline*, vol. 26 of Sixteenth Century Essays & Studies (Kirksville, Mo.: Sixteenth Century Journal Publishers, 1994), 55–86; also see Chrisman, *Strasbourg*, 201–32. For the critical text of Bucer's 1534 Short Catechism, see *BDS* 6/3.51–173.

73. *BDS* 6/3.72.2–4, 13–20.

74. See the discussions in Bornert, *Réforme protestante*, 347–49; and Stephens, *Holy Spirit*, 234–37.

75. Stephens, *Holy Spirit*, 23. In particular, see Stephens's opening chapter, "Predestination" (23–41), and chap. 4, "Sanctification and Glorification" (71–100).

76. Johannes Müller, "Die prädestinatianische Bezogenheit der Exegese," in *Martin Bucers Hermeneutik* (Gütersloh: Gütersloher Verlagshaus Gerd Mohn, 1965), 184–99.

77. Compare the comments by Karl Koch, *Studium Pietatis: Martin Bucer als Ethiker* (Neukirchen-Vluyn: Neukirchener Verlag, 1962), 81–87, esp. 83. Also see Greschat's comments on *De Regno Christi* in *Martin Bucer*, 246–48. In some disagreement, Jaques Courvoisier, *La Notion d'église chez Bucer* (Paris: Librairie Félix Alcan, 1932), 61–62, notes the practical implications of the doctrine of predestination in Bucer's theology but asserts that both Pauline and Augustinian theology are predestinarian, thus making Reformation theology essentially predestinarian from the start.

CHAPTER 2

1. The long-standing biography of Bullinger is that by Carl Pestalozzi, *Heinrich Bullinger: Leben und ausgewählte Schriften* (Elberfeld: R. L. Fridrechs, 1858). Replacing this work is the study by Fritz Blanke and Immanuel Leuschner, *Heinrich Bullinger: Vater der reformierten Kirche* (Zurich: Theologische Verlag, 1990).

2. For a recent bibliographical essay in English, see J. Wayne Baker, "The Reformation at Zurich in the Thought and Theology of Huldrych Zwingli and Heinrich Bullinger," in Maltby, ed., *Reformation Europe*, 47–73.

3. See Ernst Koch, *Die Theologie der Confessio Helvetica Posterior* (Neukirchen-Vluyn: Neukirchener Verlag des Erziehungsvereins, 1968), 387–408; idem, "Paulusexegese und Bundestheologie: Bullingers Auslegung von Gal 3:17–26," in *Histoire de l'exégèse au XVIe siècle*, ed. Olivier Fatio and Pierre Fraenkel (Geneva: Droz, 1979), 342–50; J. Wayne Baker, *Heinrich Bullinger and the Covenant: The Other Reformed Tradition* (Athens: Ohio University Press, 1980); Charles S. McCoy and J. Wayne Baker, *Fountainhead of Federalism: Heinrich Bullinger and the Covenant Tradition* (Louisville, Ky.: Westminster/John Knox Press, 1991). Note that in his otherwise quite positive review of Baker's book, Ernst Koch offers that Baker has perhaps streamlined the issue and made Bullinger's views on covenant more consistent over time than they were; see Ernst Koch, review of *Henrich Bullinger and the Covenant: The Other Reformed Tradition*, by J. Wayne Baker, in *Theologisches Literaturzeitung* 109 (1984): 43–44. Not all scholars, however, have seen Bullinger as a covenant theologian. So, for example, Edward A. Dowey Jr. criticizes the work of both Baker and Koch in "Heinrich Bullinger's Theology: Thematic, Comprehensive, Schematic," in *Calvin Studies V*, ed. John Leith (Richmond: Union Theological Seminary in Virginia, 1991), 41–60. Also see Cornelis P. Venema, "Heinrich Bullinger's Correspondence on Calvin's Doctrine of Predestination, 1551–1553," *Sixteenth Century Journal* 17 (1986): 449.

4. For more on Bullinger and baptism, see chap. 4, sec. 1, below, on the Second Helvetic Confession.

5. Heinrich Bullinger, *Catechesis* (Zurich: Froschauer, 1561), 60b. See Bullinger's comment on sign and thing signified, in his sermon "Concerning the Holy Baptism of Christ" (114 v). In that sermon Bullinger also distinguishes the "nature" (*naturam*) of baptism, that consists of the divine word and the rite that represents and seals (114 r), from the "virtue and efficacy of baptism" (*virtute enim & effectu baptismi*), that comprises themes such as forgiveness of sin, fellowship in the people of God, entrance into the church, engrafting into Christ, and regeneration by the Spirit (128 r–129r). See, Henrich Bullinger, "Concerning the Holy Baptism of Christ," ("De Sancto Christi Baptismo") *Sermonum Decasquinta*. Tomus Tertius (Zurich: Froschouer, 1551), 3:114r–129r.

6. For a summary of the issues dating this letter, see "Von dem Touff," in Heinrich Bullinger, *Heinrich Bullinger Theologische Schriften*, Ser. 3, Vol. 2, ed. Hans-Georg vom Berg, Bernhard Schneider, and Endre Zsindely (Zurich: Theologischser Verlag, 1991), 66–67.

7. Ibid., 84.

8. Heinrich Bullinger, *Summa Christenlicher Religion* (Zurich: Froschauer, 1556), 137b–57; chap. 5, "Von dem Christenlichen Touff," 145–47b.

9. Ibid., 137b–38,

10. "De sancto baptismo," in *Catechesis*, 63–65b: "in aeterno dei foedere," 64b.

11. The edition from which I worked was the Latin translation done by Josiah Simler (1530–76): *Adversus Anabaptistas* (Zurich: Froschauer, 1560) [*Heinrich Bullinger Werke* Abt. 1, Bd. 1, no. 396], book 6, "De sacrosancto Baptismo," 202b–37.

12. Ibid., 203, 216.

13. For the text of the Second Helvetic Confession (*Confessio helvetica posterior*), see *Die Bekenntnisschriften der reformierten Kirche* ed. E. F. Karl Müller (Leipzig: A. Deichert [Georg Böhme], 1903; reprint, Waltrop: Spenner, 1999), 170–221; 209.4–6. For more detail on the Second Helvetic Confession and its views on baptism, see below, chap. 4, sec. 1.

14. "Von dem Touff," 72–73. For a discussion of this Adamic covenant in Bullinger's thought, see Koch, *Confessio Helvetica Posterior*, 395–401.

15. "Von dem Touff," 73.

16. Note Koch's rhetorical question: "Who from the human side is the actual covenant partner of Adam?" to which Koch answers that it is any human being insofar as they fulfill the covenant (*Confessio Helvetica Posterior*, 397).

17. *Summa*, 158–158b.

18. Baker, *Heinrich Bullinger*, 52.

19. See, for example, *Adversus Anabaptistas*, 209–10.

20. "Iam et electio Dei ab aeterno est qua quidem alios ad vitam elegit, alios ad interitum." In "Henrici Bullengeri epistola ad Bartholomaeum Trahernum Anglum de providentia Dei eiusdemque praedestinatione electione ac reprobatione," C.O. 14.487.

21. For the state of secondary scholarship on Bullinger and predestination as of 1957, see Peter Walser, *Die Prädestination bei Heinrich Bullinger im Zusammenhang mit seiner Gotteslehre* (Zurich: Zwingli-Verlag, 1957), 9–22. For an overview and more recent bibliography, see Venema, "Bullinger's Correspondance," 435–37nn1–12. The issue generally hinges on whether the practical and pastoral views of the younger Bullinger were changed by the controversies on predestination in Geneva (between Calvin and Jerome Bolsec) or in Zurich (between Peter Martyr Vermigli and Theodor Bibliander), to which Bullinger had to respond. In his classic study on predestination in Reformed theology, Alexander Schweizer argued for the influence of Vermigli on Bullinger; see *Die protestantischen Centraldogmen in ihrer Entwicklung innerhalb der reformierten Kirche*, 2 vols. (Zurich: Orell, Fuessli, and Co., 1854), 1:285–92. Joachim Staedtke places Bullinger's change in the midst of the Vermigli-Bibliander controversy that forced Bibliander's retirement from the chair of Old Testament in the Zurich Academy; see "Die Züricher Prädestiationsstreit von 1560," *Zwingliana* 9 (1953): 536–46. Walser, *Prädestination*, 130–35, sees the change in Bullinger coming during the 1550s, although he says that he cannot find in Bullinger's thought a doctrine of reprobation that parallels the doctrine of election (135). Baker's argument that Bullinger steadfastly held to a single gracious election remains convincing (*Heinrich Bullinger*, 27–54). Note Baker's comment "During the last years of his life, Bullinger seemed increasingly like a man who had outlived his age, a nondogmatic figure in a period that was yearly growing more dogmatic" (27–28). Also see Venema, "Bullinger's Correspondence," who has some disagreement with Baker on issues of covenant and Bullinger's strict divergence from Calvin (449–50). Yet Venema finds substantial agreement with Baker on Bullinger's ideas of predestination and human freedom (438–49): Although God freely elects some for salvation, and so the primacy of divine grace is asserted, in human history God is *philanthropos*—kindly

toward humankind—wanting all to be saved. In this "limited sense," Bullinger is a "universalist." In response to such divine grace, human beings make free and responsible decisions about God and neighbor.

22. Compare the discussion in Richard A. Muller, *Christ and the Decree: Christology and Predestination in Reformed Theology from Calvin to Perkins* (Durham, N.C.: Labyrinth Press, 1986), 39–47.

23. Biographies of Calvin began as early as Theodore Beza's preface to Calvin's *Commentary on the Book of Joshua* (1564), in C.O. 21.21–50. Emil Doumergue's *Jean Calvin. Les Hommes et les choses de son temps*, 7 vols. (Lausanne: Georges Bridel, 1899–1924), is a wealth of information, though sometimes a bit hagiographic. In English, Williston Walker's *John Calvin: The Organizer of Reformed Protestantism, 1509–1564* (New York: G. P. Putnam's Sons, 1906) remains solid. Walker's work needs to be read along with T. H. L. Parker, *John Calvin: A Biography* (Philadelphia: Westminster Press, 1975); and Ronald S. Wallace, *Geneva and the Reformation: A Study of Calvin as Social Reformer, Churchman, Pastor, and Theologian* (Grand Rapids: Baker Book House, 1988). A must-read is William Bouwsma's *John Calvin: A Sixteenth Century Portrait* (New York: Oxford University Press, 1988), which places Calvin the person amid the culture that shaped him. Bouwsma's important book caused quite a stir among Calvin scholars. For entrance to the debate, see John Hesselink, "Reactions to Bouwsma's 'Portrait' of John Calvin," in *Calvinus Sacrae Scripturae Professor*, ed. Wilhelm Neuser (Grand Rapids: Wm. B. Eerdmans Publishing Co., 1994), 209–13. For overall bibliographic essays see David C. Steinmetz, "The Theology of Calvin and Calvinism," in Ozment, ed., *Reformation Europe*, 211–32; and Armstrong, "Calvin and Calvinism," 75–103. Also see the fall issue of the *Calvin Theological Journal* from 1971 onward for exhaustive bibliographies of Calvin studies each year, organized according to topics. This work extends the older Calvin bibliography found in Wilhelm Niesel, *Calvin-Bibliographie, 1901–1959* (Munich: Chr. Kaiser Verlag, 1961).

24. Parker describes the leadership at Montaigu thus: "The two rulers of Montaigu in Jean Cauvin's day were, effectively, Bédier and, nominally, Tempête, the one the most reactionary, the other the most irascible of men. Bédier was, and continued for some years to be, the leader of the conservative Paris theologians, the watchdog who barked his warning when he scented any stranger, who bit first and offered no apology afterwards. . . . Tempête, principal all the time that Cauvin was at the college, carried a name apt enough for the dullest student to perpetrate a pun, even if he did not put it so well as Rabelais: '*Horrida tempestas montem turbavit acutum.* Tempête was a great whipper of schoolboys at the Collège of Montaigu'" (*John Calvin*, 7).

25. See Alexandre Ganoczy, *The Young Calvin*, trans. David Foxgrover and Wade Provo (Philadelphia: Westminster Press, 1987), 173, 57–63, 168–78 (French ed.: *Le Jeune Calvin, Genèse et évolution de sa vocation réformatrice* [Wiesbaden: Franz Steiner Verlag, 1966]); Heiko Oberman, "*Initia Calvini*: The Matrix of Calvin's Reformation," in Neuser, ed., *Calvinus*, 117–27; Alistair E. McGrath, "John Calvin and Late Medieval Thought," *Archiv für Reformationsgeschichte* 77 (1986): 58–78 (note the cautious, general summary, 77–78); Thomas F. Torrance, *The Hermeneutics of John Calvin* (Edinburgh: Scottish Academic Press, 1988), 3–57 ("The Parisian Background"), and 73–95 ("Late Mediaeval Thought and Piety"). Also see Richard C. Gamble, "Current Trends in Calvin Research, 1982–1990," in Neuser, ed., *Calvinus*, 96–108.

26. The relationship between humanism and Calvin's theology goes beyond

this introduction. The work by William Bouwsma must be accounted for, how-ever much his Calvin "portrait" sometimes seems more iconographic than histor-ical. See not only Bouwsma's previously cited book on Calvin but also his essay "Calvin and the Renaissance Crisis of Knowing," *Calvin Theological Journal* 17 (1982): 190–211. Mary Potter Engel makes the correct point, it seems to me, when she argues that, for Calvin, the human arts were always gifts from God that, while availing nothing by way of redemption—indeed, getting in the way of God's redeeming offer because of human self-glory—rightly pointed to God as the ulti-mate source of wisdom within any human culture (*John Calvin's Perspectival Anthropology* [Atlanta: Scholars Press, 1988], 199–205). This is the corollary, I take it, to Calvin's metaphor of Scripture as spectacles: The goodness of God has spilled over into all the human arts. We just need to *see* the human arts for what they really are—gifts from God that merit our gratitude rather than our self-importance. Also see Gamble, "Current Trends," 97–101.

27. When did Calvin "convert" to the new evangelical faith? In a single pas-sage in his *Commentary on the Psalms*, written in 1557, Calvin says that he had a sudden conversion (*conversio subita*). Scholars have varied dates for Calvin's "con-version," ranging from 1527 through 1534. Perhaps we should take our cue from Oberman, who notes that the word *subita* marked the sudden way in which God worked, as compared to human efforts. *Subita* has not earthly, spatial, unit mea-surement but refers to divine intervention and agency; see Heiko A. Oberman, *The Dawn of the Reformation* (Edinburgh: T. & T. Clark, 1986), 262–64; idem, "*Initia Calvini*," 114–15n3. Calvin's conversion surely took place over the course of time. He may have read some of Luther's early works that had been translated into French in the 1520s. Calvin also had ties with evangelical and reforming French humanists. Regardless of the actual chronology, the crucial point for Calvin was that God was the one who had effected the *metanoia*. God had reigned in his heart and made him teachable—a disciple—able to hear the Word and serve God in return. This conversion was surely complete by the spring of 1534, when Calvin renounced the church benefice his father had arranged for him at the age of twelve, and which he had been receiving ever since.

28. For a thorough discussion, including Continental and Anglo-American scholarship, see B. A. Gerrish, "The Pathfinder: Calvin's Image of Martin Luther," in *The Old Protestantism and the New: Essays on the Reformation Heritage* (Chicago: University of Chicago Press, 1982), 27–48. Also see Torrance, *Hermeneutics*, who notes Calvin's indebtedness to Luther (155–59) while also noting the differences between Luther and Calvin on the relationship between the two Testaments (159). This Calvin section first appeared as an essay in *Church History*: see Riggs "Emerg-ing Ecclesiology" 29–43.

29. See Willem Balke, *Calvin and the Anabaptists*, trans. William Heynen (Grand Rapids.: Wm. B. Eerdmans Publishing Co., 1981), 40; Jacques Courvoisier, "Bucer et Calvin," in *Calvin à Strasbourg, 1538–1541*, Jean-Daniel Benoit, Jacques Cour-voisier, Pierre Scherding, D. A. Kuntz (Strasbourg: Editions Fides, 1938), 40; Ganoczy, *Young Calvin*, 137–81; Gerrish, "Pathfinder," 31; August Lang, "Luther und Calvin," in *Reformation und Gegenwart: Gesammelte Aufsätze* (Detmold: Meyer-sche Hofbuchhandlung, 1918), 76–77; idem, "Die Quellen der *Institutio* von 1536," *Evangelische Theologie* 3 (1936): 104–5; Peter Meinhold, "Calvin und Luther," *Lutherische Monatshefte* 3 (1964): 265; Doede Nauta, "Calvin and Luther," *Free Uni-versity Quarterly* 2 (1952–53): 11; François Wendel, *Calvin: Sources et évolution de sa pensée religieuse* (Paris: Presses Universitaires de France, 1950), 96.

30. See above, chap. 1.

31. W.A. 26.159.25–161.34; L.W. 40.246–48.

32. John Calvin, *Ioannis Calvini opera selecta*, ed. Peter Barth, Wilhelm Niesel, and Dora Scheuner, 5 vols. (Munich: Chr. Kaiser Verlag, 1926–52), 1.118, emphasis mine (hereafter cited as O.S. with volume and page number). In 1975, Ford Lewis Battles produced a translation of the 1536 *Institutes* along with annotations and four appendixes, which was revised and republished in 1986 to recognize the 450th anniversary of the 1536 *Institutes*. See John Calvin, *Institutes of the Christian Religion, 1536 Edition*, trans. and annotated by Ford Lewis Battles, rev. ed. (Grand Rapids: Wm. B. Eerdmans Publishing Co., 1986).

33. O.S. 1.122. Compare Zwingli's *Commentary on the True and False Religion*, Z.W. 3.758–59, 763. Calvin was perhaps influenced by Bucer: see Bornert, *Réforme protestante*, who argues that, by 1536, Bucer thought of baptism (1) as entrance into the church and instruction by the church (342–43); (2) as a time of receiving God's sign and then consecrating our faith (345–47); and (3) as needing some form of confirmation so that those baptized as children could publicly attest to their faith (361–65). The question of whether Bucer influenced Calvin's baptismal thinking is further complicated because Bucer originally developed his thinking along Zwinglian lines. On this point, see Usteri, "Stellung," 456–63; Bornert, *Réforme protestante*, 341, 356–357.

34. O.S. 1.122.

35. O.S. 1.122.

36. O.S. 1.127.

37. O.S. 1.127, 135.

38. Calvin devoted only 16 lines to this discussion (O.S. 1.132), as compared to 206 lines in his discussion of the first aspect of baptism (O.S. 1.127–32).

39. Calvin also described baptism as mortification and new life in Christ (O.S. 1.128–29), which was a regenerative washing (O.S. 1.129–30), as well as an engrafting into Christ himself, in whom all three benefits (forgiveness, regeneration, engrafting) were found (O.S. 1.132). Calvin thus described God's inviolable sacramental activity as God's promise of forgiveness (O.S. 1.134), God's promise of mortification and regeneration (O.S. 1.131), and God's offer of Christ (O.S. 1.123–24, 119–20).

40. O.S. 1.134.

41. Battles, *Institutes, 1536 Edition*, xvii–lix; Ganoczy, *Young Calvin*, 225–38.

42. O.S. 1.123. See, for example, the extended discussion in the chapter on the sacraments (O.S. 1.122–24); and note Battles's comments in *Institutes, 1536 Edition*, xxii–xxv, li–liv.

43. Battles, *Institutes, 1536 Edition*, xlv–lix. On Calvin's ecclesiology, see Balke, *Calvin*, 39–71, 97–122, 155–68, 209–11; Peter Barth, "Calvins Verständnis der Kirche," *Zwischen den Zeiten* 8 (1930): 216–33; Doumergue, *Jean Calvin*, 5:3–67; Alexandre Ganoczy, *Calvin théologien de l'église et du ministère* (Paris: Éditions du Cerf, 1964), 183–222; Harro Höpfl, *The Christian Polity of John Calvin* (Cambridge: Cambridge University Press, 1985); J. T. McNeill, "The Church in Sixteenth-Century Reformed Theology," *Journal of Religion* 22 (1942): 251–69; William Mueller, *Church and State in Luther and Calvin: A Comparative Study* (Nashville: Broadman Press, 1954), 73–163; Ray C. Petry, "Calvin's Conception of the 'Communio Sanctorum,'" *Church History* 5 (1936): 227–38; Heinrich Quistorp, "Sichtbare und unsichtbare Kirche bei Calvin," *Evangelische Theologie* 9 (1949): 83–101; H. Strohl, "La Notion d'église chez les Réformateurs," *Revue*

d'histoire et de philosophie religieuses 16 (1936): 265–319, esp. 296–311; J. S. Whale, *The Protestant Tradition: An Essay in Interpretation* (Cambridge: Cambridge University Press, 1955), 145–62.

44. O.S. 1.31. See Balke, *Calvin*, 48–49; Ganoczy, *Calvin théologien*, 184–85; Höpfl, *Christian Polity*, 19–55; Strohl, "Notion d'église," 296–303; Whale, *Protestant Tradition*,146–51. Note the parallels that Ganoczy draws between Bucer and Calvin (*Young Calvin*, 168–71).

45. Notice the unnamed reference to Cyprian in Calvin's discussion of the church outside whose walls "there is no salvation" (O.S. 1.92). Compare Cyprian, *Epistle* 72[73].21 in *The Ante-Nicene Fathers*, ed. Alexander Roberts and James Donaldson (Edinburgh, 1885– ; reprint, Grand Rapids: T. and T. Clark, 1990), 5.384.

46. O.S. 1.91

47. Compare with the strong wording in Luther's 1522 *Personal Prayer Book*: "I believe that no one can be saved who is not in this community, peacefully holding with it the same faith, word, sacraments, and love" (W.A. 10^2.394; L.W. 43.28).

48. See the discussion in O.S. 1.88–91; and note Battles's comments in *Institutes, 1536 Edition*, 265–66.

49. Balke, *Calvin*, 73–96; Ganoczy, *Young Calvin*, 106–31; Parker, *John Calvin*, 51–66; Walker, *John Calvin*, 182–215.

50. Balke, *Calvin*, 123–53; Parker, *John Calvin*, 67–81; Walker, *John Calvin*, 216–44.

51. On Strasbourg and Bucer's work, see Greschat, *Martin Bucer*, 127–38, 153–61; Gottfried Hammann, *Entre la secte et la cité: Le Project d'église du réformateur Martin Bucer* (Geneva: Labor et Fides, 1984), esp. 43–68, 175–249, 258–62; Eells, *Martin Bucer*, 127–65; François Wendel, *L'Eglise de Strasbourg, sa constitution et son organization, 1532–1535* (Paris: Presses Universitaires de France, 1942). On the Reformation's radicals in Strasbourg, see Klaus Depperman, *Melchior Hoffman. Soziale Unruhen und apokalyptische Visionen im Zeitalter der Reformation* (Göttingen: Vandenhoeck & Ruprecht, 1979), 149–93; and George H. Williams, *The Radical Reformation*, 3d ed. Sixteenth Century Essays & Studies 15 (Kirksville, Mo.: Sixteenth Century Journal Publishers, 1992), 363–431. For Bucer's efforts at the spiritual care of Strasbourg's citizens and youth, see Amy Nelson Burnett, "Church Discipline and Moral Reformation in the Thought of Martin Bucer," *Sixteenth Century Journal* 22, 3 (1991): 438–56; idem, "Martin Bucer and the Anabaptist Context of Evangelical Confirmation," *Mennonite Quarterly Review* 68 (1994): 95–122; idem, *Yoke of Christ.*

52. Robert Friedmann, *The Theology of Anabaptism* (Scottdale, Pa.: Herald Press, 1973), 115–57; William Klassen, *Anabaptism in Outline* (Kitchener, Ont., and Scottdale, Pa.: Herald Press, 1981), 101–17; Franklin H. Littell, *The Anabaptist View of the Church* (Boston: Starr King Press, 1958), 79–108.

53. Calvin, *Institutes of the Christian Religion*, 1559 ed., 4.14.19 (hereafter cited as *Inst.*, followed by book, chapter, and section); O.S. 5.277.26–7; *Inst.* 4.14.19.

54. During his stay in Strasbourg, Calvin continued his patristic readings, especially Chrysostom and Augustine. See Hughes Oliphant Old, *The Patristic Roots of Reformed Worship*, Züricher Beiträge zur Reformationsgeschichte, 5 (Zurich: Theologischer Verlag, 1975), 144–55.

55. O.S. 5.277.31–278.2; *Inst.* 4.14.19.

56. O.S. 1.125.

57. O.S. 5.278.2–6; *Inst.* 4.14.19.

58. The editors of the O.S. give a plausible explanation for the infant baptism supplement originally appearing as a separate French tract to defend the practice of infant baptism (O.S. 5.303.41, 304.16–30). This "traicte" then appeared, in altered form, in both the 1539 (Latin) *Institutes* and the 1541 (French) *Institutes*.

59. See O.S. 2.30.21–38.36 for a critical text of the *Order for Baptism*. O.S. 2.1–10 gives an introduction and literary history for the critical text of *La Forme des prieres et chantz ecclesiastiques*, in which Calvin's baptismal order can be found.

60. O.S. 2.37.5–16.

61. Balke, *Calvin*, 169–208.

62. O.S. 5.2.5–5.3.10; *Inst.* 4.1.2.

63. So, for example, O.S. 5.7.5–24; *Inst.* 4.1.4.

64. Balke, *Calvin*, 112–15; Doumergue, *Jean Calvin*, 5:29–37; Ganoczy, *Calvin théologien*, 193–200; Höpfl, *Christian Polity*, 56–90; Quistorp, "Sichtbare," 86–92; Whale, *Protestant Tradition*, 152–53.

65. Höpfl, *Christian Polity*, 84–85, pointedly says, "The first *Institutes* it will be recalled, had been completed when Calvin was quite innocent of ecclesiastical experience or responsibility. A relative abstractness in matters of detail and practice was therefore only to be expected. What borders on the inexplicable is Calvin's obscurity in such matters in 1539." Surely "inexplicable" is too harsh a word for this point in Calvin's career.

66. O.S. 5.89.14–20; *Inst.* 4.15.6.

67. O.S. 1.118.

68. O.S. 5.259.2–10; *Inst.* 4.14.1; italics added.

69. O.S. 1.127.

70. O.S. 5.285.12–16; *Inst.* 4.15.1.

71. O.S. 5.273.26–274.1, italics added; *Inst.* 4.14.16. Also see Calvin's 1540 commentary on Romans 4:10–12, in which he argued that sacraments in themselves did nothing, nor were they useful to the reprobate; yet they still had power, since unbelief does not extinguish God's truth (*Ioannis Calvini opera quae supersunt omnia*, ed. Wilhelm Baum, Edward Cunitz, and Edward Reuss, 59 vols., vols. 29–87 of *Corpus Reformatorum* [Brunswick: C. A. Schwetschke and Son (M. Bruhn), 1863–1900], 49.74; hereafter cited as C.O., with volume and page number). Compare the 1548 commentary on Galatians 5:3, where Calvin rhetorically conceded that "whatever the abuses of the ungodly might be, they nevertheless do not strip the sacred decrees of God" ("qualiscunque sit impiorum abusus, id tamen sacrosanctis Dei institutis nihil detrahere," C.O. 50.245).

72. "Multi dum illi sua pravitate viam praecludunt, efficiunt ut sibi sit inanis. Ita non nisi ad fideles solos pervenit fructus. Verum, inde nihil sacramenti *naturae* decedit" (O.S. 2.134.21–24; no. 329; emphasis mine).

73. Balke, *Calvin*, 155–60; Doumergue, *Jean Calvin*, 5:37–40; Ganoczy, *Calvin théologien*, 202–11; Höpfl, *Christian Polity*, 89–127; Whale, *Protestant Tradition*, 155–60.

74. O.S. 5.42.20–57.29, almost all of which is composed of the 1543 version; *Inst.* 4.3.1–16.

75. O.S. 5.12.24–27; *Inst.* 4.1.7.

76. On this passage, see Werner Krusche, *Das Wirken des Heiligen Geistes nach Calvin* (Göttingen: Vandenhoeck & Ruprecht, 1957), 311–16; also see Josef Bohatec, *Calvins Lehre von Staat und Kirche mit besonderer Berücksichtigung des Organismusgedankens* (Breslau: M. and H. Marcus, 1937; reprint, Aalen: Scientia, 1961), 285–86; Ganoczy, *Calvin théologien*, 202–6; Wilhelm Niesel, *Die Theologie*

Calvins (Munich: Chr. Kaiser Verlag, 1938 [English translation as *The Theology of Calvin*, trans. Harold Knight (Philadelphia: Westminster Press, 1956)]), 191–92; Quistorp, "Sichtbare," 96–99. Compare Calvin's commentary on Romans 9:6–7 (C.O. 49.175–76) and Romans 9:8–11, 15–16 (C.O. 49.175–79, 181–83).

77. Calvin wrote the dedication to Romans on October 18, 1539, about one year after his arrival in Strasbourg. Since Calvin had lectured on Romans in Geneva during 1536–37, it is probable that he had considered these ideas for several years already, perhaps working on them during the three-month stay in Basel (June–September 1538) that separated his ministries in Geneva and Strasbourg.

78. Romans 9.6 (C.O. 49.175); Romans 9:7 (C.O. 49.176). Also see Romans 9.8–11, 15–16, where Calvin discusses God's election and the three groups that can be distinguished within the covenant: (1) those who are in the covenant by birth and remain faithful to it; (2) those in the covenant by birth who truly are unfaithful; and (3) those outside the covenant who entered by faith (C.O. 49.175–79, 181–83).

79. In 1546, Calvin commented on the visible church with regard to 1 Corinthians 1:9, noting that "this is the purpose of the gospel, that Christ should become ours, and that we should be engrafted into his body" (C.O. 49.313).

80. *Inst.* 3.22.7; 3.24.5–10.

81. John Calvin, *Institution de la religion chrestienne*, ed. Jean-Daniel Benoit (Paris: J. Vrin, 1961), 2:318.

82. "This is the catholic church—the mystical body of Christ" ("Haec est ecclesia catholica, corpus Christi mysticum," O.S. 1.92).

83. *Inst.* 3.22.7; 3.24.5–10.

84. Passages such as *Inst.* 3.22.7; 3.24.5–10 remain relatively unchanged even through the 1559 *Institutes*. There Calvin moves the discussion of predestination out of the section on God's providence and into the section on the work of the Holy Spirit, a section that immediately precedes the discussion of the church.

CHAPTER 3

1. The substance of this chapter was presented to the Calvin and Calvinism section of the Sixteenth Century Conference held in St. Louis, Missouri, October 31, 1999.

2. For a short summary in English, see Parker, *John Calvin*, 107–16. Also see Walker, *John Calvin*, 281–324.

3. "Calvin to Melanchthon" (November 28 [4. Calend. Decemb.], 1552); C.O. 14.416, no. 1676.

4. C.O. 21.547.

5. Walker, *John Calvin*, 380–87; Parker, *John Calvin*, 145–49.

6. E. William Monter, *Calvin's Geneva* (New York: John Wiley & Sons, 1967), 134–35. Also see the fascinating description of the calling, training, and sending of these pastors by the church in Geneva, in Robert M. Kingdom, *Geneva and the Coming of the Religious Wars in France, 1555–1563* (Geneva: Librarie E. Droz, 1956), 1–53.

7. C.O. 14.331, 423, 469, 491, 544.

8. Bernard Gagnebin, "L'Incroyable Histoire des sermons de Calvin," *Bulletin de la société d'histoire et d'archéologie de Genève* 10, 4 (1955): 330.

9. C.O. 48.54–55.

10. O.S. 5.258.33–34; *Inst.* 4.14.1. Also see Calvin's commentaries on Acts 2:38 (C.O. 48.53) and Titus 3:5 (C.O. 52.430).

11. "Maneat interea prius illud: quia alioqui frigerent mysteria (ut visum est) nisi fidei nostrae adminicula essent, doctrinaeque appendices in eundem usum et finem destinatae" (O.S. 5.271.6–8; *Inst.* 4.14.13).

12. O.S. 5.295.9–10; *Inst.* 4.15.14.

13. O.S. 5.327.20–21; *Inst.* 4.16.22.

14. O.S. 1.118, italics added.

15. O.S. 5.260.28–29; *Inst.* 4.14.3. Likewise, to his 1536 description that sacraments attested God's goodwill and love toward humankind ("et bonam suam erga nos voluntatem testificatur"), Calvin appended the phrase "more expressly than by word" ("suamque erga nos benevolentiam et amorem expressius quam verbo testatur"); see O.S. 5.263.26–27; *Inst.* 4.14.6. Compare the 1559 causative phrase concerning sacraments, that "by attesting that good will" ("ipsam nobis obsignando") our faith was nourished, with the weak 1536 temporal phrase that it replaced, "while attesting that good will" our faith was nourished ("dum ipsam nobis obsignant"); see O.S. 5.264.28–32; *Inst.* 4.14.7. Also see *Inst.* 4.15.20, where Calvin had said, from 1536 through 1554, that the outward analogy was a good rule for the sacraments: "that we should see and ponder spiritual things in the physical" ("ut in rebus corporis spirituales conspiciamus ac cogitemus"). In 1559, Calvin made this more concrete by saying "that we should see spiritual things in the physical, as though set before our very eyes" ("ut in rebus corporis spirituales conspiciamus, perinde acsi coram oculis nostris subiectae forent"); see O.S. 5.295.21–22.

16. "Atque (ut sunt arrhae et tesserae) rata apud nos faciant," O.S. 5.275.2–3; *Inst.* 4.14.17; italics added. Also see the preceding phrase, which once read that sacraments were "messengers of glad tidings" ("rerum laetarum nuntii") but in 1559 read that sacraments were "messengers of glad tidings, or guarantees of the ratification of covenants" ("rerum laetarum nuntii, vel arrhae in pactis sanciendis"); O.S. 5.274.36–275.1; *Inst.* 4.14.17.

17. "Praestat igitur vere Deus quicquid signis promittit ac figurat: nec effectu suo carent signa, ut verax et fidelis probetur eorum author," O.S. 5.275.13–15; *Inst.* 4.14.17. Also see Calvin's 1559 addendum to the end of his section on illumination through the Holy Spirit: "Meanwhile, the Father of Lights is not able to be stopped from illuminating our minds' eyes through the sacraments with a type of intermediate brightness, just as he illuminates our physical eyes by the sun's rays" (O.S. 5.268.1–3; *Inst.* 4.14.10). See Calvin's commentaries on Genesis 3.22 (C.O. 23.79), in which he said that God "represents nothing to us with false signs, but, as they say, always speaks to us with effect." See especially Exodus 13:21 (C.O. 24.145), where Calvin argued that when Moses said God appeared in the cloud he spoke sacramentally ("notanda nobis sacramentalis loquendi ratio"): "God transfers his name to visible representations, neither to attach them to his essence (*affigat suam essentiam*), nor to restrict his boundlessness (*vel immensitatem circumscribat*), but only to teach that he does not falsely present the signs of his presence to human eyes, when, in fact, the exhibition of the thing signified is at the same time truly joined to them (*quin simul vere coniuncta sit rei signatae exhibitio*)." Compare Gerrish, who analyzed Reformed eucharistic theology and distinguished between Zwingli's "symbolic memorialism," Calvin's ("Thomistic") "symbolic instrumentalism," and Bullinger's ("Franciscan") "symbolic parallelism" ("Sign and Reality," 118–30).

18. "Neque tantum nudo spectaculo pascit oculos: sed in rem praesentem nos adducit, et quod figurat, efficaciter simul implet," O.S. 5.295.26–28; *Inst.* 4.15.14. Also see Calvin's commentary on Acts 2:38 (C.O. 48.53).

19. "Quanquam mihi animus non est baptismi vim estenuare, quin signo accedat res et veritas, quatenus per externa media Deus operatur," O.S. 5.296.7–9; *Inst.* 4.15.15.

20. O.S. 5.312.14–15; *Inst.* 4.16.9.

21. Note Calvin's comment that after the Fall, "this entire knowledge of God the creator, which we have discussed, would be useless unless faith by all means followed, showing to us God the Father in Christ (*Deum in Christo Patrem*)" (C.O. 3.320.10–13: *Inst.* 2.6.1). See Edward A. Dowey Jr., *The Knowledge of God in Calvin's Theology*, 2d ed. (New York: Columbia University Press, 1952), 205–20, 237–38; John Calvin, *The Piety of John Calvin: An Anthology Illustrative of the Spirituality of the Reformer*, trans and ed. Ford Lewis Battles, with music ed. Stanley Tagg (Grand Rapids: Baker Book House, 1978), 13–16.

22. "Hic quoque notandum est, quod externa actione figurat ac testatur minister, Deum intus peragere: ne ad hominum mortalem trahatur quod Deus sibi uni vendicat," O.S. 5.275.26–29; *Inst.* 4.14.17.

23. "Quo minus tolerabilis error est Petri Lombardi, qui diserte ea iustitiae et salutis causas facit quorum partes sunt," O.S. 5.273.17–19; *Inst.* 4.14.16. Also see *Inst.* 4.14.16, where Calvin, referring to the signs themselves as conferring the benefits of Christ, ended this section in 1559 by adding that "they are conferred indeed with the help of external signs if they encourage us to Christ; where they are twisted in another direction, their entire usefulness is unworthily destroyed" ("et quidem aiuvantibus externis signis, quae, si nos ad Christum invitant, ubi alio torquentur, indigne evertitur tota eorum utilitas," O.S. 5.274.15–17).

24. "Quae tam ab elemento illo visibili quod oculis nostris obiicitur, abstrahit, quam ab aliis omnibus mediis, ut uni Christo mentes nostras devinciat," O.S. 5.286.30–33; *Inst.* 4.15.2. For the christological telos of baptism, also see Calvin's commentaries on Matthew 3:11–12; Mark 1:7–8; Luke 3:15–18 (summary; C.O. 45.121–23); Luke 22:19 (C.O. 45.710); John 1:26 (C.O. 47.23–24); John 20:22 (C.O. 47.439); Acts 2:38 (C.O. 48:51–54); Acts 11:26 (C.O. 48.256–57); Romans 6:3–6 (C.O. 49.105–8); 1 Corinthians 1.13 (C.O. 49.318); 2 Corinthians 1:20 (C.O. 50.22–24, esp. 50.23); Ephesians 2:11–13 (C.O. 51.167–70, esp. 51.169); Galatians 3:26–27 (C.O. 50.221–22). Compare Exodus 25:9 (C.O. 24.405).

25. O.S. 5.274.18–21; *Inst.* 4.14.17.

26. O.S. 5.274.21–24; *Inst.* 4.14.17.

27. "Verum ut exigua est et imbecilla nostra fides, nisi undique fulciatur, ac modis omnibus sustentetur, statim concutitur, fluctuatur, vacillat, *adeoque labascit*," O.S. 5.260.20–23; *Inst.* 4.14.3; italics added.

28. O.S. 5.268.14; *Inst.* 4.14.11.

29. O.S. 5.278.1–2; *Inst.* 4.14.19; italics added.

30. O.S. 5.278.1–2; *Inst.* 4.14.19.

31. Thomas Aquinas, *Summa Theologica*, trans. Fathers of the English Dominican Province (London: R. & T. Washbourne; New York: Benziger Brothers, 1914), 2.1, q. 101, art. 2 (150–53).

32. O.S. 5.281.19–27; *Inst.* 4.15.23.

33. "Etsi vero tunc obscurum et paucis cognitum fuit mysterium quia tamen non alia est salutis adipiscendae ratio quam in illis duabus gratiis, noluit Deus

utriusque tessera vetustos patres, quos haeredes adoptaverat, privare," O.S. 5.292.1–4; *Inst.* 4.15.9. Also see the commentaries on Exodus 14:21 (C.O. 24.153–54); Exodus 25:9 (C.O. 24.404–5); Exodus 25:40 (C.O. 24.411); Exodus 26:30 (C.O. 24:416–17); Jeremiah 4:4 (C.O. 37.577).

34. O.S. 5.307.34–35; *Inst.* 4.16.3.

35. "Ut easdem apud nos partes obeat," O.S. 5.308.23–24; *Inst.* 4.16.4.

36. O.S. 5.316.17; *Inst.* 4.16.13.

37. O.S. 5.308.5; *Inst.* 4.16.4.

38. See Calvin's commentary on Exodus 25:9 (C.O. 24.405), in which he says that "we call to mind that all the old representations were sure testimonies of God's grace and eternal salvation; and so Christ was represented by them because all the promises of God are in him—Yes and Amen (2 Cor. 1.20)."

39. O.S. 1.83, 86–87.

40. O.S. 1.390–91; C.O. 5.332–33.

41. O.S. 1.388–93; C.O. 5.332–35.

42. "The seed of the Word of God takes root and bears fruit only in those whom the Lord has predestined, by his eternal election, to be his children and heirs of the royal kingdom. As for all the others who were condemned by the same plan of God, prior to the foundation of the world, the clear and evident preaching of truth can be nothing other than the smell of death upon death" ("la claire et evidente predication de verite ne peult estre aultre chose sinon odeur de mort en mort," O.S. 1.390).

43. The *apparatus criticus* for *Inst.* 3.21–24 (O.S. 4.368.31–432.8) shows that almost the entire content of the chapters on election was written for the 1539 *Institutes*, with major additions and revisions for the 1559 edition. In the 1539 *Institutes*, chapter 8 on predestination and providence ("De praedestination and providentia Dei") is preceded by a chapter on the relationship between the two testaments ("De similitudine ac differentia veteris ac novi testament") and is followed by a chapter on prayer ("De oratione").

44. *A Defense of the Sound and Orthodox Doctrine of the Bondage and Deliverance of the Human Will against the False Accusations of Albert Pighius*, C.O. 6.232–404.

45. *Upon the Eternal Predestination of God*, C.O. 8.249–366.

46. For brief descriptions of and primary and secondary references to the Bolsec affair, see Doumergue, *Jean Calvin*, 6:131–61; Parker, *John Calvin*, 111–14; Walker, *John Calvin*, 315–20; and J. Wayne Baker, "Jérome Bolsec," in *The Oxford Encyclopedia of the Reformation* (Oxford: Oxford University Press, 1996), 1:188–89. See C.O. 8.xvii–xxi, 141–248, especially Calvin's reply to Bolsec in the "Congregation sur l'election eternelle," C.O. 8.85–138; Calvin's argument in C.O. 8.93–118.

47. See Paul Jacobs, *Prädestination und Verantwortlichkeit bei Calvin* (Neukirchen: Kr. Moers, Buchhandlung des Erxiehungsvereins, 1937), 62–71; cf. 92, 147.

48. See Wendel, *Calvin*, 199–216; also see Jacobs, *Prädestination*, 63–65, 67–71, 119ff., who argues that, in 1559, Calvin moved the discussion of predestination into the christological section of the *Institutes* in order to secure justification as God's gracious gift and Christian ethics as grounded in that gift. In this same period, Calvin developed a limited and local teaching on the reprobate. This discussion safeguarded God's free justification by illustrating the boundary inside which God's gracious activity can be seen (50–57, 141–57, 158–59). Also see Doumergue, *Jean Calvin*, 4:355–56; John Calvin, *Concerning the Eternal Predestination of God*, trans. and ed. J. K. S. Reid (London: James Clarke, 1961), 5–6.

49. "Caeterum, ex hoc sacramento, quemadmodum ex aliis omnibus, nihil asse-quimur nisi quantum fide accipimus. Si fides desit, erit in testimonium ingratitu-dinis nostrae, quo rei coram Deo peragamur, quia promissioni illic datae increduli fuerimus," O.S. 5.296.9–13; *Inst.* 4.15.15. Note that this is the 1559 form, which shows several minor variations from its original 1536 form—see the *apparatus criti-cus* in the O.S.

50. "Non sic intelligendum quod dixi, quasi ab eius qui recipit conditione inge-nio vis et veritatem Sacramenti pendeat," O.S. 5.273.28–29; *Inst.* 4.14.16.

51. "Non sic intelligendum quod dixi, quasi ab eius qui recipit conditione aut arbitrio vis et veritas Sacramenti pendeat," O.S. 5.273.28–29; *Inst.* 4.14.16; italics added.

52. O.S. 5.260.23–28; *Inst.* 4.14.3. Compare the replacement of God's "good will" (*bona voluntati*) with God's "generosity and benificience" (*liberalitate et benefi-centia*); O.S. 5.269.25; *Inst.* 4.14.12. Also note where Calvin adds the phrase "and reconciles us to himself in his only-begotten Son" to the prior assertion that God cancels our sin, God's work is not merely forensic but that of personal reconcilia-tion (O.S. 5.277.33–278.1; *Inst.* 4.14.19). Compare O.S. 5.264.9–10 (*Inst.* 4.14.7), where Calvin had said that in the sacraments God offered mercy and "the grace of his good will" (*bonae suae voluntatis gratiam*). To reinforce the personal quality to God's grace, which was not a substance but a personal offer that could be refused, in 1559, Calvin said that God offered mercy and "the pledge of his grace" (*gratiae suae pignus*).

53. "Nos sibi confoederat," OS 5.277.29; *Inst.* 4.14.19.

54. "Quia hic mutua inter Deum et nos interponitur stipulatio," O.S. 5.277.31–32; *Inst.* 4.14.19.

55. "Hic mira se profert Dei benignitas, quod familiariter paciscitur cum Abram: quemadmodum solent homines cum sociis et paribus suis. Haec enim solennis est foederum inter reges et alios formula, ut eosdem sibi fore hostes et amicos mutuo promittant. Hoc certe inaestimabile est rari pignus, quod Deus se eosque nostra causa demittit," commentary on Genesis 17:3; (C.O. 23.177). As should be obvious here, the relational language Calvin used to describe the per-sonal relationship between God and humankind spoke of a *strictly asymmetrical relationship*: God as ever initiating, faithful, and gracious; humankind as ever responding, weak in faith, and failing in gratitude.

56. "Nec satis apposite ratiocinantur, dum ex eo contendunt non esse testimo-nia gratiae Dei, quia et *ab impiis saepe accipiuntur*, qui tamen Deum nihilo sibi magis propitium inde sentiunt, sed graviorem potius damnationem contrahunt," O.S. 5.263.28–31; *Inst.* 4.14.7; italics added.

57. "Nec satis apposite ratiocinantur, dum ex eo contendunt non esse testimo-nia gratiae Dei, *quia impiis quoque porriguntur*, qui . . . ," O.S. 5.263.28–30; *Inst.* 4.14.7; italics added.

58. "Sed obiiciunt, non posse hominum ingratitudine quicquam detrahi vel intercidere de fide promissionum Dei. Fateor sane, et vim mysterii integram manere dico, quantumvis impii eam, quoad in se est, exinanire studeant. Aliud tamen est offerri, aliud recipi," O.S. 5.393.16–20; *Inst.* 4.17.33.

59. As early as 1543, Calvin not only admitted but insisted on this point when he cited Augustine that "[i]n the elect alone the sacraments effect what they rep-resent" (O.S. 5.272.21–22; *Inst.* 4.14.15). See the references and larger discussion in *Inst.* 4.14.15–16. To be fair to Calvin, it is clear that he did not want the issue of election to be a pastoral problem for the church. Despite the numerous addi-

tions to and editing of the election material for the 1559 *Institutes*, Calvin made little reference to election in his baptismal material apart from this one (1543) reference to Augustine. Calvin was surely intentional when he bracketed the sacramental chapters of the *Institutes*, keeping the election material outside. His *Second Defense against Westphal* (1556) showed his desire not to disturb people's piety with technical material that would distract them from God's offer of grace. There Calvin noted that he had "made a passing mention of secret election; but for what end? Was it to lead pious minds from hearing the promise or contemplating the signs? There was nothing I was more careful about than to engross them completely in the word. What? While so many times I inculcate that grace is offered by the sacraments, do I not invite them to seek the seal of their salvation from that source?" (C.O. 9.119; English translation in John Calvin, *Tracts and Treatises on the Reformation of the Church*, ed. T. F. Torrance, trans. Henry Beveridge, 3 vols. (Edinburgh: The Calvin Translation Society, 1844–51; reprint, Edinburgh and London: Oliver and Boyd, 1958), 2:343.

60. O.S. 5.274.18–24; *Inst.* 4.14.17. For other examples of Calvin's insistence that baptism, like all sacraments, requires faith for the fulfillment of that which is promised, see O.S. 5.261.21–28 *(Inst.* 4.14.4); 5.264.9–16 (4.14.7); 5.271.28–272.1 (4.14.14); 5.273.8–13 (4.14.15); 5.273.20–26 (4.14.16); 5.296.9–13 (4.15.15). Also see the commentaries on Genesis 17:14 (C.O. 23.244); Jeremiah 4:4 (C.O. 37.578); Jeremiah 9.25 (C.O. 38.56); Acts 8:13 (C.O. 48.180); and Acts 15:9 (C.O. 48.346–47).

61. For example, O.S. 5.265.31–266.10 *(Inst.* 4.14.8); 5.266.17–267.5 (4.14.9); 5.267.28–268.3 (4.14.10); 5.268.4–16 (4.14.11); 5.274.24–275.26 (4.14.17); and see the commentaries on Deuteronomy 30:6 (C.O. 25.54); John 20:22 (C.O. 47.439–40); Acts 16:14 (C.O. 48.377–78). See also the 1560 French *Institution (Inst.* 4.14.9), where, concerning the gift that opens the eyes and ears of our faith, Calvin says that "the Holy Spirit has that very office, in our hearts, of a special grace outside the course of nature" ("mais le sainct Esprit a ce mesme office en nos âmes d'une grâce speciale outre le course de nature"); see Calvin, *Institution de la religion chretienne*, ed. Benoit, 4:298. The 1559 Latin *Institutio* had had a christological reference there: "Christ by a special grace outside the measure of nature does the same thing in our hearts" ("Christus autem praeter naturae modum speciali gratia idem in animis nostris agit," O.S. 5.267.4–5).

62. Egil Grislis, "Calvin's Doctrine of Baptism," *Church History* 3 (1962): 55.

63. Krusche, *Wirken*, 235, 241, 343; Grislis, "Calvin's Doctrine," 55. Also note the comment by Joachim Beckmann, *Vom Sakrament bei Calvin* (Tübingen: J. C. B. Mohr [Paul Siebeck], 1926), 51; and see the criticism that Hans Grass makes about Calvin's teaching on the Lord's Supper in *Die Abendmahlslehre bei Luther und Calvin* (Gütersloh: C. Bertelsmann Verlag, 1954), 217, 227.

64. Beginning with his 1543 *Institutio*, Calvin steadfastly argued against emergency baptism and baptism by women (O.S. 5.300.21–303.31; *Inst.* 4.15.20–22): the former because God's power was by no means limited by baptism and God saves those whom God chooses, especially those born into God's covenant; the latter because God's ordinances should be obeyed, and God ordained only ministers to baptize (Matt. 28:19). Calvin reinforced both these opinions in the 1559 *Institutes*; see the addition in O.S. 5.301.17–26 *(Inst.* 4.15.20) and the bulk of sections 21–22 (O.S. 5.301.17–303.19; *Inst.* 4.15.21–22). Also see Calvin's (1553) commentary on John 20:17 (C.O. 47.434).

65. John Calvin to John Clauberger (June 24, 1556), in C.O. 16.203–7, esp. 206 (no. 2484). Italics added.

66. Compare here Calvin's 1550 addition. From 1539 through 1545, Calvin had said, "I wish not to affirm rashly that they [i.e., infants] are endowed with the same faith we experience in ourselves—I prefer to leave this undetermined." In 1550, Calvin amended this to read "endowed with the same faith, *or have entirely the same knowledge of faith,* as we experience in ourselves—I prefer to leave this undetermined ("non quod eadem esse fide praeditos, temere affirmare velim, quam in nobis experimur, *aut onnino habere notitiam fidei similem*: quod in suspenso relinquere malo," O.S. 5.323.27–28; *Inst.* 4.16.19. Italics added.

67. So, in 1545, Calvin insisted that children were baptized not so that strangers to the church could become God's children but so that those who already belong to the body of Christ might receive its sign (O.S. 5.303.19–25; *Inst.* 4.15.22). Note Calvin's (1546) commentary on 1 Corinthians 7:14–15, in which he argued that Christian children already belonged to the covenant (C.O. 49.411–13).

68. Compare Calvin's (1541) commentary on Romans 9:6 (C.O. 49.175) and Romans 9:7 (C.O. 49.176). Compare Romans 9:8–11, 15–16, where Calvin discusses God's election and the three groups that can be distinguished within the covenant: (1) those who are in the covenant by birth and remain faithful to it; (2) those in the covenant by birth who truly are reprobate; and (3) those outside the covenant who entered by faith (C.O. 49.175–79, 181–83).

69. "Addendus est secundus gradus restrictor, vel in quo conspicua fuit Dei gratia magis specialis: quando ex eodem genere Abrahae alios repudiavit Deus, alios in Ecclesia fovendo, se inter filios retinere ostendit," O.S. 4.376.23–26; *Inst.* 3.21.6.

70. O.S. 5.272.6–14; *Inst.* 4.14.14.

71. *Inst.* 4.16.17; see Benoit, ed., *Institution,* 4.355. Compare the 1539 Latin text given in O.S. 5.321.10–12.

72. "Le Seigneur donc sanctifiera bien ceux que bon luy semblera, comme il a sanctifié sanct Iean, puisque sa main n'est pas accourcie" (*Inst.* 4.16.17; Benoit, ed., *Institution,* 4.355).

73. Later Reformed orthodoxy, as chap. 4 shows, was very clear here. Also see the comments by Grislis, "Calvin's Doctrine," 56–57.

74. "But they object that human ingratitude is not able to detract from or hinder anything of the trustworthiness of God's promises. Yes, of course, I agree; and I say that the power of the mystery remains unaffected however much the wicked are eager to enervate it, as far as it is *in se.* For all that, it is one thing to be offered, and another to be received" (O.S. 5.393.16–20; *Inst.* 4.17.33).

75. O.S. 5.325.17; 326.22–23; *Inst.* 4.16.21.

76. Commentary on Acts 3:25 (C.O. 76.76). Compare Calvin's discussion on Romans 9:8–11, 15–16 (C.O. 49.175–79, 181–83).

77. Commentary on Romans 9:6 (C.O. 49.175), italics added.

78. See, for instance, *Inst.* 4.15.15.

79. O.S. 5.295.9–11; *Inst.* 4.15.14. Also see Calvin's definitions of a sacrament and of baptism: O.S. 1.122, 125, 127, 135; O.S. 5.259.2–10 (*Inst.* 4.14.1); O.S. 5.278.2–6 (*Inst.* 4.14.19).

80. O.S. 5.296.9–13; *Inst.* 4.15.15.

81. Commentary on Acts 3:25 (C.O. 76.76).

82. Calvin had a section in his 1536 *Institutes* (4.23) that defended the concept of *fides infantium* (infant faith). See O.S. 1.135–36; Battles, ed., *Institution, 1536 Edition,* 101–2. This material did not appear in later editions of the *Institutes.* Also see above, n. 68.

83. O.S. 5.324.20–3; *Inst.* 4.16.20.

84. "Denique nullo negotio solvi potest obiectio haec, baptizari in futuram poenitentiam et fidem: quae etsi nondum in illis formatae sunt, arcana tamen spiritus operatione utriusque semen in illis latet," O.S. 5.324.24–7; *Inst.* 4.16.20. Compare Calvin's version of this addendum made for the 1560 French *Institution:* "Bref ceste obiection est solue en un mot, quand nous disons qu'ils sont baptisez en foy et pénitence pour l'advenir, desquelles combien qu'on ne voye point d'appearance, toutesfois la semence y est plantée par l'operation secrete du sainct Esprit" (Benoit, ed., *Institution*, 4.357).

85. Grislis, "Calvin's Doctrine," 56.

86. Just prior to the seed metaphor, Calvin was discussing how the sacrament of circumcision benefited Jewish children at the moment of administration (*quo circuncidebantur momento*). There he says that "as in all God's acts, so *in this very act* there also shines enough wisdom and righteousness to thwart the detractions of the wicked. For although infants, *at the very moment* (*quo circuncidebantur momento*) they were circumcised . . ." (O.S. 5.324.20; *Inst.*4.16.20; emphasis mine). Perhaps what we see here is an instance of "sacramental parallelism" rather than the more usual "sacramental instrumentalism" that Calvin applied to the signs for the Lord's Supper, and which Grislis finds missing here. See Gerrish, "Sign and Reality."

87. Ronald S. Wallace, *Calvin's Doctrine of the Word and Sacrament* (London: Oliver and Boyd, 1953), 190.

88. O.S. 5.297.25–298.1; *Inst.* 4.15.17

89. Krusche, *Wirken*, 235, 241, 343.

90. Note Calvin's 1559 addendum to the end of the chapter of the *Institutes* that discussed the sacraments (4.14.26): "Thus it follows that by receiving the sacraments they [i.e., the faithful] do nothing there to merit praise, and that even in this activity (which for their part is merely passive) no work can be ascribed to them" (O.S. 5.285.8–10). Calvin here stood in a long line of medieval theologians (Lombard, Scotus, Gregory of Rimini, and Luther) who insisted, in various ways, that God's grace did not depend on or need any human activity. For a summary of this discussion, with secondary references and notes, see Ozment, *Age of Reform*, 22–42.

91. Note Calvin's explanation, added to the 1560 French *Institutes*, that clarified his 1559 addendum to the end of the sacramental section: "I call the act passive because God does everything, and we only receive" ("J'appelle Acte passif, pource que Deau fait le tout, et seulement nous recevons," *Inst.* 4.14.26; Benoit, ed., *Institution*, 4.402). No "work" may be ascribed to the person, meaning (as the context shows) no *meritorious* work, but there is, of course, the normal activity of receiving an offer.

92. Calvin certainly considered the 1559 *Institutes* to be the definitive edition. He says to the reader that even though previous editions of the *Institutes* were enriched with some passages, "I never was satisfied until it had been organized in the order now proposed." See "John Calvin to the Reader" (1559), in O.S. 3.5.14–15.

93. O.S. 5.393.16–20; *Inst.* 4.17.33.

CHAPTER 4

1. The principal collection of Reformed confessions remains that by Müller, ed., *Bekenntnisschriften der reformierten Kirche*. Two earlier critical collections

should be mentioned: *Collectio confessionum in ecclesiis reformatis publicatarum*, ed. H. A. Niemeyer (Leipzig: Klinkhardt, 1840); and, *Bibliotheca Symbolica Ecclesiae Universalis: The Creeds of Christendom, with a History and Critical Notes*, 3 vols. 4th ed., ed. Philip Schaff (New York: Harper & Brothers, 1919). More recent is the collection edited by Wilhelm Niesel, *Bekenntnisschriften und Kirchenordnungen der nach Gottes Wort reformierten Kirchen*, 3d ed. (Zollikon-Zurich: Evangelischer Verlag, 1940). For an introduction to the complex issues concerning the Reformed confessions, see B. A. Gerrish, "The Confessional Heritage of the Reformed Church," *McCormick Quarterly* 19 (1966): 120–34, including nn1–18 for further resources; idem, *The Faith of Christendom: A Source Book of Creeds and Confessions* (Cleveland and New York: World Publishing Company, 1963), 17–46, 126–50, 354–60. Also see *Reformed Confessions of the 16th Century*, ed. Arthur C. Cochrane (Philadelphia: Westminster Press, 1966), 11–31; and Jan Rohls, *Reformed Confessions: Theology from Zurich to Barmen*, trans. John Hoffmeyer, introduction by Jack L. Stotts (Louisville, Ky.: Westminster John Knox Press, 1998), xi–xxiii, 3–28.

2. See Gerrish, "Confessional Heritage," 125–29.

3. For example, see the discussions in Cochrane, *Reformed Confessions*, 15–31; and Gerrish, "Confessional Heritage," 122–25.

4. The First Helvetic Confession (*Confessio helvetica prior*) can be found in Müller, *Bekenntnisschriften*, 101–9 (German); for the Latin and German, see Schaff, *Bibliotheca Symbolica* 3:211–31.

5. "Die gantze krafft, würkung, and frucht der Sacramenten" (Müller, *Bekenntnisschriften*, 106.36); the Latin has "Num in rebus ipsis totus fructus sacramentorum est" (Schaff, *Bibliotheca Symbolica*, 3:223).

6. Note the discussion of free will (article 9) and God's eternal will to save humankind (article 10), in which human beings do evil through their free will, and yet, in response, God never stopped bearing concern for humankind ("der gnedig vatter, nie uffgehört, sorg für jnn zetragenn"); Müller, *Bekenntnisschriften*, 102–3, 103.8–9.

7. The Geneva Confession (*Confession de la Foy*) can be found in Müller, *Bekenntnisschriften*, 11–116; C.O. 9.693–700.

8. C.O. 9.697.

9. The 1545 Geneva Catechism (*Catechismus ecclesiae Genevensis*) Latin text can be found in Müller, *Bekenntnisschriften*, 117–53; for the French text (1541), see Niesel, *Bekenntnisschriften*, 3–41. The French text has supplied the numbers for the questions.

10. See above, chap. 2.

11. Müller, *Bekenntnisschriften*, 146.31–147.25; Niesel, *Bekenntnisschriften*, 35.8–36.4.

12. Müller, *Bekenntnisschriften*, 148.24–49; Niesel, *Bekenntnisschriften*, 37.12–35.

13. Müller, *Bekenntnisschriften*, 149.7–149.36; Niesel, *Bekenntnisschriften*, 38.1–38.25.

14. See chap. 2, above.

15. The Second Helvetic Confession (*Confessio helvetica posterior*) can be found in Müller, *Bekenntnisschriften*, 170–221. For a theological analysis, see Koch, *Confessio Helvetica Posterior*. Also see the essays in Joachim Staedtke, ed. *Glauben und Bekennen: Vierhundert Jahre Confessio Helvetica Posterior* (Zurich: Zwingli Verlag, 1966); Edward A. Dowey Jr., *A Commentary on the Confession of 1967 and an Introduction to* The Book of Confessions (Philadelphia: Westminster Press, 1968), 201–13; Cochrane, *Reformed Confessions*, 220–23; and Jack Rogers, *Presbyterian*

Creeds: A Guide to the Book of Confessions (Philadelphia: Westminster Press, 1985), 116–35.

16. Chapter 19 ("De Sacramentis Ecclesiae Christi"); Müller, *Bekenntnisschriften*, 205.29–38.

17. Müller, *Bekenntnisschriften*, 206.11–14, 25–32.

18. "Ut signis communibus, non sanctificatis aut efficacibus" (ibid., 208.11); see ibid., 207.13–208.14.

19. Ibid., 206.33–207.2.

20. "Baptisari quid sit?" (ibid., 209.4).

21. Ibid., 209.4–7.

22. Ibid., 209.7–18.

23. Ibid., 209.42–49. There is a brief section on the Anabaptists that concludes with the terse sentence "Therefore we are not Anabaptists and have no commerce with them whatsoever."

24. For a helpful introduction to the French Confession (*Confessio gallicana*), see Gerrish, *Faith of Christendom*, 126–50.

25. For a history of the French Confession and its sources, see Jacques Pannier, *Les Origines de la confession de foi et de la discipline des église réformées de France* (Paris: F. Alcan, 1936). Also see Hannelore Jahr's *Studien zur Überlieferungsgeschichte der Confession de foi von 1559* (Neukirchen-Vluyn: Neukirchener Verlag des Erziehungsvereins, 1964). Jahr does careful textual work on the confession (19–29), discusses the spread and influence of the French Confession (29–57), and has more recent bibliographical material (156–62). The French text of the confession can be found in Müller, *Bekenntnisschriften*, 221–32; for the Latin text, see Niemeyer, *Collectio*, 327–39.

26. Articles 34–35, 38; Müller, *Bekenntnisschriften*, 230.1–7, 11–15; 231.15–17.

27. Müller, *Bekenntnisschriften*, 230.18–22.

28. For the text of the Belgic Confession (*Confession belgica*), see Müller, *Bekenntnisschriften*, 233–49; the French version can be found in Schaff, *Bibliotheca Symbolica*, 3:383–436, who used the official version from the Synod of Dort (1618–19), which differed from the original French confession in several areas. For an overview of the Belgic Confession and literature, see Cochrane, *Reformed Confessions*, 185–88; Niesel, *Bekenntnisschriften*, 119. Also see Michael A. Hakkenberg, "Belgic Confession," in *The Oxford Encyclopedia of the Reformation*, ed. Hans J. Hillerbrand (Oxford: Oxford University Press, 1996), 1:137–39.

29. Müller, *Bekenntnisschriften*, 245.35–246.1.

30. Ibid., 246.14–29.

31. Ibid., 246.30–247.2.

32. "Baptismum infantium, fidelibus parentibus natorum, damnant" (ibid., 246.3–7).

33. For the text of the Heidelberg Catechism (*Der Heidelberger Katechismus*), see Müller, *Bekenntnisschriften*, 682–719. The structure of the catechism follows an earlier catechism of Zacharias Ursinus, who had studied at Wittenberg with Melanchthon. The threefold structure of law–gospel–new life comes from Melanchthon, yet the final section on new life reflects Calvin's so-called third use of the law. The sacramental theology has been taken to be Calvinist (Müller, *Bekenntnisschriften*, iii; Schaff, *Bibliotheca Symbolica*, 1:543), although Gerrish has employed a supple method and argued that the eucharistic doctrine owes more to Bullinger. See Gerrish, "Sign and Reality," 125–26. In a careful textual analysis of the catechism, Wilhelm Neuser has argued that the baptismal material is indebted

primarily to Melanchthon, although it shows its own unique and synthetic reworking of material from Luther, Calvin, and Melanchthon. See Wilhelm H. Neuser, *Die Tauflehre des Heidelberger Katechismus: Eine aktuelle Lösung des Problems der Kindertaufe* (Munich: Chr. Kaiser Verlag, 1967). For introduction to the catechism, see Dowey, *Commentary*, 187–200; Rohls, *Reformed Confessions*, 20–21; Rogers, *Presbyterian Creeds*, 96–112; *The Heidelberg Catechism: 400 Anniversary Edition*, trans. Allen O. Miller and M. Eugene Osterhaven (New York: United Church Press, 1962), 5–8.

34. Qq. 69 (Müller, *Bekenntnisschriften*, 700.25–28); 71 (701.14–16); 73 (701.33–36).

35. Q. 73 (Müller, *Bekenntnisschriften*, 701.30–36).

36. See above, chap. 2.

37. See above, chap. 1.

38. In "Sign and Reality," Gerrish notes that the Heidelberg Catechism has the repeated sacramental pattern of "so gewiß·. . . so gewiß": As certainly as the external washing occurs, so certain am I that the internal washing occurs (125). For Gerrish, this "symbolic parallelism" indicates the influence of Bullinger's sacramental theology.

39. Neuser, *Tauflehre*, 22, 23–29, 33–37.

40. Ibid., 20–27, 36–38.

41. Ibid., 31–33. "A covenant theology is just as distant to the Heidelberg Catechism as to its predecessor, the Catechesis minor" (32).

42. Ibid., 14, 22–27.

43. For the text of the Scots Confession, see Niesel, *Bekenntnisschriften*, 79–117, who gives the Scots text and the Latin text on opposing pages. For an overview and basic bibliography, see Cochrane, *Reformed Confessions*, 159–62; Dowey, *Commentary*, 173–86; and Rogers, *Presbyterian Creeds*, 79–91. Also see Alex Cheyne, "The Scots Confession of 1560," *Theology Today* 17 (1960): 323–38; and, W. Ian P Hazlet, "The Scots Confession 1560: Context, Complexion and Critique," *Archiv für Reformationsgeschichte* 78 (1987): 287–320.

44. Note Dowey's comment that "this great Confession is as craggy, irregular, powerful, and unforgettable as the hills of north Scotland" (*Commentary*, 175).

45. Hazlet, "Scots Confession," 294–306.

46. Niesel, *Bekenntnisschriften*, 106.40–45; 108.1–11.

47. Ibid., 108.37–46; 110.1–3.

48. Ibid., 108.35–37.

49. Ibid., 106.45; 108.6—note the plural in the Latin text (109.5)—108.17, 27.

50. Ibid., 106.42–45.

51. Here a curious variation occurs: The Scots text then reads "or into quhose mouthis God hes put sum sermon of exhortation," implying the possibility of non-appointed, charismatic, yet still lawful preaching. The Latin text omits the word *or*. See ibid., 110.8; 111.7.

52. Ibid., 110.10–20.

53. Ibid., 112.19–26. Here we see what will become a standard Protestant solution to the medieval development in which first communion and confirmation spun off from the patristic rite of initiation and floated unattached in the Western liturgical sea. Confirmation became a rite of Christian passage and first communion was held off until after confirmation. For Bucer's pioneering efforts in Strasbourg, see the works by Amy Nelson Burnett. In the Roman Church, confirmation

and first communion continued in varying relation to baptism and each other until Pius X, wanting to increase eucharistic participation among the laity, set the twentieth-century Roman Catholic pattern of baptism–first communion–confirmation.

54. For the Latin texts of the 1552 Forty-two Articles and the 1562 (1563) Thirty-nine Articles, in parallel columns, see Müller, *Bekenntnisschriften*, 505–22. See Schaff, *Bibliotheca Symbolica*, 3:486–516, for the Latin text of the 1563 Articles, the English text of the 1571 Articles, and the 1801 American Revision (which mainly emends the sections on royal supremacy), all three in parallel columns. For a general introduction, see E. J. Bicknell, *A Theological Introduction to the Thirty-nine Articles of the Church of England*, 3d ed., rev. H. J. Carpenter (London: Longman, 1961); B. J. Kidd, *The Thirty-nine Articles: Their History and Explanation*, 5th ed. (London: Rivingtons, 1925); and William P. Haugaard, *Elizabeth and the English Reformation* (Cambridge: Cambridge University Press, 1968). For overviews and select bibliographies, see William P. Haugaard, "From the Reformation to the Eighteenth Century," in *The Study of Anglicanism*, ed. Stephen Sykes and John Booty (London: SPCK, 1988; Philadelphia: Fortress Press, 1988), 3–28; and Peter Toon, "The Articles and Homilies," in Sykes and Booty, eds., *Anglicanism*, 133–43.

55. For the text, see Müller, *Bekenntnisschriften*, 522–25; for an overview of catechisms in the Anglican tradition, see James Hartin, "Catechisms," in Sykes and Booty, eds., *Anglicanism*, 154–63. Also see Francis Procter, *A New History of the Book of Common Prayer*, rev. and rewritten by Walter Howard Frere (London: Macmillan & Co., 1955), 597–602.

56. Müller, *Bekenntnisschriften*, 524.21–23.

57. Ibid., 524.34–36; 525.1–2.

58. Ibid., 524.30–33.

59. Ibid., 524.33–40.

60. For a brief introduction to the Westminster Assembly, with notes and a select bibliography, see John H. Leith, *Assembly at Westminster: Reformed Theology in the Making* (Richmond: John Knox Press, 1973).

61. For overviews of the Westminster Confession and catechisms, see Dowey, *Commentary*, 214–50; Leith, *Assembly at Westminster*, 65–107; and Rogers, *Presbyterian Creeds*, 140–65. The text for the two catechisms can be found in Müller, *Bekenntnisschriften*, 612–52, who gives the English version of the Shorter Catechism and the Latin version of the Larger Catechism. I have used Müller's English text for the Shorter Catechism and translated from the Larger Catechism.

62. See above, chap. 2.

63. Dowey's comment on "faith" in the Westminster Confession hits the mark: "The catchword of the Reformation, 'By faith alone!' has been practically replaced with another, 'By divine decree!'" (*Commentary*, 223–24).

64. Müller, *Bekenntnisschriften*, 636.33–36.

65. Of course, in this case the word *given* could only connote a divine subject acting toward an object who was an *object*—like "giving" spin to a ball. The word *give* could not mean acting toward an object who was truly a *subject*, in which case what was "given" could *in principle* be refused.

66. Müller, *Bekenntnisschriften*, 637.19–36.

67. For an introduction to Protestant orthodoxy, see the essay on "Orthodoxie" (I. Lutherische Orthodoxie, by Markus Mattias; II. Reformierte Orthodoxie, by Olivier Fatio), in *Theologische Realenzyklopädie* (Berlin and New York: Walter de Gruyter, 1995), 25:464–97; for numerous and accessible English essays on

Reformed orthodoxy, see the bibliography to that essay (25:496–97). For a survey of scholarly views on orthodoxy and a very brief definition of orthodoxy, see Muller, *Christ and the Decree*, 1–13.

68. See the comments by Barth in Heinrich Heppe, *Reformed Dogmatics*, foreword by Karl Barth, rev. and ed. Ernst Bizer, trans. G. T. Thompson (London: Allen & Unwin, 1950), v–vii; for Tillich, see his strong assertion that Protestant orthodoxy must be studied and understood to understand later Protestant theology (Tillich, *Christian Thought*, 276–78).

69. Heinrich Schmid, *The Doctrinal Theology of the Evangelical Lutheran Church*, 3d ed., rev. and trans. Charles A. Hay and Henry E. Jacobs (Minneapolis: Augsburg Publishing House, 1961); Heppe, *Reformed Dogmatics*. Although an invaluable sourcebook, Heppe's work (in arrangement, selection, and discussion) sometimes shows his own theological perspective, as scholars have noted. See, for instance, the comments by Barth, *Reformed Dogmatics*, v–vii; and Muller, *Christ and the Decree*, passim.

70. So Heidegger and Gulielmus Bucanus; see Heppe, *Reformed Dogmatics*, 613.

71. So Johannes Wollebius, Heidegger, Polanus; see Heppe, *Reformed Dogmatics*, 611–12; also chap. 24, "Sacraments in General," esp. sec. 17.

72. Heppe, *Reformed Dogmatics*, 613–14.

73. Ibid., 619–20.

74. Ibid., 617–18.

75. Note also that Heidegger asserted that "it is admitted that many baptized persons are neither elect nor glorified, as many unbaptized persons are both elect and glorified.—The causes and means of salvation are far deeper than earthly things and elements, namely eternal foreknowledge, predestination, etc." (ibid., 617).

76. Ibid., 624–25.

77. So Heidegger; see ibid., 620–21.

78. So Leiden Synopsis, Bucanus, Riissen, Wollebius, Wallaeus, and others; see ibid., 621–22.

79. So Heidegger; see ibid., 622–23.

80. Ibid., 611–26.

81. This position is to be distinguished from the "Bullinger type" of Reformed sacramental theology, in which the sacraments were a means of grace and by divine decree what happened outwardly also happened inwardly. See Gerrish, "Sign and Reality," 123–30.

82. Schleiermacher bibliographies can be found in Terrence N. Tice, *Schleiermacher Bibliography: With Brief Introductions, Annotations, and Index* (Princeton, N.J.: Princeton Theological Seminary, 1966); idem, *Schleiermacher Bibliography (1784–1984): Updating and Commentary* (Princeton, N.J.: Princeton Theological Seminary, 1985); idem, "Schleiermacher Bibliography: Update 1987," *New Athenaeum/Neues Athenaeum* 1 (1989): 280–350; idem, "Schleiermacher Bibliography: Update 1990," *New Athenaeum/Neues Athenaeum* 2 (1991): 131–65; idem, "Schleiermacher Bibliography: Update 1994," *New Athenaeum/Neues Athenaeum* 4 (1995): 139–94; idem, *Schleiermacher's Sermons: A Chronological Listing and Account* (Lewiston, N.Y.: E. Mellen Press, 1997). For those not familiar with Schleiermacher, by far the best introduction to his theology is the work by B. A. Gerrish, *A Prince of the Church: Schleiermacher and the Beginnings of Modern Theology* (Philadelphia: Fortress Press, 1984). Martin Redeker's *Schleiermacher: Life and Thought*, trans. John Wallhauser (Philadelphia: Fortress Press, 1973), remains a standard introduction to Schleiermacher's life and thought. Richard R. Niebuhr gives a more

complete introduction to Schleiermacher's theology in his book *Schleiermacher on Christ and Religion* (New York: Charles Scribner's Sons, 1964). As for baptism, so far as I can tell there is no substantial monograph on Schleiermacher's theology of baptism, nor on the sacraments in general for that matter. Such a monograph would go well beyond the scope of this study and would need to include not only the corpus of Schleiermacher's writings but a careful study of ecclesial and sacramental issues that formed the context of his thought on this subject.

83. See Redeker, *Schleiermacher*, 94–100, 151–208.

84. Friedrich Schleiermacher, *The Christian Faith* (Philadelphia: Fortress Press, 1976), sec. 106.1, 476 (*Der Christliche Glaube nach den Grundsätzen der evangelischen Kirche im Zusammenhange dargestellt*, 7th ed., ed. Martin Redeker [Berlin: Walter de Gruyter, 1960], 2:147). Here and following cited according to propositions and subsections, followed by the page number in the English edition and, in parentheses, the volume and page number in Redeker's critical edition. Unless otherwise noted, I have used the English translation.

85. "The difference is simply that the self-revelation of Christ is now mediated by those who preach Him; but they being appropriated by Him as His instruments, the activity really proceeds from Him and is essentially His own." *Christian Faith*, sec. 108.5, 490–91 (2:165).

86. Ibid., sec. 127.3, 589–90 (2:127–28).

87. Ibid., sec. 136, 619 (2:318).

88. Ibid., sec. 137.1–2, 628–29 (2:328–30).

89. Ibid., sec. 137.2, 629–31 (2:330–32).

90. "Denn wird die Taufe schlecht empfangen, wenn sie ohne Glauben empfangen wird; so ist sie auch nicht gut gegeben." Ibid., sec. 137.2, 630 (2:331).

91. Ibid., sec. 137.2, 631 (2:332).

92. For Schleiermacher, *regeneration* was that turning point in which the continuity of the old self ceased and the new self began. Seen from the other side, *sanctification* was the "growing continuity of the new life," in which the old life slowly receded (ibid., sec. 106.1, 476 [2:148]). Schleiermacher then parsed regeneration into justification and conversion: The one represented the person's changed relationship to God, the other represented the person's changed relationship to the old life (sec. 107, 478 [2:150]). Justification and conversion were thus "utterly inseparable" (*unzertrennlich voneinander*) and "simultaneous" (*gleichzeitig*) (sec. 107.1, 479 [2:151]). Also see sec. 109.2, 498 (2:175).

93. "Now of course it is by the very same act that the individual is regenerated and that he becomes a spontaneously active member of the Christian Church." Ibid., sec. 114.2, 531 (2:214).

94. Ibid., sec. 136.3, 622–23 (2:321–23).

95. Ibid., sec. 137.2, 630 (2:331).

96. Ibid., sec. 138.2, 636 (2:338).

97. Ibid., sec. 138.1, 635 (2:337–38).

98. Ibid., sec. 138.2, 637 (2:339–40).

99. Ibid., sec. 138.2, 637 (2:339).

100. See Dale Moody, *Baptism: Foundation for Christian Unity* (Philadelphia: Westminster Press, 1967), 45–112, to which this section is indebted. I have chosen to discuss only some of the Reformed responses to Karl Barth's influential book on baptism. The much-overlooked work by Leenhardt is clear and to the point, working closely with the New Testament texts. Marcel's work was picked because he consciously tried to represent Calvin, the Reformed tradition, and covenant. The Dutch

material is mentioned because of the connection to Reformed orthodoxy, the Reformed confessions (such as the Belgic Confession and Synod of Dort), and Calvin and his treatment of election and baptism. Finally I refer to the essay by Wilhelm Neuser, who worked from the Heidelberg Catechism, a document also examined in this chapter.

101. See Emil Brunner, *Truth as Encounter*, trans. A. W. Loos and David Cairns (Philadelphia: Westminster Press, 1964), 181–85. The original text (*Wahrheit als Begegnung*) stemmed from the Olavus Petri Lectures, whose theme was the relationship between the subjective and objective in Christianity. Brunner believed that this dichotomy stemmed from Greek philosophy and that the biblical view was "truth as encounter." Thus, in the baptism section (181–85), Brunner talked about the objective and subjective aspects of baptism, which roughly correlated to the issues of validity and efficacy.

102. Ibid., 184.

103. See Emil Brunner, *The Misunderstanding of the Church*, trans. Harold Knight (Philadelphia: Westminster Press, 1965), where he makes the covenant argument for infant baptism, linking circumcision and baptism (65–66).

104. Karl Barth, *The Teaching of the Church regarding Baptism*, trans. E. A. Payne (London: SCM Press, 1948).

105. Ibid., 9–18.

106. Ibid., 14, 20–21.

107. Ibid., 26–33.

108. Ibid., 34–54, esp. 36, 40–47.

109. Ibid., 16.

110. Ibid., 55–64, esp. 55–56.

111. Barth, *Church Dogmatics*, IV/4.

112. Markus Barth, *Die Taufe—Ein Sakrament?* (Zollikon-Zurich: Evangelischer Verlag, 1951).

113. Barth, *Church Dogmatics*, IV/4, 3–40.

114. Ibid., 50–68.

115. Ibid., 68–100.

116. Ibid., 100–164.

117. Barth and Cullmann debated the topic of infant baptism in lectures, in writings, and in academic seminars. Their conversation represented one of the most spirited and well-known discussions of baptism in twentieth-century Protestantism. Cullmann's foundational doctrine was that of the "general baptism" effected by Jesus Christ through his death and resurrection and offered to all, regardless of their ability to know or respond (Oscar Cullman, *Baptism in the New Testament*, trans. J. K. S. Reid [Philadelphia: Westminster Press, 1950], 9–22). Such general baptism made one a member of the "Reign of Christ," in which God's prevenient grace was offered to all people. Within this outer circle lay an "inner circle," the body of Christ, or the church, which was the realm of a special manifestation of God's prevenient grace, the grace of baptism (Cullman, *Baptism*, 27–44). As for faith, Cullmann argued for a threefold perspective on faith: Before baptism, faith was demanded of adults; during baptism, faith was demanded from the congregation; and after baptism, faith was demanded of all who were baptized (51–55). Finally, Cullmann made a detailed and revitalized defense of infant baptism by arguing for baptism as the continuation and fulfillment of infant circumcision (57–69).

118. Franz J. Leenhardt, *Le Baptême chrétien, son origine, sa signification* (Neuchâtel and Paris: Delachaux & Niestlé, 1946).

119. Ibid., 42

120. Ibid., 66. It should be noted that when Joachim Jeremias and Kurt Aland intensely debated whether the early church baptized infants, the general consensus emerged that no one could tell. Perhaps the apostolic church did baptize infants; perhaps not. See Kurt Aland, *Did the Early Church Baptize Infants?* trans. and with an introduction by G. R. Beasely-Murray (Philadelphia: Westminster Press, 1963); Joachim Jeremias, *Infant Baptism in the First Four Centuries*, trans. David Cairns (Philadelphia: Fortress Press, 1960).

121. Leenhardt, *Baptême chrétien*, 71.

122. Ibid., 71–72.

123. Pierre Charles Marcel, *The Biblical Doctrine of Infant Baptism: Sacrament of the Covenant of Grace*, trans. Philip Edgcumbe Hughes (London: James Clarke & Company, 1953).

124. Ibid., 13, 22–23.

125. Ibid., 72–98.

126. Ibid., 106–23.

127. Ibid., 187–203.

128. For a detailed summary of the issues within the Dutch Reformed Church, as well as bibliography for the Dutch Reformed theologians and for the South African theologians, see Moody, *Baptism*, 73–77.

129. Neuser, *Tauflehre*, in particular 5–6, 11–16, 23–33.

130. Ibid., 6–23.

131. Ibid., 23–29.

132. Ibid., 33–38. Neuser corrected Barth's reading of the Heidelberg Catechism, showing where Barth misread the text (29). Neuser also showed that Marcel misunderstood the catechism and its scriptural references (6). There is some irony here because, as we have seen, Marcel critiqued Leenhardt for *not* doing a dogmatic exegesis of infant baptism. By returning to the Reformed tradition and doing exegesis from there, argued Marcel, he would show that infant baptism was biblically sound and that Leenhardt was mistaken to say that those who exegetically justified infant baptism were "persistently scraping scraps of text in order to make weapons of them" (so Leenhardt, *Baptême chrétien*, 67).

CHAPTER 5

1. For helpful entrance to the Calvin and Schleiermacher material, see B. A. Gerrish, *Tradition and the Modern World: Reformed Theology in the Nineteenth Century* (Chicago: University of Chicago Press, 1978), 99–150; idem, *Old Protestantism*, 131–49; B. A. Gerrish, ed., *Reformers in Profile* (Philadelphia: Fortress Press, 1967), 142–64. Also see Charles Partee, "Calvin's Central Dogma, Again," *Sixteenth Century Journal* 18 (1987): 191–99, who argues that union in Christ is Calvin's organizing center. But see Muller, *Christ and the Decree*, 17–38, who argues for the strict interconnection of Christology and election.

2. Niebuhr, *Schleiermacher*, 210–14.

3. B. A. Gerrish, *Grace & Gratitude: The Eucharistic Theology of John Calvin*

(Minneapolis: Fortress Press, 1993). Also see Pamela Ann Moeller, *Calvin's Doxology* (Allison Park, Pa.: Pickwick Publications, 1997).

4. Old, *Reformed Baptismal Rite*, 83, 124, 129, 135–40, 178, 286.

5. It is possible that Calvin learned a covenant theology for baptism from reading Augustine. By 1539, Calvin had read widely in the church fathers, and Augustine could have been a source for and support of covenant theology. As a parallel, note Bullinger's frequent citing of Augustine in his *One and Eternal Covenant of God*, as well as Bucer's use of Augustine in his 1533 essay on infant baptism. See McCoy and Baker, *Fountainhead of Federalism*, 99–138.

6. For an introduction to covenant theology, see McCoy and Baker, *Fountainhead of Federalism*, 11–44, 63–79. On the issue of Bullinger and the covenant, see chap. 2, section 2, above, esp. nn. 3, 21. McCoy and Baker also have interesting sections on covenant and political theology; see *Fountainhead of Federalism*, 45–62, 80–98.

7. But see the next note concerning Bullinger, Barth, and Schleiermacher.

8. Karl Barth, *Church Dogmatics* II/2, trans. G. W. Bromiley (Edinburgh: T. & T. Clark, 1957). The discussion of covenant in Bullinger and Barth raises an interesting connection to Schleiermacher. Although Schleiermacher was not interested in covenant language, his discussion of election did what covenant did for Bullinger and Barth: The work of Christ was for all humanity, not merely for some chosen few.

9. See above, particularly chap. 3.

10. See McCoy and Baker, *Fountainhead of Federalism*, 24–26, 65–69. Note that this double covenant presents a distinctly different covenant theology from what we have seen in Zwingli, who in his late writings against the Anabaptists described a single, true covenant of God (chap. 1, above). It also differs from what we have seen in Calvin, who spoke of a covenant unity, comprised of old and new, which related as shadow to reality or promise to fulfillment (chap. 2). And it differs from the single, bilateral covenant of Bullinger (chap. 2).

11. See above, chap. 3.

12. Philip I. Devenish, "The Sovereignty of Jesus and the Sovereignty of God," *Theology Today* 53 1 (1996): 63–73.

13. See, in particular, Luther's *Von der Wiedertaufe*, W.A. 26.144–74; *Concerning Rebaptism*, L.W. 40.229–62.

14. O.S. 5.393.16–20; *Inst.* 4.17.33.

15. *Concerning Rebaptism* (Von der Widdertauffe an zween Pfarherrn), W.A. 26.144–74; L.W. 40.229–62.

16. W.A. 26.154.3–11; L.W. 40.239–40.

17. As we have seen, this was fundamentally the response to Barth by the French Reformed theologians.

18. Recall the comments by Schleiermacher (chapter 4, section 3, above), and by Leenhardt, Marcel, and Neuser (chap. 4).

19. Here Schleiermacher's careful comments about infant baptism being allowed to continue and about the role of confirmation seem eminently sensible.

20. *Book of Common Worship* (Louisville, Ky.: Westminster/John Knox Press, 1993), 403–17.

21. Perhaps no Reformed theologian has said this better than Karl Barth: "Hence not the sacrament alone nor preaching alone, nor yet, to speak meticulously, preaching and the sacrament, but preaching with the sacrament, with the visible act that confirms human speech as God's act, is the constitutive element,

the perspicuous centre of the Church's life" (*Church Dogmatics* I/1, trans. G. W. Bromiley [Edinburgh: T. & T. Clark, 1975], 70).

22. See the Introduction, above.

23. See the Introduction, above.

24. See the Introduction, above.

25. Barth, *Church Dogmatics*, I/1, 69–70; italics added.

26. See Old, *Reformed Baptismal Rite*, 51–76, 145–78.

27. See Dawn DeVries, *Jesus Christ in the Preaching of Calvin and Schleiermacher* (Louisville, Ky.: Westminster John Knox Press, 1996), esp. 14–25, 48–70, and 95–107. Also see Moeller, *Calvin's Doxology*, 53–83.

28. Note Gerrish's comment in *Grace & Gratitude* (82): "It is not too difficult to see how the cognitive strand in Calvinism could lead to an arid intellectualism that turns the worshiping community into a class of glum schoolchildren. Heavy didacticism has always been the bane of Reformed worship, and sometimes the point of it—to let God's fatherly face become visible—is less than obvious." Also see the chapter on Reformed worship in White, *Protestant Worship*.

CONCLUSION

1. O.S. 5.274.18–20; *Inst.* 3.14.17

2. Neuser rightly commented in his study of the Heidelberg Catechism that the baptismal sections of the various confessions must always be read in light of the sacramental section that precedes them; Neuser, *Tauflehre*, 5.

3. Müller, *Bekenntnisschriften*, 208.22–29. Compare Calvin's comments in the opening of *Inst.* 3.14.7.

4. Rohls, *Reformed Confessions*, xi.

5. *Inst.* 3.14.13

6. Note the comment by Gerrish: "To be saved, in the teaching of the confessions, is precisely to look outside of ourselves to Christ, in whom we are to recover all that we lack in ourselves (cf., Geneva Confession, parts V, VI, IX). The doctrine of justification is so presented as to turn us away from ourselves—even from our faith!—to Christ alone" ("Confessional Heritage," 130).

7. So, for example, Moeller, *Calvin's Doxology*.

8. *Christian Faith*, sec. 137.2, 632 (2:333): "Auf der andern Seite kann man sagen, ist auch der Glaube bei der Taufe noch nicht gewesen, so wird er doch nicht nur *nach* der Taufe, sondern, da diese der Anfang der ganzen Reihe von Tätigkeiten ist, welche die Kirche auf den Getauften richten, *durch* die Taufe enstehen . . ." (italics added).

9. See the comments by Gerrish, "Sign and Reality," 128–30.

10. *Inst.* 4.17.5

11. Jill Raitt, "Roman Catholic New Wine in Reformed Old Bottles? The Conversion of the Elements in the Eucharistic Doctrines of Theodore Beza and Edward Schillebeeckx," *Journal of Ecumenical Studies* 8 (1971): 581–604.

12. Negatively put, the failure to hold the means of grace in intimate proximity to the divine presence is to have worship fall from grace and lapse into seemingly endless forms of pseudo-worship: memorialism, moralism, didactic teaching, or entertainment, and so on. All too often Reformed worship has forgotten its own insights and lapsed into these worship practices.

13. See Bultmann's classic essay "The Concept of Revelation in the New Testament," in Schubert M. Ogden, selected, translated, and introduced, *Existence and Faith: Shorter Writings of Rudolf Bultmann* (New York: Meridian Books, 1960), 58–91. Also see the essay "The Historicity of Man and Faith," in Ogden, ed., *Existence and Faith*, 92–110. While a detailed argument cannot be recounted here, two citations can summarize Bultmann's exegetical assessment of revelation in the New Testament. From "Concept of Revelation," Bultmann says, "There is no other light shining in Jesus than has always already shined in the creation. Man learns to understand himself in the light of the revelation of redemption not a bit differently than he always already should understand himself in face of the revelation in creation and the law—namely, as God's creature who is limited by God and stands under God's claim, which opens up to him the way to death or to life" (86). To the question, then, of what more one knows in the event of revelation through Jesus, Bultmann says by analogy, "What 'more,' then, do I know when I am in an actual relationship of friendship? Nothing!—at any rate, nothing more *about* friendship. What 'more' I do know is that I now know my friend and also know myself anew, in the sense that, in understanding my friend, my concrete life in its work and its joy, its struggle and its pain, is qualified in a new way" ("Historicity of Man and Faith," 100).

14. In this study, the most notable expressions of Christ himself being present were Calvin, Bullinger, the French Confession and the Scots Confession, and Schleiermacher.

15. Chapter 4 outlined how Schleiermacher carefully argued much the same point about the baptizing church being the body of Christ.

16. Luther's position on Scripture immediately comes to mind here. On the one hand, Scripture is the queen that rules over all religious authorities (W.A. 40^1.119, L.W. 26.57; W.A. 40^1. 120, L.W. 26.58). No one validates Scripture, which validates itself and interprets itself by always pointing toward Christ, who is the center of Scripture. By contrast, Christ is the king who authorizes Scripture. Relative to Christ, who is the source of authority, both the authority (Scripture) and the one under authority (the Christian) stand on equal footing. And so, for instance, Luther can say straightforwardly to his adversaries that if they push Scripture on him, then he will push Christ on them (W.A. 40^1.459, L.W. 26.295; W.A. 39^1.47, L.W. 34.112). Also see Paul Bradshaw's criticism of primary and secondary theology as used by Kavanagh and others, "Difficulties in Doing Liturgical Theology," *Pacifica* 11 (1998): 190–93.

17. Although somewhat dated, the best introduction to the wide variety of worship forms in the New Testament church remains Ferdinand Hahn, *The Worship of the Early Church*, ed. John Reumann, trans. David E. Green (Philadelphia: Fortress Press, 1973). For discussions of liturgical diversity in the early church, see Paul Bradshaw *The Search for the Origins of Christian Worship* (London: SPCK/New York: Oxford University Press, 1992); Bradshaw, "Doing Liturgical Theology"; Paul V. Marshall, "Reconsidering 'Liturgical Theology': Is there a *Lex Orandi* for all Christians?" *Studia Liturgica* 25 (1995): 129–51; James F. White, "How Do We Know It Is Us?", pp. 55–65 in *Liturgy and the Moral Self*, ed. E. Byron Anderson and Bruce T. Morrill, S.J. (Collegeville, Minn.: Liturgical Press, 1998).

18. Morton Smith, "Pauline Worship as Seen by Pagans," *Harvard Theological Review* 73 (1980): 241–49.

19. Elizabeth Schüssler Fiorenza, *In Memory of Her* (New York: Crossroad, 1988), 323–34. For footwashing as the possible entrance rite to some Johannine communities, see Martin Connell, "'*Nisi Pedes*' Except for the Feet: Footwashing in the Community of John's Gospel" *Worship* 70 (1996): 20–30.

20. Among New Testament scholars of recent generations, Willi Marxsen was the most clear on this point: *The New Testament as the Church's Book*, trans. James E. Mignard (Philadelphia: Fortress Press, 1972).

BIBLIOGRAPHY

1. PRIMARY SOURCES

The Ante-Nicene Fathers. Edited by Alexander Roberts and James Donaldson. Edinburgh, 1885–. Reprint, Grand Rapids: 1990.

Aquinas, Thomas. *Summa Theologica.* Translated by the Fathers of the English Dominican Province. London: R. & T. Washbourne; New York: Benziger Brothers, 1914.

Die Bekenntnisschriften der reformierten Kirche. Edited by E. F. Karl Müller. Leipzig: A. Deichert (Georg Böhme), 1903. Reprint, Waltrop: Spenner, 1999.

Bekenntnisschriften und Kirchenordnungen der nach Gottes Wort reformierten Kirchen. 3d ed. Edited by Wilhelm Niesel. Zollikon-Zurich: Evangelischer Verlag, 1940.

Bibliotheca Symbolica Ecclesiae Universalis: The Creeds of Christendom, with a History and Critical Notes. 4th ed. Edited by Philip Schaff. 3 vol. New York: Harper & Brothers, 1919.

Book of Common Worship. Louisville, Ky.: Westminster/John Knox Press, 1993.

Bucer, Martin. *Martin Bucers Deutsche Schriften.* Gütershloh: Gütershloher Verlaghaus Gerd Mohn, 1960.

Bullinger, Heinrich. *Adversus Anabaptistas.* Translated by Josiah Simler. Zurich: Froschouer, 1560.

———. *Catechesis.* Zurich: Froschauer, 1561.

———. The Decades of Heinrich Bullinger. Translated by H. I; edited for the Parker Society by Thomas Harding. Cambridge: University Press, 1849–1852.

———. *Heinrich Bullinger Theologische Schriften.* Edited by Hans-Georg vom Berg, Bernhard Schneider, and Endre Zsindely. Zurich: Theologischser Verlag, 1991.

———. *Sermonum Decades Quinque.* Tomus 1–3. Zurich: Froschouer, 1549–1551.

———. *Summa Christenlicher Religion.* Zurich: Froschouer, 1556.

Calvin, John. *Calvin: Institutes of the Christian Religion.* Edited by John T. McNeill. Translated and indexed by Ford Lewis Battles. 2 vols. Library of Christian Classics 20–21. Philadelphia: Westminster Press, 1960.

———. *Institutes of the Christian Religion, 1536 Edition.* Translated and annotated by Ford Lewis Battles, rev. ed. Grand Rapids: Wm. B. Eerdmans Publishing Co., 1986.

———. *Concerning the Eternal Predestination of God*. Translated and edited by J. K. S. Reid. London: James Clarke, 1961.

———. *Ioannis Calvini opera quae supersunt omnia*. Edited by Wilhelm Baum, Edward Cunitz, and Edward Reuss. 59 vols. Volumes 29–87 of *Corpus Reformatorum*. Brunswick: C. A. Schwetschke and Son (M. Bruhn), 1863–1900.

———. *Ioannis Calvini opera selecta*. Edited by Peter Barth, Wilhelm Niesel, and Dora Scheuner. 5 vols. Munich: Chr. Kaiser Verlag, 1926–52.

———. *Institution de la religion chrestienne*. Edited by Jean-Daniel Benoit. 5 vols. Paris: J. Vrin, 1957–63.

———. *Institution of the Christian Religion (1536)*. Translated by Ford Lewis Battles. Atlanta: John Knox Press, 1975.

———. *The Piety of John Calvin: An Anthology Illustrative of the Spirituality of the Reformer*. Translated and edited by Ford Lewis Battles. Music edited by Stanley Tagg. Grand Rapids: Baker Book House, 1978.

———. *Theological Treatises*. Translated, with introductions and notes, by J. K. S. Reid. Library of Christian Classics 22. Philadelphia: Westminster Press, 1954.

———. *Tracts and Treatises on the Reformation of the Church*. Edited by T. F. Torrance. Translated by Henry Beveridge. 3 vols. Edinburgh: The Calvin Translation Society, 1844–51. Reprint, Edinburgh and London: Oliver and Boyd, 1958.

Collectio confessionum in ecclesiis reformatis publicatarum. Edited by H. A. Niemeyer. Leipzig: Klinkhardt, 1840.

The Heidelberg Catechism: 400 Anniversary Edition. Translated by Allen O. Miller and M. Eugene Osterhaven. New York: United Church Press, 1962.

Luther, Martin. *D. Martin Luthers Werke: Kritische Gesamtausgabe*. Weimar: Hermann Böhlaus, 1883–.

———. *D. Martin Luthers Werke: Kritische Gesamtausgabe. Die Deutsche Bibel*. Weimar: Hermann Böhlaus, 1906.

———. *Luther's Works*. Edited by Jaroslav Pelikan and Helmut T. Lehmann. 55 vols. St. Louis: Concordia Publishing House; Philadelphia: Fortress Press, 1955–1986.

Reformed Confessions of the 16th Century. Edited by Arthur C. Cochrane. Philadelphia: Westminster Press, 1966.

Schleiermacher, Friedrich. *The Christian Faith*. Philadelphia: Fortress Press, 1976.

———. *Der Christliche Glaube nach den Grundsätzen der evangelischen Kirche im Zusammenhange dargestellt*. 7th ed. Edited by Martin Redeker. Berlin: Walter de Gruyter, 1960.

Theologische Realenzyklopädie. s.v. "Orthodoxie." Berlin and New York: Walter de Gruyter, 1995.5: 464–97.

Zwingli, Huldrych. *Huldreich Zwinglis sämtliche Werke*. Edited by Emil Egli, Georg Finsler, et al. 14 vols. Volumes 88–101 of *Corpus Reformatorum*. Vol. 1: Berlin: C. A. Schwetschke und Sohn, 1905. Vols. 2–5, 7–12: Leipzig: M. Heinsius Nachfolger, 1908– . Vols. 6/1, 6/2, 13–14: Zurich: Verlag Berichthaus, 1944– .

———. *Huldrych Zwingli Writings*. Translated and edited by H. Wayne Pipkin. Allison Park, Pa.: Pickwick Press, 1984.

———. *The Latin Works of Huldreich Zwingli*. Edited by Clarence Nevin Heller. Philadelphia: Heidelberg Press, 1929.

———. *Selected Works of Huldreich Zwingli*. Edited by Samuel Macauley Jackson. Philadelphia: University of Pennsylvania Press, 1901.

2. SECONDARY STUDIES

Aland, Kurt. *Did the Early Church Baptize Infants?* Translated and with an introduction by G. R. Beasely-Murray. Philadelphia: Westminster Press, 1963.

Althaus, Paul. "Martin Luther über die Kindertaufe." *Theologische Literaturzeitung* 3 (1948): 705–14.

Armstrong, Brian G. "Calvin and Calvinism." Pp. 75–103 in *Reformation Europe: A Guide to Research II*, edited by William S. Maltby. St. Louis: Center for Reformation Research, 1992.

Bainton, Roland. *Here I Stand!* New York: Abingdon-Cokesbury Press, 1950.

Baker, J. Wayne. *Heinrich Bullinger and the Covenant: The Other Reformed Tradition*. Athens: Ohio University Press, 1980.

———. "Jérome Bolsec." In *The Oxford Encyclopedia of the Reformation*. Oxford: Oxford University Press, 1996.

———. "The Reformation at Zurich in the Thought and Theology of Huldrych Zwingli and Heinrich Bullinger." Pp. 47–73 in *Reformation Europe: A Guide to Research II*, edited by William S. Maltby. St. Louis: Center for Reformation Research, 1992.

Balke, Willem. *Calvin and the Anabaptists*. Translated by William Heynen. Grand Rapids: Wm. B. Eerdmans Publishing Co., 1981.

Barth, Karl. *Church Dogmatics*. I/1. Translated by G. W. Bromiley. Edinburgh: T. & T. Clark, 1975.

———. *Church Dogmatics*. II/2. Translated by G. W. Bromiley. Edinburgh: T. & T. Clark, 1957.

———. *Church Dogmatics*. IV/4: *The Christian Life* (fragment). Translated by G. W. Bromiley. Edinburgh: T. & T. Clark, 1969.

———. *The Teaching of the Church Regarding Baptism*. Translated by E. A. Payne. London: SCM Press, 1948.

Barth, Markus. *Die Taufe—Ein Sakrament?* Zollikon-Zurich: Evangelischer Verlag, 1951.

Barth, Peter. "Calvins Verständnis der Kirche." *Zwischen den Zeiten* 8 (1930): 216–33.

Beauduin, Lambert. *La Piété de l'église*. Brussels: Vromant & Co., 1914.

Beckmann, Joachim. *Vom Sakrament bei Calvin*. Tübingen: J. C. B. Mohr (Paul Siebeck), 1926.

Bicknell, E. J. *A Theological Introduction to the Thirty-nine Articles of the Church of England*. 3d ed. Revised by H. J. Carpenter. London: Longman, 1961.

Bizer, Ernst. "Die Entdeckung des Sakraments durch Luther." *Evangelische Theologie* 17 (1957): 64–90.

———. *Fides ex auditu: Eine Untersuchung über die Entdeckung der Gerechtigkeit*

Gottes durch Martin Luther. 2d ed. Neukirchen Kreis Moers: Verlag der Buchhandlung des Erziehungsvereins, 1961.

Blanke, Fritz, and Immanuel Leuschner. *Heinrich Bullinger: Vater der reformierten Kirche.* Zurich: Theologische Verlag, 1990.

Bohatec, Josef. *Calvins Lehre von Staat und Kirche mit besonderer Berücksichtigung des Organismusgedankens.* Breslau: M. and H. Marcus, 1937. Reprint, Aalen: Scientia, 1961.

Bornert, René. *La Réforme protestante du culte a Strasbourg au XVIᵉ siècle (1523–1598).* Leiden: E. J. Brill, 1981.

Bouwsma, William. "Calvin and the Renaissance Crisis of Knowing." *Calvin Theological Journal* 17 (1982): 190–211.

———. *John Calvin: A Sixteenth Century Portrait.* New York: Oxford University Press, 1988.

Bradshaw, Paul. "Christian Initiation." Pp. 601–12 in *The New Dictionary of Sacramental Worship.* Edited by Peter E. Fink, S.J. Collegeville, Minn.: Liturgical Press, 1990.

———. "Difficulties in Doing Liturgical Theology," *Pacifica* 11 (1998): 181–94.

———. *The Search for the Origins of Christian Worship.* London: SPCK/New York: Oxford University Press, 1992.

Brand, Eugene. "New Rites of Initiation and Their Implications in the Lutheran Churches." *Studia Liturgica* 12, 2–3 (1977): 151–65.

Brecht, Martin. "Herkunft und Eigenart der Tauferanschauung der Züricher Täufer." *Archiv für Reformationsgeschichte* 64 (1973): 147–65.

———. *Martin Luther: His Road to Reformation, 1483–1521.* Translated by James L. Schaaf. Philadelphia: Fortress Press, 1985.

———. *Martin Luther: The Preservation of the Church, 1532–1546.* Translated by James L. Schaaf. Minneapolis: Fortress Press, 1993.

———. *Martin Luther: Shaping and Defining the Reformation, 1521–1532.* Translated by James L. Schaaf. Minneapolis: Fortress Press, 1990.

Brinkel, Karl. *Die Lehre Luthers von der fides infantium bei der Kindertaufe.* Berlin: Evangelische Verlagsanstalt, 1958.

Brinkoff, L., O.F.M. "Chronicle of the Liturgical Movement." Pp. 40–67 in *Liturgy in Development.* New York: Sheed and Ward, 1965.

Bromiley, Geoffrey W. *Historical Theology: An Introduction.* Grand Rapids: Wm. B. Eerdman's Publishing Co., 1978.

Brunner, Emil. *The Misunderstanding of the Church.* Translated by Harold Knight. Philadelphia: Westminster Press, 1965.

———. *Truth as Encounter.* Translated by A. W. Loos and David Cairns. Philadelphia: Westminster Press, 1964.

Bullinger, Heinrich. *Sermonum Decades Quique.* 3 vol. Zurich: Froschouer, 1549–1551.

———. *The Decades of Heinrich Bullinger.* Translated by H. I; edited for the Parker Society by Thomas Harding. Cambridge: Cambridge University Press, 1849–1852.

Burnett, Amy Nelson. "Church Discipline and Moral Reformation in the Thought of Martin Bucer." *Sixteenth Century Journal* 22, 3 (1991): 438–56.

———. "Martin Bucer and the Anabaptist Context of Evangelical Confirmation." *Mennonite Quarterly Review* 68 (1994): 95–122

————. *The Yoke of Christ: Martin Bucer and Christian Discipline.* Vol. 26 of Sixteenth Century Essays & Studies. Kirksville, Mo.: Sixteenth Century Journal Publishers, 1994.

Chandlee, H. Ellsworth, "The Liturgical Movement." Pp. 307–14 in *The New Westminster Dictionary of Liturgy and Worship,* edited by J. G. Davies. Philadelphia: Westminster Press, 1986.

Cheyne, Alex. "The Scots Confession of 1560." *Theology Today* 17 (1960): 323–38.

Chrisman, Miriam Usher. *Strasbourg and the Reform: A Study in the Process of Change.* New Haven, Conn.: Yale University Press, 1967.

Connell, Martin. "'Nisi Pedes' Except for the Feet: Footwashing in the Community of John's Gospel." *Worship* 70 (1969): 20–30.

Cottrell, Jack Warren. "Covenant and Baptism in the Theology of Huldreich Zwingli." Unpublished Th.D. dissertation, Princeton Theological Seminary, 1971.

Courvoisier, Jacques. "Bucer et Calvin." Pp. 37–66 in *Calvin à Strasbourg, 1538–1541,* edited by Jean-Daniel Benoit, Jacques Courvoisier, Pierre Scherding, D. A. Kuntz, *Calvin à Strasbourg,* 1538-1541. Strasbourg: Editions Fides, 1938.

————. *La Notion d'église chez Bucer.* Paris: Librairie Félix Alcan, 1932.

Crichton, J. D. "A Theology of Worship." Pp. 3–31 in *The Liturgy of the Church,* 2d ed., edited by Cheslyn Jones, Geoffrey Wainwright, Edward Yarnold, and Paul Bradshaw. London: Oxford University Press, 1992.

Cullmann, Oscar. *Baptism in the New Testament.* Translated by J. K. S. Reid. Philadelphia: Westminster Press, 1950.

Depperman, Klaus. *Melchior Hoffman. Soziale Unruhen und apokalyptische Visionen im Zeitalter der Reformation.* Göttingen: Vandenhoeck & Ruprecht, 1979.

Devenish, Philip I. "The Sovereignty of Jesus and the Sovereignty of God." *Theology Today* 53, 1 (1996): 63–73.

DeVries, Dawn. *Jesus Christ in the Preaching of Calvin and Schleiermacher.* Louisville, Ky.: Westminster John Knox Press, 1996.

Doumergue, Emil. *Jean Calvin. Les Hommes et les choses de son temps.* 7 vols. Lausanne: Georges Bridel, 1899–1924.

Dowey, Edward A., Jr. *A Commentary on the Confession of 1967 and an Introduction to* The Book of Confessions. Philadelphia: Westminster Press, 1968.

————. "Heinrich Bullinger's Theology: Thematic, Comprehensive, Schematic." Pp. 41–60 in *Calvin Studies V,* edited by John Leith. Richmond: Union Theological Seminary in Virginia, 1991.

————. *The Knowledge of God in Calvin's Theology.* 2d edition. New York: Columbia University Press, 1952.

Edwards, Mark U., Jr. "Luther's Biography." Pp. 5–20 in *Reformation Europe: A Guide to Research II,* edited by William S. Maltby. St. Louis: Center for Reformation Research, 1992.

Eells, Hasting. *Martin Bucer.* New Haven, Conn.: Yale University Press, 1931.

Engel, Mary Potter. *John Calvin's Perspectival Anthropology.* Atlanta: Scholars Press, 1988.

Fagerberg, David W. *What Is Liturgical Theology?* New York: Pueblo Publishing Company, 1992.

Farner, Oskar. *Huldrych Zwingli.* 4 vols. Zurich: Zwingli-Verlag, 1946–60.

———. *Zwingli the Reformer: His Life and Work.* Translated by D. G. Sear. Hamden, Conn.: Archon Books, 1968.

Fatio, Olivier. "Orthodoxie" (II. Reformierte Orthodoxie). In *Theologische Realenzyklopädie.* Vol. 25. Berlin and New York: Walter de Gruyter, 1995.

Ferel, Martin. *Gepredigte Taufe: Eine homilitische Untersuchung zur Taufpredigt bei Luther.* Tübingen: J. C. B. Mohr (Paul Siebeck), 1969.

Finsler, Georg. *Zwingli-Bibliographie: Verzeichnis der Gedruckten Schriften von und über Ulrich Zwingli.* Nieuwkoop: B. de Graaf, 1968.

Fiorenza, Elizabeth Schüssler. *In Memory of Her.* New York: Crossroad, 1988.

Fischer, J. D. C. *Christian Initiation in the Medieval West.* London: SPCK, 1965.

Fischer, J. D. C., and E. J. Yarnold, S.J. "The West from about AD 500 to the Reformation." Pp. 144–52 in *The Liturgy of the Church,* 2d ed., edited by Cheslyn Jones, Geoffrey Wainwright, Edward Yarnold, and Paul Bradshaw. London: Oxford University Press, 1992.

Friedmann, Robert. *The Theology of Anabaptism.* Scottdale, Pa.: Herald Press, 1973.

Friedrich, Reinhold. "Martin Bucer—Ökumene im 16. Jahrhundert." Pp. 1:257–68 in *Martin Bucer and Sixteenth Century Europe,* 2 vols., edited by Christian Krieger and Marc Lienhard. Leiden: E. J. Brill, 1993.

Funk, Virgil C. "The Liturgical Movement (1830–1969)." Pp. 695–715 in *The New Dictionary of Sacramental Worship,* edited by Peter E. Fink, S.J. Collegeville, Minn.: Liturgical Press, 1990.

Gäbler, Ulrich. *Huldrych Zwingli: His Life and Work.* Translated by Ruth L. C. Gritsch. Philadelphia: Fortress Press, 1986.

———. *Huldrych Zwingli im 20. Jahrhundert: Forschungsbericht und annotierte Bibliographie, 1897–1972.* Zurich: Theologischer Verlag, 1975.

———. "Die Zwingli-Forschung seit 1960." *Theologische Literaturzeitung* 96, 7 (1971): 481–90.

Gagnebin, Bernard. "L'incroyable histoire des sermons de Calvin." *Bulletin de la société d'histoire et d'archéologie de Genève* 10, 4 (1955): 311–34.

Gamble, Richard C. "Current Trends in Calvin Research, 1982–1990." Pp. 96–108 in *Calvinus Sacrae Scripturae Professor,* edited by Wilhelm Neuser. Grand Rapids: Wm. B. Eerdmans Publishing Co., 1994.

Ganoczy, Alexandre. *Calvin théologien de l'église et du ministère.* Paris: Éditions du Cerf, 1964.

———. *The Young Calvin.* Translated by David Foxgrover and Wade Provo. Philadelphia: Westminster Press, 1987.

Gerrish, B. A. "The Confessional Heritage of the Reformed Church." *McCormick Quarterly* 19 (1966): 120–34.

———. *The Faith of Christendom: A Source Book of Creeds and Confessions.* Cleveland and New York: World Publishing Company, 1963.

———. *Grace and Gratitude: The Eucharistic Theology of John Calvin.* Minneapolis: Fortress Press, 1993.

———. *The Old Protestantism and the New: Essays on the Reformation Heritage.* Chicago: University of Chicago Press, 1982.

———. *A Prince of the Church: Schleiermacher and the Beginnings of Modern Theology.* Philadelphia: Fortress Press, 1984.

———. *Tradition and the Modern World: Reformed Theology in the Nineteenth Century.* Chicago: University of Chicago Press, 1978.

———. *Saving Faith and Secular Faith.* Minneapolis: Fortress Press, 1992.

———, ed. *Reformers in Profile.* Philadelphia: Fortress Press, 1967.

Grass, Hans. *Die Abendsmahlslehre bei Luther und Calvin.* Gütersloh: C. Bertelsmann Verlag, 1954.

Greschat, Martin. *Martin Bucer: Ein Reformator und seine Zeit.* Munich: Verlag C. H. Beck, 1990.

———. "Das Profil Martin Bucers." Pp. 1:9–17 in *Martin Bucer and Sixteenth Century Europe,* 2 vols., edited by Christian Krieger and Marc Lienhard. Leiden: E. J. Brill, 1993.

Grislis, Egil. "Calvin's Doctrine of Baptism." *Church History* 3 (1962): 46–65.

Grönvik, Lorenz. *Die Taufe in der Theologie Martin Luthers.* Göttingen and Zurich: Vandenhoeck & Ruprecht, 1968.

Hahn, Ferdinand. *The Worship of the Early Church.* Edited by John Reumann. Translated by David E. Green. Philadelphia: Fortress Press, 1973.

Hakkenberg, Michael A. "Belgic Confession." In *The Oxford Encyclopedia of the Reformation.* Edited by Hans J. Hillerbrand. Oxford: Oxford University Press, 1996.

Hamman, Gottfried. "La Démarche théologique de Bucer." Pp. 1:71–81 in *Martin Bucer and Sixteenth Century Europe,* 2 vols., edited by Christian Krieger and Marc Lienhard. Leiden: E. J. Brill, 1993.

———. *Entre la secte et la cité: le project d'église du réformateur Martin Bucer.* Geneva: Labor et Fides, 1984.

Hartin, James. "Catechisms." Pp. 154–63 in *The Study of Anglicanism,* edited by Stephen Sykes and John Booty. London: SPCK, 1988; Philadelphia: Fortress Press, 1988.

Haugaard, William P. *Elizabeth and the English Reformation.* Cambridge: Cambridge University Press, 1968.

———. "From the Reformation to the Eighteenth Century." Pp. 3–28 in *The Study of Anglicanism,* edited by Stephen Sykes and John Booty. London: SPCK, 1988; Philadelphia: Fortress Press, 1988.

Hazlet, W. Ian P. "The Scots Confession 1560: Context, Complexion and Critique." *Archiv für Reformationsgeschichte* 78 (1987): 287–320.

Hemmann, Carl. "Zwingli's Stellung zur Tauffrage im literarischen Kampf mit den Anabaptisten." *Schweizerische Theologische Zeitschrift* 36 (1919): 29–33, 79–85.

Heppe, Heinrich. *Reformed Dogmatics.* Foreword by Karl Barth. Revised and edited by Ernst Bizer. Translated by G. T. Thompson. London: Allen & Unwin, 1950.

Hesselink, John. "Reactions to Bouwsma's 'Portrait' of John Calvin." Pp. 209–13 in *Calvinus Sacrae Scripturae Professor,* edited by Wilhelm Neuser. Grand Rapids: Wm. B. Eerdmans Publishing Company, 1994.

Hillerbrand, Hans J. "The Origin of Sixteenth Century Anabaptism: Another Look." *Archiv für Reformationsgeschichte* 53 (1962): 152–80.

Hopf, Constantin. *Martin Bucer and the English Reformation.* Oxford: Basil Blackwell, 1946.

Höpfl, Harro. *The Christian Polity of John Calvin*. Cambridge: Cambridge University Press, 1985.

Irwin, Kevin. "Liturgical Theology." Pp. 721–33 in *The New Dictionary of Sacramental Worship*, edited by Peter E. Fink, S.J. Collegeville, Minn.: Liturgical Press, 1990.

Jacobs, Paul. *Prädestination und Verantwortlichkeit bei Calvin*. Neukirchen: Kr. Moers, Buchhandlung des Erziehungsvereins, 1937.

Jahr, Hannelore. *Studien zur Überlieferungsgeschichte der Confession de foi von 1559*. Neukirchen-Vluyn: Neukirchener Verlag des Erziehungsvereins, 1964.

Jeremias, Joachim. *Infant Baptism in the First Four Centuries*. Translated by David Cairns. Philadelphia: Fortress Press, 1960.

Jetter, Werner. Review of *Die Taufe in der Theologie Martin Luthers*, by Lorenz Grönvik. In *Lutherische Rundschau* 19 (1969): 249.

———. *Die Taufe beim Jungen Luther*. Tübingen: J. C. B. Mohr (Paul Siebeck), 1954.

Johnson, Maxwell E. "The Role of *Worship* in the Contemporary Study of Christian Initiation: A Select Review of the Literature" *Worship* 75 (2001): 20–35.

Jordahn, Bruno. "Der Taufgottesdienst im Mittelalter bis zum Gegenwart." Pp. 350–425 in *Leiturgia: Handbuch des evangelischen Gottesdienstes*, vol. 5: *Taufgottesdienstes*, edited by Karl Ferdinand Müller and Walter Blankenburg. Kassel: Johannes Stauda Verlag, 1970.

Kavanagh, Aidan. *Confirmation: Origins and Reform*. New York: Pueblo Publishing Company, 1988.

———. "Initiation: Baptism and Confirmation." *Worship* 46 (1972): 262–76.

———. *On Liturgical Theology*. New York: Pueblo Publishing Company, 1984.

———. "The Role of Ritual in Personal Development." Pp. 148–49 in *The Roots of Ritual*, edited by James D. Shaughnessy. Grand Rapids: Wm. B. Eerdmans Publishing Co., 1973.

———. *The Shape of Baptism: The Rite of Christian Initiation*. New York: Pueblo Publishing Company, 1978.

Kawerau, Gustav. "Liturgische Studien zu Luthers Taufbüchlein von 1523." *Zeitschrift für kirchliche Wissenschaft und kirchliches Leben* 10 (1898): 407–31, 466–77, 519–47, 578–99, 625–43.

Kidd, B. J. *The Thirty-nine Articles: Their History and Explanation*. 5th ed. London: Rivingtons, 1925.

Kilmartin, Edward J., S.J. *Christian Liturgy: Theology and Practice*. Vol. 1: *Systematic Theology of Liturgy*. Kansas City, Mo.: Sheed and Ward, 1988.

Kingdom, Robert M. *Geneva and the Coming of the Religious Wars in France, 1555–1563*. Geneva: Librarie E. Droz, 1956.

Kittleson, James. *Luther: The Story of the Man and His Career*. Minneapolis: Augsburg Publishing House, 1986.

Klassen, William. *Anabaptism in Outline*. Kitchener, Ont., and Scottdale, Pa.: Herald Press, 1981.

Koch, Ernst. "Paulusexegese und Bundestheologie: Bullingers Auslegung von Gal 3:17–26." Pp. 342–50 in *Histoire de l'exégèse au XVIe siècle*, edited by Olivier Fatio and Pierre Fraenkel. Geneva: Droz, 1979.

———. Review of *Heinrich Bullinger and the Covenant: The Other Reformed Tradition*, by J. Wayne Baker. *Theologisches Literaturezeitung* 109 (1984): 43–44.

———. *Die Theologie der Confessio Helvetica Posterior*. Neukirchen-Vluyn: Neukirchener Verlag des Erziehungsvereins, 1968.

Koch, Karl. *Studium Pietatis: Martin Bucer als Ethiker*. Neukirchen-Vluyn: Neukirchener Verlag, 1962.

Kretschmar, Georg. "Die Geschichte des Taufgottesdienstes in der alten Kirche." Pp. 59–273 in *Leiturgia: Handbuch des evangelischen Gottesdienstes*, vol. 5: *Taufgottesdienstes*, edited by Karl Ferdinand Müller and Walter Blankenburg. Kassel: Johannes Stauda Verlag, 1970.

Krusche, Werner. *Das Wirken des Heiligen Geistes nach Calvin*. Göttingen: Vandenhoeck & Ruprecht, 1957.

Künzli, Edwin. "Aus der Zwingli-Forschung." *Theologische Rundschau* n.s. 37, 4 (1972): 361–69.

Lang, August. "Luther und Calvin." In *Reformation und Gegenwart: Gesammelte Aufsätze*. Detmold: Meyersche Hofbuchhandlung, 1918.

———. "Die Quellen der *Institutio* von 1536." *Evangelische Theologie* 3 (1936): 104–5.

Leenhardt, Franz J. *Le Baptême chrétien, son origine, sa signification*. Neuchâtel and Paris: Delachaux & Niestlé, 1946.

Leith, John H. *Assembly at Westminster: Reformed Theology in the Making*. Richmond: John Knox Press, 1973.

Littell, Franklin H. *The Anabaptist View of the Church*. Boston: Starr King Press, 1958.

Locher, Gottfried. *Zwingli's Thought: New Perspectives*. Leiden: E. J. Brill, 1981.

Lohse, Bernard. *Martin Luther: An Introduction to His Life and Work*. Translated by Robert C. Schultz. Philadelphia: Fortress Press, 1986.

———, ed. *Der Durchbruch der reformatischen Erkenntnis bei Luther*. Darmstadt: Wissentschaftliche Buchgesellschaft, 1968.

———, ed. *Der Durchbruch der reformatischen Erkenntnis bei Luther—Neuere Untersuchungen* Stuttgart: F. Steiner Verlag Wiesbaden, 1988.

Lutterjohann, Rudolf. "Die Stellung Luthers zur Kindertaufe." *Zeitschrift für systematische Theologie* 11 (1934): 188–224.

Made Not Born: New Perspectives on Christian Initiation and the Catechumenate. Notre Dame, Ind.: University of Notre Dame Press, 1976.

Marcel, Pierre Charles. *The Biblical Doctrine of Infant Baptism: Sacrament of the Covenant of Grace*. Translated by Philip Edgcumbe Hughes. London: James Clarke & Company, 1953.

Marshall, Paul V. "Reconsidering 'Liturgical Theology': Is there a *Lex Orandi* for all Christians?" *Studia Liturgica* 25 (1995): 129–151.

Marxsen, Willi. *The New Testament as the Church's Book*. Translated by James E. Mignard. Philadelphia: Fortress Press, 1972.

Mattias, Markus. "Orthodoxie" (I. Lutherische Orthodoxie). In *Theologische Realenzyklopädie*, Vol. 25. Berlin and New York: Walter de Gruyter, 1995. 5: 464–97.

McCoy, Charles S., and J. Wayne Baker, *Fountainhead of Federalism: Heinrich Bullinger and the Covenant Tradition*. Louisville, Ky.: Westminster/John Knox Press, 1991.

McGrath, Alistair E. "John Calvin and Late Medieval Thought." *Archiv für Reformationsgeschichte* 77 (1986): 58–78.

McNeill, J. T. "The Church in Sixteenth-Century Reformed Theology." *Journal of Religion* 22 (1942): 251–69.

Meinhold, Peter. "Calvin und Luther." *Lutherische Monatshefte* 3 (1964): 264–69.

Moeller, Pamela Ann. *Calvin's Doxology.* Allison Park, Pa.: Pickwick Publications, 1997.

Molwitz, P. "Luther's Lehre von der Kindertaufe." *Neue Kirchliche Zeitschrift* 38 (1917): 359–72.

Monter, E. William. *Calvin's Geneva.* New York: John Wiley & Sons, 1967.

Moody, Dale. *Baptism: Foundation for Christian Unity.* Philadelphia: Westminster Press, 1967.

Mueller, William. *Church and State in Luther and Calvin: A Comparative Study* Nashville: Broadman Press, 1954.

Müller, Johannes. *Martin Bucers Hermeneutik.* Gütersloh: Gütersloher Verlagshaus Gerd Mohn, 1965.

Muller, Richard A. *Christ and the Decree: Christology and Predestination in Reformed Theology from Calvin to Perkins.* Durham, N.C.: Labyrinth Press, 1986.

Nauta, Doede. "Calvin and Luther." *Free University Quarterly* 2 (1952–53): 1–17.

Neuser, Wilhelm. *Die Tauflehre des Heidelberger Katechismus: Eine aktuelle Lösung des Problems der Kindertaufe.* Munich: Chr. Kaiser Verlag, 1967.

Niebuhr, Richard R. *Schleiermacher on Christ and Religion: A New Introduction.* New York: Charles Scribner's Sons, 1964.

Niesel, Wilhelm. *Calvin-Bibliographie, 1901–1959.* Munich: Chr. Kaiser Verlag, 1961.

———. *Die Theologie Calvins.* Munich: Chr. Kaiser Verlag, 1938. English translation as *The Theology of Calvin.* Translated by Harold Knight. Philadelphia: Westminster Press, 1956.

Nümann, K. "Zur enstehung des lutherischen Taufbüchleins von Jahre 1523." *Monatsschrift für Gottesdienst und kirchliche Kunst* 33 (1928): 214–19.

Oberman, Heiko A. *The Dawn of the Reformation.* Edinburgh: T & T Clark, 1986.

———. *"Initia Calvini:* The Matrix of Calvin's Reformation." Pp. 117–27 in *Calvinus Sacrae Scripturae Professor,* edited by Wilhelm Neuser. Grand Rapids: Wm. B. Eerdmans Publishing Co., 1994.

———. *Luther: Man between God and the Devil.* New Haven, Conn.: Yale University Press, 1989.

Ogden, Schubert M., ed. selected, translated, and introduced. *Existence and Faith: Shorter Writings of Rudolf Bultmann.* New York: Meridian Books, 1960.

Old, Hughes Oliphant. *The Patristic Roots of Reformed Worship.* Züricher Beiträge zur Reformationsgeschichte, 5. Zurich: Theologischer Verlag, 1975.

———. *The Shaping of the Reformed Baptismal Rite in the Sixteenth Century.* Grand Rapids: Wm. B. Eerdmans Publishing Co., 1992.

Ozment, Steven. *The Age of Reform*. New Haven, Conn.: Yale University Press, 1980.

———. *The Reformation in the Cities*. New Haven, Conn.: Yale University Press, 1975.

Pannier, Jacques. *Les origines de la Confession de foi et de la discipline des Église réformées de France*. Paris: F. Alcan, 1936.

Parker, T. H. L. *John Calvin: A Biography*. Philadelphia: Westminster Press, 1975.

Partee, Charles. "Calvin's Central Dogma, Again." *Sixteenth Century Journal* 18 (1987): 191–99.

Pelikan, Jaroslav J. "Luther's Defense of Infant Baptism." Pp. 200–218 in *Luther for an Ecumenical Age*, edited by Carl S. Meyer. St. Louis: Concordia Publishing House, 1967.

Pestalozzi, Carl. *Heinrich Bullinger: Leben und ausgewählte Schriften*. Elberfeld: R. L. Fridrechs, 1858.

Petry, Ray C. "Calvin's Conception of the 'Communio Sanctorum.'" *Church History* 5 (1936): 227–38.

Pfatteicher, Philip H., and Carlos R. Messerli. *Manual on the Liturgy— Lutheran Book of Worship*. Minneapolis: Augsburg Publishing House, 1979.

Pipkin, H. Wayne. *A Zwingli Bibliography*. Bibliographia Tripotamopolitana no. 7. Pittsburgh: The Clifford E. Barbour Library, Pittsburgh Theological Seminary, 1972.

Pollet, J.-V.-M. "Zwinglianisme." In *Dictionnaire de Theologie Catholique*. Paris: Librairie Letouzey et Ané, 1950.

Potter, G. R. *Zwingli*. Cambridge: Cambridge University Press, 1976.

Procter, Francis. *A New History of the Book of Common Prayer*. Revised and rewritten by Walter Howard Frere. London: Macmillan & Co., 1955.

Quistorp, Heinrich. "Sichtbare und unsichtbare Kirche bei Calvin." *Evangelische Theologie* 9 (1949): 83–101.

Raitt, Jill. "Roman Catholic New Wine in Reformed Old Bottles? The Conversion of the Elements in the Eucharistic Doctrines of Theodore Beza and Edward Schillebeeckx." *Journal of Ecumenical Studies* 8 (1971): 581–604.

Redeker, Martin. *Schleiermacher: Life and Thought*. Translated by John Wallhauser. Philadelphia: Fortress Press, 1973.

Riggs, John W. "Emerging Ecclesiology in Calvin's Baptismal Thought, 1536–1543." *Church History* 64, 1 (1995): 29–43.

———. "Normative Shape for Christian Worship." *Prism* 3, 2 (1988): 34–36.

———. "The Sacred Food of *Didache* 9 and 10 and Second-Century Ecclesiologies." Pp. 256–83 in *The Didache in Context*, edited by Clayton Jefford. Leiden: E. J. Brill, 1995.

Rogers, Jack. *Presbyterian Creeds: A Guide to the* Book of Confessions. Philadelphia: Westminster Press, 1985.

Rohls, Jan. *Reformed Confessions: Theology from Zurich to Barmen*. Translated by John Hoffmeyer. Introduction by Jack L. Stotts. Louisville, Ky.: Westminster John Knox Press, 1998.

Schmid, Heinrich. *The Doctrinal Theology of the Evangelical Lutheran Church*.

3d ed. Revised and translated by Charles A. Hay and Henry E. Jacobs. Minneapolis: Augsburg Publishing House, 1961.

Schmidt-Clausing, Fritz. *Zwingli als Liturgiker*. Göttingen: Vandenhoeck & Ruprecht, 1952.

———. "Zwingli und die Kindertaufe." *Berliner Kirchen-Briefe* 6 (1962): 4–8.

Schweizer Alexander. *Die protestantischen Centraldogmen in ihrer Entwicklung innerhalb der reformierten Kirche*. 2 vols. Zurich: Orell, Fuessli, and Co., 1854.

Searle, Mark, O.F.M. *Christening: The Making of Christians*. Essex: Kevin Mayhew Ltd., 1977.

———. "The Journey of Conversion." *Worship* 54 (1980): 35–55.

Seeberg, Reinhold. *Text-Book of the History of Doctrines*. Translated by Charles F. Hay. Grand Rapids: Baker Book House, 1983.

Senn, Frank. "The Shape and Content of Christian Initiation: An Exposition of the New Lutheran Liturgy of Holy Baptism." *Dialog* 14 (1975): 97–107.

Smith, Morton. "Pauline Worship as Seen by Pagans." *Harvard Theological Review* 73 (1980): 241–49.

Staedtke, Joachim. "Die Züricher Prädestiationsstreit von 1560." *Zwingliana* 9 (1953): 536–46.

———, ed. *Glauben und Bekennen: Vierhundert Jahre Confessio Helvetica Posterior*. Zurich: Zwingli Verlag, 1966.

Steinmetz, David C. "The Theology of Calvin and Calvinism." Pp. 211–32 in *Reformation Europe: A Guide to Research*, edited by Steven Ozment. St. Louis: Center for Reformation Studies, 1982.

Stephens, W. P. *The Theology of Huldrych Zwingli*. Oxford: Clarendon Press, 1986.

———. *The Holy Spirit in the Theology of Martin Bucer*. London: Cambridge University Press, 1970.

Stookey, Lawrence. "Three New Initiation Rites." *Worship* 51 (1977): 33–49.

Strohl, H. "La Notion d'église chez les Réformateurs." *Revue d'histoire et de philosophie religieuses* 16 (1936): 265–319.

Tappert, Theodore G., ed. *The Book of Concord: The Confessions of the Evangelical Lutheran Church*. Philadelphia: Fortress Press, 1959.

Tice, Terrence N. *Schleiermacher Bibliography: With Brief Introductions, Annotations, and Index*. Princeton, N.J.: Princeton Theological Seminary, 1966.

———. *Schleiermacher Bibliography (1784–1984): Updating and Commentary*. Princeton, N.J.: Princeton Theological Seminary, 1985.

———. "Schleiermacher Bibliography: Update 1987." *New Athenaeum/Neues Athenaeum* 1 (1989): 280–350.

———. "Schleiermacher Bibliography: Update 1990." *New Athenaeum/Neues Athenaeum* 2 (1991): 131–65.

———. "Schleiermacher Bibliography: Update 1994." *New Athenaeum/Neues Athenaeum* 4 (1995): 139–94.

———. *Schleiermacher's Sermons: A Chronological Listing and Account*. Lewiston, N.Y.: E. Mellen Press, 1997.

Tillich, Paul. *A History of Christian Thought*. New York: Simon & Schuster, 1968.

Toon, Peter. "The Articles and Homilies." Pp. 133–43 in *The Study of Anglicanism*, edited by Stephen Sykes and John Booty. London: SPCK, 1988; Philadelphia: Fortress Press, 1988.

Torrance, Thomas F. *The Hermeneutics of John Calvin*. Edinburgh: Scottish Academic Press, 1988.

Tracy, James D. "Humanism and the Reformation." Pp. 33–57 in *Reformation Europe: A Guide to Research*. Edited by Steven Ozment. St. Louis: Center for Reformation Research, 1982.

Usteri, Johann Martin. "Calvins Sakraments und Tauflehre." *Theologische Studien und Kritiken* 3 (1884):419–56.

———. "Darstellung der Tauflehre Zwinglis." *Theologische Studien und Kritiken* 3 (1884): 205–84.

———. "Die Stellung der Strassburger Reformatoren Bucer und Capito zur Tauffrage." *Theologische Studien und Kritiken* 3 (1884): 456–524.

Venema, Cornelis P. "Heinrich Bullinger's Correspondence on Calvin's Doctrine of Predestination, 1551–1553." *Sixteenth Century Journal* 17 (1986): 449.

von Geusau, Alting. *Die Lehre von der Kindertaufe bei Calvin*. Bilthoven: Uitgeverij H. Nelissen, 1963.

Walker, Williston. *John Calvin: The Organizer of Reformed Protestantism, 1509–1564*. New York: G. P. Putnam's Sons, 1906. Reprint, New York: Schocken Books, 1969.

Wallace, Ronald S. *Calvin's Doctrine of the Word and Sacrament*. Edinburgh: Oliver and Boyd, Ltd., 1953.

———. *Geneva and the Reformation: A Study of Calvin as Social Reformer, Churchman, Pastor, and Theologian*. Grand Rapids: Baker Book House, 1988.

Walser, Peter. *Die Prädestination bei Heinrich Bullinger im Zusammenhang mit seiner Gotteslehre*. Zurich: Zwingli-Verlag, 1957.

Wendel, François. *Calvin: sources et évolution de sa pensée religieuse*. Paris: Presses universitaires de France, 1950.

———. *L'Eglise de Strasbourg, sa constitution et son organization, 1532–1535*. Paris: Presses Universitaires de France, 1942.

Whale, J. S. *The Protestant Tradition: An Essay in Interpretation*. Cambridge: Cambridge University Press, 1955.

White, James F. *Protestant Worship: Traditions in Transition*. Louisville, Ky.: Westminster John Knox Press, 1989.

Williams, George H. *The Radical Reformation*. 3d ed. Sixteenth Century Essays & Studies 15. Kirksville, Mo.: Sixteenth Century Journal Publishers, 1992.

———. "How Do We Know It Is Us?" Pp. 55–65 in *Liturgy and the Moral Self*, edited by E. Byron Anderson and Bruce T. Morrill, S.J. Collegeville, Minn.: Liturgical Press, 1998.

Yoder, John Howard. "The Turning Point in the Zwinglian Revolution." *Mennonite Quarterly Review* 32 (1958): 128–40.

INDEX OF NAMES

INDEX OF SUBJECTS

LaVergne, TN USA
24 March 2011
221461LV00004B/3/P